THE pagan Anthology
of short fiction

PRESENTED BY LLEWELLYN AND *PanGaia* Magazine
Introduction by Diana Paxson

THE Pagan Anthology
of short fiction

13 Prize Winning Tales

Llewellyn Publications
Woodbury, Minnesota

First Edition
First Printing, 2008

Book design by Steffani Sawyer
Cover design by Lisa Novak
Cover image of tree © 2008 by George Ostertag/SuperStock
Cover image of pen © 2008 by Photodisc/SuperStock
Editing by Brett Fechheimer
Llewellyn is a registered trademark of Llewellyn Worldwide, Ltd.

The Library of Congress Cataloging-in-Publication Data for *The Pagan Anthology of Short Fiction: 13 Prize Winning Tales* is pending.

ISBN: 978-0-7387-1269-7

Llewellyn Publications
A Division of Llewellyn Worldwide, Ltd.
2143 Wooddale Drive, Dept. 978-0-7387-1269-7
Woodbury, Minnesota 55125-2989, U.S.A.
www.llewellyn.com

Printed in the United States of America

Contents

Contents

The Search for Pagan Fiction

WHAT DO WE MEAN BY "PAGAN FICTION"?
BY DIANA L. PAXSON

When I agreed to be one of the judges for the first Pagan Fiction Awards, sponsored by *PanGaia* magazine and presented at Panthea-Con in February 2008, the question "What do we mean by 'Pagan fiction'?" didn't even occur to me. Anne Newkirk Niven, editor of *PanGaia*, asked me if I would rather write a story or judge the contest, and in my innocence I thought that reading a lot of other people's stories would be easier than writing one of my own, and certainly more fun. This is not to say that I don't get great satisfaction out of writing, but one puts almost as much effort into planning a short story as into setting up a novel, so the former is a far less efficient use of time and energy. Bear that in mind as you read the stories included in this volume—their authors not only worked well, they worked *hard*.

Anne had also told me that Llewellyn was going to publish the finalists. This would be the first anthology of Pagan short stories ever, a chance to define what is effectively a new subgenre of short fiction. As both a writer and a Pagan, the chance to help shape this anthology was an opportunity that I could hardly resist.

Having sold more than seventy-five short stories over the years, I figured I knew what a story was. As Marion Zimmer Bradley used to define it, the basic story plot is, "Joe has his fanny in a bear trap, and this is how he gets it out . . . " The bear trap doesn't need to be physical, but there does have to be some kind of problem—physical, psychological, or spiritual—that Joe, or Josephine, must solve. The story has to have a beginning, a middle, and an end, and by the time we reach the conclusion, something in the situation should have changed.

But even that is not enough unless Josephine, or Joe, is the kind of character who can engage the reader's sympathy, or at least stimulate enough interest to keep her reading. We don't have to like the protagonists, but we have to care what becomes of them. Stories are about people (not always human people, but beings that think and feel). Whether we wish we could share their adventures, or whether we thank the gods we don't have to, in their struggles we see our own.

And then of course the writing has to be readable—which to my mind is the bottom line. The word-handling needs to be good enough for the reader to keep turning the pages. If the reader can't figure out what is going on, it won't matter how sympathetic the characters are or how intriguing the plot is.

But what defines a story as *Pagan*?

That's the point at which things got really interesting, as it became apparent that none of the judges really knew. Figuring out how to evaluate the stories was a learning experience for everyone.

Nor had we realized that our community includes so many writers. The response to the call for submissions was almost overwhelming. Hope springs eternal in an author's breast, and Robert Heinlein (author of *Stranger in a Strange Land*) once advised writers to keep sending a story out, because somewhere, someday, an editor would be desperate enough to buy it. It works, too. Many years after I sold my first short story, the editor told me he bought it because he and his assistant had agreed that " . . . the next short story that's not absolutely awful we'll take." Thus, I can't fault the people who submitted stories that I would have expected to see in *Fantasy & Science Fiction* instead. And perhaps one day I will see some of the stories that didn't make our final cut in that magazine—many of the stories were very good indeed.

We did agree that our selections should not be limited by genre. Currently in popular fiction, anything set in the future or with a lot of technology is, by definition, science fiction; anything set in an alternate world, especially one with a medieval culture, or in a setting, past or present, in which magic works, is generally classed as fantasy. Mainstream fiction encompasses mainstream reality, the world that Main Street USA (if there even is such a thing anymore) would recognize as real. Fantasy is the genre label under which my own work has been marketed for the past twenty-seven years. I recall one editor commenting that the book I had just turned in had "a lot of rituals, but they work." My (unvoiced) response was that they ought to, since I had actually done most of them. That, of course, was the problem. To my editor, what I was writing was fantasy. To me, it was realism. This may explain why authors who submitted stories for this contest assumed that anything with elements of the supernatural, paranormal, mythological, or spiritual could be classed as a Pagan story.

The challenge to the judges was to figure out which element was which. Our judging team was nicely balanced. Elizabeth Barrette was looking for stories with literary merit, and Anne Newkirk Niven wanted stories that people would enjoy. I agreed that we should choose stories that were not only Pagan but also had literary value, and that would keep people turning pages long enough to appreciate their deeper meaning. But as I worked my way through the submissions, I began to realize that I was also looking for something more. What would distinguish Pagan fiction from a story that might appear in *Fantasy & Science Fiction* or *The New Yorker*? It eventually became clear to me that I was looking for stories in which the spirituality was real, stories in which the actions and reactions of the protagonist were motivated by Pagan beliefs, experience, and ethics.

This is exemplified by the winning story, April's "A Valkyrie Among Jews," which directly addresses the question of Pagan identity. I've known many witches whose birth-religion was Judaism, and I've sympathized with their struggles to reconcile the beliefs and practices of their old religion with those of their new one. When the Pagan culture in question is Germanic, the conflict can be even more acute. Working with the Jewish residents of a retirement home, the valkyrie of the title, a Pagan and a fan of Wagner's operas, is forced to confront her feelings about her own Jewish heritage.

Taking the remaining stories thematically rather than in the order in which they appear in this book may clarify what I mean. "The Bitter Herbs of Camelot," by A. C. Fisher Aldag, also has contemporary relevance, and is particularly poignant to those of us who watched so many friends die when the AIDS epidemic was at its height. When is death a gift and how do we face our choices? We all call on the Goddess, but will we be willing to accept her gifts if she comes? In "Under a Double Rainbow," by Sophie Mouette, the Goddess shows herself as splendid and as varied as the rainbow of the title. "Selk River," by Melodie Bolt, is also set in the world we know, although even contemporary Iceland can be an uncanny place—as a woman devastated by grief learns, and in doing so begins her healing.

In "A Nose for Magic," by Eugie Foster, a guy with an unusual talent meets a woman with an unusual familiar to solve a problem involving magical ethics. What sets this one apart is its humor and charm. "Draw Down," by Alex Bledsoe, gives us the age-old choices in a classic Western setting. You may think you've seen the characters before—a feisty Irish witch, a bigoted preacher, and a laconic sheriff—but their portrayal shows us something new.

Some of the stories, like Vylar Kaftan's "Black Doe," are set in the kind of legendary past that could be classed as fantasy. Trayja's world is a tribal culture from some unknown time and place. What makes it outstanding is the mythic depth, the careful detail with which the setting is presented, and the sensitivity of the characterization. In "The Rune Hag's Daughter," by Linda Steele, the society is neolithic, but the conflict between the demands of family tradition and individual need is eternal, as is the search to heal the soul.

I was surprised to discover how many of the best stories could be classed as science fiction. Deborah Blake's "Dead and (Mostly) Gone" takes place in a near-future setting, proving that in a world in which Paganism is an accepted part of the social scene there may be some new careers for witches, but the quest to find meaning in one's job is the same. Reading "From Our Minds to Yours," by C. S. MacCath, we wonder if this is the future, or a present we just haven't heard about yet. The problem is scientific, but the story is less about a solution than about the ways our faith helps us to respond. "Seabird," by Paula R. Stiles, is set in another dystopian future, in which the magical north exists in an uneasy peace with the industrial south. The setting frames a story of a father's love for his child, the problem of survival in an alien world.

"Silkie's Diary," by A. C. Fisher Aldag, features another special little girl. Growing up is hard even, or especially, when you can turn into a seal. Aldag's second story is as bright as the first was shadowed, a "young adult" story that could easily be the first in a best-selling series. One is left wanting to read more of Silkie's adventures. "We Have Come Home," by A. L. Waldron, also focuses on children, in a bittersweet story in which the mythology of the stars both creates and helps the characters deal with a kind of tragedy that is eternal.

So what do we mean by "Pagan fiction"? Clearly it is constrained neither by time nor by space. In whatever world these stories take place, the world of the spirit is real. The characters strive to find healing, faith, and meaning for their lives, and in reading these stories we are aided to find that meaning in our own lives as well.

Deborah Blake is a Wiccan High Priestess who has been lead-
ing her current group, Blue Moon Circle, for four years. She is
the author of Circle, Coven & Grove: A Year of Magickal
Practice *(Llewellyn, 2007) and* Everyday Witch A to Z: An
Amusing, Inspiring & Informative Guide to the Wonderful World of Witchcraft *(Llewellyn, 2008). She is cur-*
rently working on her third nonfiction book and looking for a
home for her first novel (about a Witch, of course). When not
writing, Deborah runs The Artisans' Guild, a cooperative shop
she founded with a friend, and works as a jewelry maker, tarot
reader, ordained minister, and intuitive energy healer. She lives
in a hundred-year-old farmhouse in rural upstate New York
with five cats who supervise all her activities, both magickal and
mundane.

Dead and (Mostly) Gone

BY DEBORAH BLAKE

It was the end of another long shift, and Donata's stomach roiled with a combination of too much bad coffee and too many frustrations. Her room in the basement of the police building was damp and cold, and smelled vaguely of sweat, stale air, and despair. By the end of the day, she no longer noticed the smell. She figured it came with the territory, so to speak. Nobody wanted her upstairs with the rest of the gang, and that suited her just fine. The sign on the door said *Witness Retrieval Specialist*—that sounded so much more official than *Witch*.

Donata sighed and looked at her watch again. The chief had called down an hour ago, pleading with her to stay past shift-end to deal with an important case. A crisis, he'd called it. Time-critical.

Yeah, right. Then why was she still sitting here? Half past seven on a Friday night, there were lots of places she'd rather be. Well, all right, not lots—let's face it, cops weren't all that popular except with other cops, and Witch-cops weren't all that popular even with them. Oh, the Pagan community tried to be supportive of all its members (a bit like cops, if you thought about it), but it was an old habit for Witches to be leery of the law, and old habits die hard.

Donata had been at this job for fifteen years, which she figured was about twelve years too many. When she'd started in March of 2018, badge shiny, eyes bright with the fervor of the righteous, she'd had visions of days spent in glorious success—the triumph of law over lawlessness. After fifteen years, she knew better. They didn't just relegate her to the basement because she was an embarrassment in the eyes of the public (and most of her colleagues). The miasma of anguish, gloom, and regrets that emanated from her area of the building could drive even the most hardened cop to drink at the end of the day. She knew she'd been doing the job too long when she'd realized that she no longer noticed that either.

When Witchcraft had finally come out of the broom closet, as Pagans liked to say, there was a period of adjustment for everyone involved. Then the Catholic Church settled most of the lawsuits for religious persecution out of court, admitting to centuries of lying to the public for the greater glory of God and his coffers. It hadn't hurt that the latest pope's mother turned out to be the last in a long line of Stregas, traditional Italian Witches. And the scientific community had sheepishly conceded that it had concrete proof that the human brain was capable of such "unscientific" feats as clairvoyance and other psychic powers. Pagan pride days became as commonplace as gay marches, and life resumed its normal course. More or less.

So now Witches were an accepted part of the community, just another once-oppressed group struggling to find its place in a society that had reluctantly admitted Witches to the status of equals without ever becoming quite comfortable with their presence. For most, it made surprisingly little difference in their lives. Other than the fact that they could post ritual times in the paper and practice their nature-based religion openly, without fear of losing their jobs or their children, life went on much as it had before.

That is, except for a gifted few, for whom society had a use. Dowsers, for instance, saved the trouble of drilling exploratory holes for water or oil wells. Now, there was a nice job. Reasonable hours, good pay, true appreciation for your work. Donata often thought she should have become a dowser. She sighed again. She was willing to bet that dowsers were all home on Friday nights, or out doing whatever dowsers did for fun. And to think that she once thought her job was glamorous. Of course, she had been much younger then.

When they first came up with the position of Witness Retrieval Specialist, it had seemed like the perfect solution to one of the most frustrating situations in police work. Someone is murdered, but there are no witnesses. If there were no major clues at the scene of the crime, and nothing to tie any particular suspect to the murder, the police hit a dead end.

After the dust of the societal changes had settled, some bright young cop on a murder case came up with an unconventional idea at the end of a frustrating week of fishing for clues and banging his head against a wall of alibis. He convinced his superiors to bring in a Witch to call in the one witness to the crime that no one had been able to talk to—the victim himself.

And so it began. The Witch, a fairly obscure psychic (who went on to write a book about the case and spent a few years on the talk-show circuit, before the phenomenon became too commonplace to catch the public's interest), called forth the spirit of the dead man, who promptly pointed the finger at his best friend, who quickly recanted his alibi in the face of such an incontrovertible witness.

While it's true that ghosts can lie, it turned out that most murdered folk would much rather point the finger at whomever it was that actually cut their lives short than waste this once-in-a-death-time opportunity by blaming someone else, no matter how much that person might have pissed them off during their days among the living. Besides, with a little training and practice, a Witch could almost always tell if one of the dearly departed was lying.

So the police academy added a new specialization to their curriculum, albeit one requiring candidates to pass some pretty unusual tests to qualify for selection. And Donata Santori had been a proud member of the first-ever graduating class of Witness Retrieval Specialists, more commonly referred to by their less-talented peers as "ghost yankers."

At first, it really had been all that she'd expected. She'd helped to solve the "unsolvable" crimes, brought hardened criminals to long-delayed justice, aided families in finding closure. For the first few years, she'd gone home at the end of the day with a feeling of satisfaction, and the knowledge that she'd helped in a way that few others could. It had seemed as though her "gift" had a real purpose, and the job had given her life meaning and glory.

But the satisfaction she'd felt slowly started to fade in the face of the grinding realities of the job. It wasn't just the lack of acceptance by other, more conventional cops, although she'd truly expected that to pass away after they'd seen how much help she could be. It wasn't the nagging of her friends and family to get a better, "normal" job—one that paid more and had fewer irregular hours. It wasn't even the way the job seemed to eat her life until it was all that was left.

No, the thing that finally wore her down was the job itself. Day after day of talking to the dead, instead of to the living. One tragic tale after the other. "My husband killed me because I overcooked the roast one too many times." "My partner killed me after he embezzled all the money from our business." "Some druggie mugged me in an alley for twenty bucks and my watch. Oh, yes, I know where to find him; I've been haunting him for weeks. Too bad he's too strung out to be able to tell I'm there."

After a while, it all started to sound the same. And fifteen years later, Donata had to admit to herself that her friends and family were right; it was time to quit and find a better job. It didn't matter that she was good at this one, or that there were few people with the talent and inclination to take her place. The truth was, she just didn't care any more. The dead had gotten along fine without her before, and they could do so again.

Donata put her head down on her desk, next to the remains of the pastrami on rye that had been her dinner. She was so tired. Tired of the job, tired of death and the pettiness that seemed to plague the human condition. Maybe she could get a job as an Avon Lady, peddling beauty instead of wallowing in ugliness.

The rap of a fist on her half-closed door jarred her out of her reverie. She looked up, expecting to see the clerk who usually brought the case files down from the more rarefied air upstairs. Instead, she saw the weary, grizzled face of the chief himself. Intrigued in spite of herself, Donata sat up straighter behind her desk and pushed the pungent scraps of her sandwich over the corner of her desk and into the trash. As far as she could recall, the chief hadn't come down here since Donata's first day at the precinct. She saw him in the hallway, of course, and at the occasional meetings where he actually felt a need for her presence, but to the best of Donata's knowledge, Chief O'Malley had never set foot in the basement since the day he'd personally escorted her down to her new office. This case must be something big.

The police chief dragged the only other chair in the office out of a corner, and sat down heavily. A big, graying man on the verge of retirement, with only a slight gut to show for his years behind a desk eating bad food at odd hours, the chief always looked tired and a little grumpy. It came with the position, she supposed. But tonight the tired was more obvious than the grumpy, and Donata thought that she detected an edge of desperation on top of it all. Well, it didn't take a psychic to figure that out—he wouldn't have come to her if this were some normal case, one that he could solve by normal means. Still, it was a little disconcerting to see the boss-man looking so worried.

Donata cleared her throat before she spoke. "Got something for me, Chief?" As if that weren't obvious.

O'Malley hitched his chair a little closer to her desk and carefully set down a folder in the space vacated by her dinner. One stubby, nicotine-stained finger tapped the top of the folder, but he didn't open it right away. Donata saw him glance around, taking in the paint peeling off the walls, the lack of windows, the stacks of paperwork from cases both old and pending. She could feel his long-delayed realization of how dreary her job really was and his guilt over his lack of appreciation for her work—all of it overlaid with that sense of desperation and fear.

"A bad one," he finally said. "We've got nothing, and we're running out of time. For a while there we thought we had a lead, but it turned out to be a case of mistaken identity." He scratched the end-of-the-day stubble on his chin absently, which reminded Donata of the sounds mice made as they scrabbled through the wall behind her desk. "You're all we've got, I'm afraid." He shifted uncomfortably on the hard wooden chair, clearly not happy about being there, with her.

Donata finally snapped. Hell, it was late, she was tired, and she was going to quit this damn job anyway. She wasn't going to sit there and play games with someone who clearly didn't like her, or the job she did.

"For the gods' sake, spit it out, Chief," she said, slumping back in her seat. "You're telling me how serious this is and how little time we have. It's way past quitting time—why don't you just tell me what's so damn important that it brought you all the way down here to my little slice of heaven, so we can both go home."

O'Malley glared at Donata, but he didn't respond with the lecture on respect that she'd expected. Instead, he flipped open the file and turned it toward her. On top was a picture of a towheaded little girl, maybe four or five years old. She was wearing a pink tutu and flashing a set of dimples as she posed in mid-twirl. The little girl looked happy and alive, in a way that only small children can. Donata felt the acids in her stomach churning in response.

She looked at the chief with dismay. She never got used to the children. "This is the victim?" she asked.

The chief hung his head. "That's my granddaughter, Lacey. She was five last week." Donata thought she saw the glint of tears in his eyes.

"She's dead?" she asked quietly. It seemed as though she could feel something after all. All the more reason to quit this damn job. She hated to see this tough man brought down like everyone else. Death, the great equalizer. Damn.

Unexpectedly, O'Malley shook his head. "No, not yet. At least we don't think so." He pushed the picture of the little girl aside, to reveal the one underneath.

This new photo contained none of the joy of the previous one. It featured a scruffy man, clearly unhappy. Dead, in fact. The hole in the middle of his forehead made that clear. Strangely, he didn't seem to look any worse than he must have before the unsightly hole was added to the various scars and prison tattoos already decorating what could only have been a homely face to begin with. A face only a mother could love—although in this case, Donata thought even that was unlikely.

She picked up the photo. "So who is he? Or who *was* he, I should say."

The chief grimaced. "Michael Franco. Rap sheet as long as your arm: robbery, extortion, beating up little old ladies in alleys. You name it; if there was money in it, and it didn't require actual work, Franco did it. Spent a couple of short stretches in prison, didn't seem to teach him anything. Got out a week ago on parole. Good behavior. Huh." They looked at each other for a minute, their differences temporarily negated by their common disgust with the system. O'Malley turned back to the photos.

"He kidnapped my granddaughter this morning, on her way to the park. Knocked down her mother, picked her up, and ran. Sped off in a car and was gone before anyone could do a thing. Two blocks from her house. We got the call from him an hour later."

Donata looked at her boss intently. "He called you, or her mother?"

O'Malley looked, if possible, wearier than he had when he'd entered her office. "Me. He knew who I was, who she was. We figure it was personal, although we haven't figured out why yet. If he was still alive, that might matter. But he's dead, so it doesn't."

"What happened?" she asked.

He sighed. "The usual screw-ups. Tip-off by a neighbor, overeager young beat cop new to the job. The guy got cornered, then he got shot. No big loss to society. Under normal circumstances, we'd be happy to save the expense of a trial."

Donata knew it couldn't be that simple, or O'Malley wouldn't be sitting in her dismal little office playing show-and-tell. "Your granddaughter wasn't with him when they found him?"

"No," the police chief said heavily, "she wasn't." He squeezed his fists together so hard the knuckles showed white. "When the bastard called, he told us that he'd buried her someplace where we'd never find her, and that her air would run out by midnight. Our only hope was to capture him alive, and force him to tell us where he'd hidden her." He looked grim. "Now he's dead, and our only hope is you."

Donata didn't feel any better about that than the man seated across the desk from her did. She pushed her hair back from her face and tried to gather up the scattered remains of her energy.

"You know, Chief, the reason that my job works is that most of the time the dead folks I talk to are eager to give me the information on who killed them. Your guy, on the other hand, isn't likely to be all that enthusiastic about sharing. He doesn't strike me as the type who'd be overwhelmed by remorse just because he's crossed over to the other side."

O'Malley nodded. "Yeah, I know. More likely to gloat than anything else. But the department psychic who usually handles finding missing persons is out of town, on some kind of damn retreat, and we haven't been able to find anyone who's able to make a connection with Lacey." He swallowed hard. "They think that she's probably unconscious. You're all we've got, Donata."

To her surprise, the older man reached out and took her hand, an unspoken plea written clearly across his face.

"I know it's a long shot, Donata," the chief said, "and it's late, and you're tired, and you don't like me much. But I'm asking you to try. Please."

What was she going to say? "No, go home, forget about your granddaughter"? Donata pushed her chair away from her desk and, along with the two photographs, picked up the small box of magical supplies she always kept handy. The chief followed her down the hallway to the room reserved for official magical workings, where she spent much of her daily grind immersed in the sacred rituals required to communicate with the recently dead. Somehow she didn't think that this one was going to be easy.

She glanced up in surprise as O'Malley followed her through the doorway. She wasn't used to an audience.

"Are you sure you want to be here for this?" she asked.

O'Malley nodded solemnly, suddenly respectful. "If it won't interfere with anything."

Donata shrugged. "Don't see why it should. Just keep back out of the way, and don't say anything, okay? It's important not to interrupt me."

"Got it." The chief settled his considerable bulk against a back wall, and watched her set up the quarter candles at north, south, east, and west, and the small altar table in the middle. Donata used incense, salt, and water to cleanse the space, then cast the circle, and she called the protective spirits of the elements to their quarters. First Air to the east, then Fire to the south, Water to the west, and finally Earth to the north. With their powers to protect her, along with her own focus and will, it was safe to call the spirit of the dead man back into the land of the living. As long as she stood within that circle, there was nothing the dead could do to harm her. That didn't make them fun to deal with, though.

She focused on the picture of the now-deceased Michael Franco, and invoked the aid of the gods in drawing him back to the earthly plane one more time. She spoke the words of the spell she used for these rituals, with a few minor alterations to fit the circumstances, and called the name of the dead man three times. For a few moments there was only silence, and the feeling of the air growing heavier in the space around her. She could sense the chief shifting restlessly behind her; she held up a hand, without looking, to remind him not to move.

The incense seemed to swirl and eddy in a nonexistent breeze, and then slowly it solidified into the image of a man. Transparent and wavery, it was nonetheless clearly recognizable as Franco, down to the sneer on his unhandsome face.

Unlike many of the recently dead, Franco showed no signs of confusion or fear. He clearly knew who and where he was. All his focus was on Donata; in his place outside the circle, the chief might as well have been invisible.

His voice came like a distant whisper, clear and quiet. "What do you want, Witch?"

"The child," replied Donata evenly. "Tell me where the child is, before it is too late."

"Or what," the shade mocked, "you're going to kill me? A little late for that, don't you think?"

Donata smiled at him. It wasn't a nice smile. She thought it was probably just as well for the chief's piece of mind that he couldn't see it from where he stood.

"Oh, no, Michael," she said. "I don't have to do that. All I have to do is make sure you can never be reborn."

The dead man looked at her, uncertainty a glimmer in his shadow eyes. "What are you talking about, Witch? I'm dead. That's it. If my old sainted mother was right, then I'm going to hell. If she was wrong, then I'm just plain dead. Either way, there's nothin' you can do to me. As far as I'm concerned, that little girl can rot where she lies."

Donata pulled in all the power that came with her gift—much more than she used in her day-to-day work, more than most other people ever saw. Drawing on her connection to the gods she believed in beyond any doubt, she let the dead man see her assurance as she ripped away his.

"Well, Michael, that's where you're wrong," she whispered. "There is no heaven, no hell. There is only the cycle of birth, growth, death, and rebirth. Into each lifetime we come with the ability to learn from our previous mistakes, and make ourselves anew—better, wiser, happier. Even you have that chance." She ignored the slight sounds coming from behind her, and focused all her energy on the dead man, seeing him mesmerized by her words.

"You're just sayin' that to get me to tell," he retorted in an agonized mumble. "I'm not fallin' for it."

She opened her arms wide, so that the light spilled out into the candlelit room. "Look," she said to him. "Look deep inside. You will see that your soul knows I speak the truth." She took a deep breath. "You have a chance at a new life. A dozen new lives. Unless I take that chance away from you."

She heard his gasp, remarkable since he could no longer take in air.

"You wouldn't," he said. "You couldn't. Nobody has that kind of power."

Donata gazed serenely through the curls of incense. "I can, actually. We have rules about doing no harm to the living. But you're not living, not anymore. And you're threatening the life of a little girl who never hurt anyone. So, yes, Michael, there is something I can do to you. And I will, unless you tell me how to find that little girl, right now."

The ghost gave a sob—of grief, frustration, anger, and hope. "Promise me you'll let me move on," he pleaded, his misshapen face further distorted by fear. "I want another chance! Promise me!"

Donata nodded slowly. "Tell me the truth, and I swear that you will get your chance. Now—tell me!"

"The old bus depot, on Fifth Street. It's scheduled for demolition tomorrow. She's in the janitor's closet in the basement. I drugged her, but she's okay. I swear!" She could see the ghost's demeanor change as he gave up his burden.

Donata stepped up to the altar and raised her arms above her head. "You are free to go, dead one. Go, and do better in your next life." Quietly and efficiently, she sent his spirit back to the limbo from which it had come, dismissed the quarters, and opened the circle.

Only then did she turn around and face the police chief, standing open-mouthed behind her.

"Don't you think you'd better go get your granddaughter?" she said, with a smile only a little twisted by tiredness and irony.

O'Malley pushed himself away from the wall and moved toward the door. Then he turned back to her.

"Thanks, Donata," he said. "For helping with my granddaughter. And for . . . the education. I'll try and make sure you have things a little easier around here."

"That would be nice, Chief," she replied. "And you're welcome. I'm glad it worked. I wasn't sure it would."

He turned to leave, then swiveled back to her one more time. She cocked an eyebrow at him, inviting the question she knew was coming.

"Can you really do that," he asked, "keep someone from moving on to their next life?" He tried, almost successfully, to keep the fear out of his voice.

The precinct Witch looked back at him and laughed. "No way. I'm a witch, not a god. But there's no rule that says you can't lie to a dead guy—at least not in the line of duty."

A. C. Fisher Aldag is a wife, mother, Pagan clergyperson, writer, environmental activist, and small-time farmer who lives in Michigan. She is one of the founders of Caer na Donia y Llew, a legal Pagan church with a Cymri (Welsh, Celtic) tradition. For the past several years, she has been researching historic systems of magick, Witchcraft, folklore, and Paganism from different regions in the United Kingdom.

Silkie's Diary

(as told to A. C. Fisher Aldag)

18th September, season of Alban Elfed

After Jacky broke up with me, I was terribly sad and Ms. Vonda the librarian said that I had symptoms of depression, so she gave me this Diary to write down my innermost thoughts. She said maybe that would help me feel better. So far it isn't working very well. For days afterward, I cried and cried, but of course there weren't any tears, since I can't shed water from my eyes like real people do. Maybe Sadie Dylan is right, and it's like I'm a werewolf or something.

But that's not why Jacky broke up with me. It was because he feels emasculated. I had to look that word up in the dictionary. It means the same as unmanned. I don't understand why, because

I gave him plenty of loving, but Jacky said it was because I was always doing stuff for myself, and he couldn't do anything for me. It's true that I rescued those sailors in the shipwreck, but I got a commendation award from the mayor, and everybody said they were proud of me, even Jacky. Maybe it was because of the pirates. Jacky was all set to save me, but I'd already beat up three of those scalawags, jumped overboard, and swam down the coast, all the way home by myself. Or maybe it's because he was so afraid during the storm last summer, when he broke his leg and I actually had to rescue *him*.

Ms. Vonda says that I am not responsible for any man feeling emasculated, and that I am a strong and empowered woman. She says I should write down all the things that I am good at, and all the people whom I love, and all the qualities which I like in myself. That will help show me my capabilities. I guess that it's worth a try.

Things I Am Good At:
- Swimming
- Fishing
- Taking tests at school
- Helping the animals at the shelter
- Magick

That was a really short list. The "people I love" list is much longer.

People I Love:
- Mam and Da, the Lady Mildred Llewellyn, and Captain Howard Morgan
- My biological mother, who is in the Summerland, may she swim free always
- Brothers and sisters: Moira, Brenda, Howie, Geoffrey (even though he fell asleep on watch and let me get captured by those stupid pirates), Glenna called Pudding, and last but not least, wee Laura called Lily
- All my nieces and nephews
- Denita Washington, my Best Friend Forever!

- Ms. Vonda Washington, the librarian
- Mrs. LeDux, my teacher at Southwestern Michigan ISD special education
- Rigoberto and Maricella, my kitty cats
- The real Rigoberto and Maricella, who are Jacky's parents
- Buck, the mule
- Joachim Hernandez, called Jacky. I wish I didn't love him anymore, but I still do.

Qualities I Like in Myself:
- I can hold my breath for 15 minutes
- I can use my sonar to find big schools of fish, which nobody else in our whole tribe can do
- I have good hair
- I can swim at 12 miles per hour
- I am patient with tourists, even the real snotty ones

To be fair, Ms. Vonda says that I can also write down all the things and people that I do *not* like, here in this Diary, which should help me to be able to deal with my feelings on a realistic level. This makes me feel horribly mean, because there is a whole lot of stuff that I don't like, much.

Things and People that I do NOT Like:
- Stupid nasty rotten stinky pirates
- Tourists who think they own the whole lake all for themselves
- Sukie Dylan and Sadie Dylan
- Wearing clothes
- Big growly dogs
- Guns
- Taking out the garbage
- The Lady Sheila Todd, what a grump! I asked her for a love potion and she almost bit my head off. She said it's the worst kind of evil magick and that it was enslaving someone, and

that I had no morals for even suggesting it. She is probably right, but she could have said it nicer.

- My brother Geoffrey. Yes I love him, but he is on my bad side right now.
- Whoever Jacky is dating. I'm sure she is a perfectly nice girl, BUT she has pretty yellow hair and blue eyes. I bet she cooks tacos for him, and does not eat live minnows. And I bet she doesn't *ever, ever* turn into a seal.

20th September

Tomorrow is our holiday, Alban Elfed, the autumnal equinox. We will bless all the boats and thank Manannon, the God of the lake, and Morgana, the Goddess of the waters, for their many blessings and bounty. Everyone will eat a big feast, and we'll have a harvest dance and play games. Mam and Da are happy because we caught tons of fish this year, and we took more tourists out sailing than ever before, despite the attack by those pirates.

The U.S. Coast Guard says there aren't any buccaneers on Lake Michigan, but they're wrong, because some pirates took me prisoner for almost a week. They also captured Jacky and my big brother Howie and the CEO of the Nagamini Corporation, but the Coast Guard said that it was an isolated incident and they didn't really take us seriously.

Ms. Vonda says that naturally I would experience depression after such a traumatic experience, and that if I want to talk to her, she will always be there. But when I started to tell her about getting chained in a flea-ridden brig, and there weren't any live fish so I had to eat rats, she looked so awfully shocked that I stopped talking. Or using sign language, that is, because I can't exactly talk, not speaking with my mouth, anyway. The rats weren't really so bad, they were plump because they'd been eating all the food those pirates spilled on the floor. The worst part was that the Coast Guard thought we were fibbing, and that Jacky broke up with me afterward.

Howie says that Jacky is a lame coward and a scurvy dog, and that I am well rid of him. But that doesn't make me feel any better. Tomorrow is a sacred holiday, so I'm supposed to be happy. So I will write another list, of all my favorite things, and that might help cheer me up.

My Very Favorite Things:
- Fish
- Other good things to eat—crawdads eggs blueberries snails frogs & minnows
- Sailing
- Dancing on the beach under a full moon
- Beltane
- Playing pool, even though I am not very good at it
- Fireworks
- Sunshine
- Kitties and doggies
- Mam telling me stories, also reading stories in books. But Mam's stories are best.
- Riding downhill on a sled really fast
- Finding agate stones on the beach
- Making love with Jacky

Ms. Vonda suggested that I write down some of the stories of our people, for posterity. Some day the children might want to read them. So here goes:

In the first days, all of the ice was melting, and so there was a great flood across the old country. Most of the human people drowned, but one little girl with shape-shifting powers turned herself into a seal person and survived. Her name was Murgen. She ate lots of delicious fish: trout, perch, and salmon. And eggs. And mussels fresh in the shell. She was an excellent swimmer. One day some evil men heard Murgen singing, and they were so impressed by her voice that they captured her in a net. They told her that she would have to convert to their religion, and they put her on display in a big glass tank for everyone to stare at. They made her sing just for them. She was terribly sad. I read in a book that Murgen became a saint. But Mam told me a different version of the story, about how Murgen escaped and returned to the sea. And she lived happily ever after.

Sadie Dylan said that Murgen wasn't really a real person, and so she had no soul. I wonder if that is true?

25th September, season of Samhain

Today I got a letter in the mail from Denita. She is at Spelman College in Atlanta, Georgia, learning how to be an attorney. I really miss my BFF, though I am glad that she has this wonderful opportunity. She will be able to help her people, who are African Americans, by making sure the law is enforced equally for everyone. Mam noticed that I was kind of mopey, so she asked if I would like to go away to college, too. "You are smart enough, truly," Mam said.

"Don't know if I can," I told her in sign language.

"Surely, if Denita can go off to school, then you could as well," Mam said. She means because Denita is in a wheelchair and needs help to get around. "You might like to further your studies. Look at the Auldwedd daughter, the first Cymri girl to attend an American college. You could do that, Silkie . . ."

Mam honestly means well, and she loves me, but she just doesn't understand. If I went away to a university, the first time I ate a live fish all the other students would probably freak out. Plus I'd be so far away from the lake and our tribe. So I signed, "Da needs me on the ship next spring to help fish for perch." I was thinking: Mam won't let me out of doing my chores—she never has before! It's the perfect excuse.

Both Mam and Da looked really sad, like they felt guilty because they thought that the Llewellyn Shipping Company was the reason I couldn't attend college. "You must do what is right for you, Silkie, and not let us stand in your way," Mam said.

But Mam and Da and the shipping business aren't preventing me from going to school; it's just that I wouldn't fit in with anyone there, because I am not a real person like them. Other people can accept a little difference, like Denita using a wheelchair, or the Auldwedd girl being from a Cymri tribe. But people won't accept a great, big, fat, glaring difference like mine. Which is probably why Jacky broke up with me.

27th September

Today I had a really close call. If I told Mam or Da or even my big brother Howie, they would likely all have a collective heart attack. They would probably never let me anywhere near the water again, and that would be like torture. So I will keep it to myself.

This afternoon, I jumped off the ship gunwale into the lake to hunt for salmon. They swim down the inland rivers to spawn offshore, which means lay eggs. So everyone is catching salmon, and salting away fish for the winter, or selling them to the frozen food companies. Anyway, I was swimming around using my sonar to find the salmons' location, when all of a sudden, something grabbed onto my tailfin. It was horribly scary. I thought for a minute that it was the lake monster, or the giant beaver called an *Afanc* from the old lands, or even that blighter Davy Jones, trying to drag me down to his locker with all the sailors who have drowned in Lake Michigan.

It wasn't a monster or anything. But it was just as deadly. It was an old piece of plastic sheeting, wrapped around some sunken logs, and I got myself all tangled up in it. It was just like the fishnet that caught Murgen. I can hold my breath longer than most people, but not forever. I didn't know what to do. If I transformed back into my human body, the water pressure might have crushed me into ooze. But in my animal form, I didn't have any fingers to unwind myself from the mess.

At first I panicked, and probably wasted half my oxygen struggling. Then it was like a peace came over me, and I became very calm. I saw mind-pictures, like my biological mother used to send to me when she was alive. She told me to trust in the Gods. My Mam says the same thing, and it's true. So I prayed, and then I got the image of turning my body over counterclockwise in the water. Finally, the horrid plastic came loose, and I swam for the surface.

We didn't catch any salmon, but I am incredibly grateful to Manannon and Morgana, so I'm making a sacrifice anyway, some fresh tender bass fillets and my specialest agate stone, the green one with white markings. Now I know that I am *not* clinically depressed, because I am very, *very* glad to still be alive.

The 30th, the last day of September

Hurrah, the Samhain holy day is only a month away! I CAN'T WAIT!!!

> *My Very Favorite Things about Samhain:*
> * Having a bonfire on the beach
> * Telling spooky stories
> * Big sister Brenda comes home to visit
> * Wearing a costume. This year I am being a Star Princess and I get to wear a sequined dress and high heels and I even have a gold tiara.
> * Carving pumpkins
> * TP-ing the Dylans' house

This year I will teach my nieces and nephews how to make wax paper leaf pictures. You heat up a clothes iron. You place some pretty colored autumn leaves flat on top of the wax paper. You put another sheet of wax paper on top of the leaves. With the hot iron, press down on the wax paper so that the wax sticks together, preserving the leaves between the sheets of paper. It looks like stained glass. You can hang leaf pictures up in your windows.

Last year for trick-or-treat, Da gave me a whole lake sturgeon all my very own that I didn't have to share with anybody. It must have weighed thirty-five pounds. I couldn't even eat the whole thing. It would have made me as sick as Geoffrey got that one year, when he gulped down all the Halloween candy in his entire goody bag before the sun came up in the morning. He had a tummy ache for nearly a week.

2nd October

Yesterday I was in the library, and found a new book on Celtic legends. It was a modern version of some older stories of my people. Well, I always knew where I came from, because Mam told me about my adoption, around the same time as she talked about sperms, eggs, mating, and all of that stuff. I am a Silkie, also called a Selchie, Murdhuacha, Kelpie, Rón, or Merrow. My people lived in the waters around the old country, and when the humans sailed here to America, the Selchie folk swam across the ocean along with them. We are supposed to protect the sailors, rescue human people from shipwrecks, and lead them to big schools of tasty fish. But my biological mother got killed by a gun, and so I came to live with the Llewellyn tribe.

Only this story that I read was very sad. It was about a human guy who fell in love with a Selchie lady when he saw her sunning herself on the beach. To capture her, he stole her sealskin cloak so that she couldn't transform and swim away. He married her and they had three children. Yet she always missed the ocean and her own people, so she was terribly lonely. One day the man was out fishing, and the Selchie wife found her seal-fur cape hidden in the rafters of the cottage, so she grabbed it. She took her three kids down to the water, put on her sealskin cloak, and jumped into the ocean to escape with her children. Only they were half human, and they all three drowned.

I was so upset by this story that the book fell out of my hands. Ms. Vonda noticed, and came over to pick it up. She instantly knew what I had been reading. Her mouth was moving but I wasn't watching her lips. Because I was wondering if everyone else knew about this legend but just hadn't told me. Ms. Vonda gave me a long, warm hug and took my face in her hands, so that I would look at her and know what she was saying.

"You've read *Stuart Little*, right?" I nodded, wondering what that had to do with anything. "Well, you remember the part where his parents changed the words to 'The Night Before Christmas,' so that it didn't contain the word 'mouse'? That was because they didn't want Stuart to hear a negative stereotype about a mouse and feel maligned. It's the same reason I didn't want Denita to read *Little Black Sambo*."

I understand why Mam, Da, and Ms. Vonda wished to protect me from an unpleasant stereotype of the Selchie people. But I still have to wonder if some of those legends are really true. I do not cry with real tears. I have rescued nine people from drowning. I help sailors to find schools of fish. And I turn into a seal. All of that stuff is written about in the story books. But I don't need a seal-fur cloak to transform, and I can't talk, let alone sing. So maybe not everything that is written about us is true.

I wonder if I have a soul?

7th October

This weekend is the Harvest Festival in our town. Most of the tourists go back home after Sunday. It is a very big deal to Maricella and Rigoberto Hernandez, because they are farmers, and they will sell a lot of their crops during the festival. Da and Howie will take people out sailing on the tall ships, not for a long fishing trip or up to the Indian casino or to Sleeping Bear Dunes, because it's too cold for most everyone to go swimming. We'll just sail up and down the channel and around the harbor for half an hour at a time. Buck the mule will be grumbling because he has to haul the ships up the river, and he hates to work. But I love every minute. Soon we'll have to put the ships in dry dock and we won't be able to go sailing all winter long. Lake Michigan ices over and the season comes to a close.

The Coolest Things about Morgana Bay, Michigan:
- Lake Michigan
- Climbing up inside the lighthouse to look at the view
- Sailing with the Llewellyn Shipping Company
- The library
- Watching the drawbridge go up and down

- The Harvest Festival
- Riding down the toboggan runs
- Going camping in the forest, where there are real coyotes. Not everybody knows that there are coyotes living in Michigan.
- Playing pool at the Docksider Tavern

Maybe I will see Jacky at the autumn harvest picnic. He doesn't work on our ship anymore, since he took a job minding the lighthouse. After that furious storm last summer, he might have lost his sea legs. That's what some of the crewmen said. His leg did get broken, but he's all better now, not even walking with a cane. Maybe Jacky will realize how much he misses sailing with the Llewellyn Shipping Company.

Maybe he misses me, too.

12th October

I! Saw! Jacky! He was at the seafarers' picnic on our private beach. Most everybody who works in shipping turned up. Jacky even said hi to me, but he was being awfully distant. So I mostly hung out with my family. Lily and a bunch of the other kids were tending the cauldron full of seafood chowder. Mam said that it reminded her of the magick kettles in the Celtic legends, which never ran out of food. Da told us that some of those cauldrons could resurrect fallen warriors. The spell would not work in the presence of a coward.

Some of the sailors began talking about things that frightened them. Many of them said drowning. Others said the lake monster. Most everybody said they were scared of pirates. Selwyn Jones is afraid of the giant beaver, the Afanc. "'Tis because I have a wooden leg, and beavers like to chew wood," he explained. "But we must face our fears, so that we aren't branded cowards." Maybe his advice was directed at Jacky, who hasn't set foot on the deck of a ship since the storm. Right after Selwyn said that, Jacky made an excuse to leave.

Which means he didn't hear what else Selwyn had to say, which was especially interesting to me. "Speakin' o' beavers, Silkie m' lass, I heard tell as there's some o' your people up around Beaver Island." Selwyn made a quick warding gesture that he thought I didn't see, but I was so excited by his news that I wasn't offended. "You know. The mer-folk."

"*We* are Silkie's people," said Da, looking as if he'd bit into something rotten. Selwyn actually took a step back. He knows Da carries a big cutlass.

Mam was dismayed, but she quickly covered it with a smile. "Aye, that we are, but Silkie might wish to visit with her first family sometime."

So right then, I knew my parents' greatest fear. They were afraid that I would leave them forever. Not like big sister Brenda going to Chicago, because she returns twice a year, on Samhain and Beltane. Not like going away to college, because I'd be home for the summer. No, Mam and Da are afraid that I will swim away from them, and never come back.

"Mayhap we will take a little sail up the coast, before the season is over," Da said, looking right at me, so that I could plainly read his lips. "See if we can find Silkie's other kinfolk." He still acted like he was in pain. But I knew Da wasn't the kind of person who would hide away anyone's sealskin cloak.

Things That I Am Afraid of:
- Dogs that bite
- Guns
- Pirates
- Drowning
- Monsters
- Being all by myself, alone, forever

15th October

My little sister Lily has been helping me pack for my sailing trip to Beaver Island. "It used to be a pirate hideout," she said. "I read about it in Michigan History class. Maybe you'll find their buried treasure."

"If you found a pirate hoard, how would you spend it?" I asked her.

Her little face scrunched up with thought. "I'd buy twenty yards of taffeta fabric, and chocolate, and hair ribbons, and a kite. And purple nail polish. And the house needs a new roof, Da said. And the ships could all use new mainsails . . . " She glanced at me. "And I would give a million dollars to the animal shelter, so you'd never have to put down any more of the kitties and doggies." This made me smile, because Lily is so kindly and good.

Most of the time. Lily held up my new orange string bikini and said, "If you wear *this* out in public, Da will have heart failure! I'm *telling!*"

Da always says that I have to wear clothes so the men don't get bad ideas in their heads and try to take advantage of me. He says that bikinis do not qualify as real clothing. But I was wearing clothes when those pirates took me prisoner, and it didn't seem to make any difference. They ravished me anyway.

"Must have clothes that I can wear in my seal form," I told my father in sign language. "Otherwise when I turn back into a human, I will be butt-naked."

Believe it or not, Da actually thought my bikini was a good idea. "You will need to wear *some*thing," he said.

Mam had an even better idea. She gave me an iron talisman in the shape of a pentagram, a pretty star with five points. "'Tis called the Witches' Shield," she told me. We unhooked one of the bikini strings, put the good-luck charm on it, and refastened the string. Mam didn't say why she did this, but I knew anyway. Magickal folks are very often afraid of iron. If any spirit tried to cause mischief, or even harm me, the pentagram talisman would keep me safe.

"You're coming back home, aren't you, Silkie?" asked Lily anxiously.

"Will be home in time for Samhain," I promised.

17th October

I love, love, *love* to go sailing! It's like the Native American Indian story about the boy who rides on the back of the giant turtle. I love to stand up in the crow's nest with the wind in my face, where I can see for a hundred miles. I love to dive off the gunwale into the water. Even doing the chores isn't so bad. We have to swab the decks, polish the wooden brightwork, shine the brass, unfurl the sails, position them to catch the winds, crank the anchor chain up and down, caulk everyplace that might develop a leak, and wash out the live-safe so it doesn't smell of dead fish. Today there weren't any tourists aboard so we didn't have to cook their meals, make their beds, answer questions, or hold their hands so they don't fall overboard. It's only Da, Howie, me, and four crewmen.

Of course we couldn't just take a pleasure trip, because time is money. We also had to catch fish. This involves unfolding the nets, putting weights on one side and glass floats on the other, and lowering the nets into the water just so, so that they don't get tangled. We have to pull them back up, throw the little fishes overboard, and put the edible fish into the live-safe. We have to ice them down, so they don't spoil. This is how we make our living.

Our vessel, the *Annie*, is the only tall ship on the water today. In fact, we are the only folk out on the lake, except for this huge, gy-normous cabin cruiser which passed us going about sixty. They were throttling so fast, their wake made us bob in the water. I waved at the people on her deck, but they didn't wave back. Darn snotty tourists. As they stormed by, I could clearly see the name "Pleazure Cruize, Chicago" painted in red on the fiberglass stern. "They think they own the whole bloody lake," Howie grumbled.

But I'm not going to pay one more minute of attention to them. Because Da says if the fair wind keeps up, we should make Beaver Island by tomorrow morning. And then I will see my first family again!

17th October (later)

I just had the scariest, most awfullest thing happen to me *ever*. Worse than being ravished by pirates. Worse than nearly drowning. Almost even worse than my biological mother dying. This was horrible.

We were somewhere between Manistee and Big Sable. There aren't a lot of human people's homes nearby; it's mostly forests and stony beaches. I was up in the crow's nest, acting as lookout and sniffing for fish. All of a sudden, the *Annie* turns about and starts heading for shore. But there isn't any port there, not even a channel. In fact, the coastline is terribly rocky. There are boulders scattered around like a giant's pool balls. Jagged granite poking out of the water. Rocks like that can really cause serious damage to a ship. So I wonder, what the heck is Da doing?

I stomp my foot hard on the floor of the crow's nest, which is my signal for the crew to pay attention. Nobody even glances up. I can see the men on deck, and they're all standing on the port side, staring out at the water. I've got really good eyesight, but I don't see anything there. Yet all of the crew seem fascinated. Even Da, who has abandoned the wheel, and is standing with everybody else, shading his eyes and gazing over the horizon. Meanwhile the ship is crossways to the wind, slowly running for the shore.

I make my noise to get them to look at me. Howie always says that I sound just like a barking dog; I don't know, because I can't hear myself. Yet my noise has never failed to get someone to look up, so I can sign to them. But nobody is looking. Nobody notices me at all.

I know something is really wrong. Quickly, I slide down the rope rigging and land on the deck. I race to the gunwale and peer across the lake, but there's just water. Nothing else. I nudge Howie in the ribs, hard, but he doesn't look at me. He is just staring out at the empty lake. His mouth is hanging open. I snap my fingers in front of his face. He doesn't budge. If I didn't know any better, I'd swear that he's asleep.

Everyone else acts the same. It's as if they are in a trance. Including Da, who is always the most practical, levelheaded man on the planet. My father is gazing over the water as if he is hypnotized. I shake him, bark at him, wave my hands, and he is still completely out of it. His eyes are wide open and staring. And in a minute, the ship is going to run aground.

I know what I have to do. I gallop to the stern, leap to the windlass, and slam both my hands down on the lever. It trembles for a minute, then releases the anchor chain. You are supposed to crank the windlass slowly and carefully, because the chain can rip things up, like the wooden side of the ship. If the chain breaks, it can go crack like a whip, and maybe injure somebody. Fortunately, the windlass spins like it's supposed to, and the chain flows smoothly down without doing anything worse than tearing some splinters out of the wood. When the anchor hits bottom, the ship comes to an abrupt halt, throwing some of the men off their feet. For a minute, everything shudders, and the *Annie* pitches and rolls in the water, because nobody has furled any of her sails. This is kinda bad for her, but running aground on those rocks would be way worse.

I know good and well if my father was conscious, he would be hollering at me about casting the anchor like that. But Da, and everyone else, are still staring, captivated by the water. Or whatever is out there.

I look again. At first I don't see anything. Just a little rocky shoal, like a sandbar that is only visible at low tide. It is covered with seaweed and garbage and stinky dead fish. If we had kept sailing north-northeast, in a few minutes the *Annie* would have sailed between this mini-island and the shore, and she would have gotten stuck. Then oh, would Da be awfully mad at me, because we'd have to attach ropes to the lifeboats, and row hard to pull her out of there, and it would likely damage her hull. Maybe even break off the rudder. Which would cost me my allowance until I was fifty. So even though there was a risk involved in casting the anchor, it's a good thing I did!

I don't have time to sit and congratulate myself, though. Because that's when this sailor called Taylor Dylan jumps overboard, wearing all his clothes. He begins to swim, desperately thrashing toward that shoal, as if he is starving and the little island is covered with tasty fresh salmon and trout.

What the blazes is he doing?

Then I see the broken shards of fiberglass, scattered over the rocky shoal with all the other garbage. One of the larger pieces has red letters on it. Not much is left. Just "eazure Cruize, Chi." But I realize that is what little remains of the fancy cabin cruiser that passed us this morning. The tourists who didn't wave back are now shipwrecked.

Although they were a bit rude, I hadn't wished for anything bad to happen to them. And though I don't much care for the Dylan family, I sure didn't want horrible things to befall any of them, either. Not like what happened to Taylor.

The seaweed moves. Something large splashes into the water. And suddenly, Taylor Dylan goes under. He's just—gone. Vanished. Only a trail of bubbles marks where he went down.

Since I am a Selchie, it is my duty to rescue human sailors from drowning. I begin to strip off my blouse. Clothes get tangled in my flippers when I transform. This makes it difficult to swim. But before I can change into my seal body, another crewman begins to clamber over the gunwale. It is Selwyn Jones, the old guy with the wooden leg, who'd told me that he'd seen my people at Beaver Island. Good old Selwyn, who was so frightened of the Afanc. He'd been the one who'd prompted this trip. And now he's fixing to get himself drowned, or eaten alive by whatever horrid creature is out there.

I grab Selwyn by the back of his collar. The fabric tears in my hands. As Selwyn lifts his wooden leg over the gunwale, I catch hold of it. Luckily his leg is strapped on real tight. Yanking hard, I tug Selwyn backward onto the deck. He falls flat on his butt, yet I'm sure that didn't hurt him. The old salt actually looks disappointed, as if I was preventing him from attending the best, *best* vacation ever. He even takes a swing at me. That is how bad Selwyn wants to jump overboard, and swim toward whatever monstrous fate awaits him on that little shoal.

Then I hear it. I actually, truly, really *hear* it. Me, who has never heard anything in my whole life.

Intellectually, I realize that human people enjoy music. It's what makes them dance. I know that songbirds make pretty sounds. People create joyful music when they laugh, and when they make love, and when they sing. Although I have never heard any sound before. Not even really loud noises, like the bang of a gun, or fireworks, or the ambulance siren.

This sound isn't at all like those frightening things . . . it's more like the music that humans adore so much. It resembles sweet poetry combined with the wind in the trees and the lapping of waves on a warm, sandy beach. I take a step closer to the railing. Along with Da, Howie, and the rest of the crew. They hear it too! And I can hear! I'd never even heard the fire truck siren, telling me to get out of the road . . .

Siren.

Siren!

That is *not* a pile of seaweed clumped there on the shoal. It is a person. She is part human, part sea-creature, but she does not have a silvery fish tail, like the mermaids of fairy stories. She doesn't resemble the lovely picture of Murgen in the library book. This person is ugly, pinch-faced, and sickly green. Her long, scaly tail resembles a water snake. Her wide mouth is overflowing with sharp, pointy teeth, like a biting dog. I can smell her, too: reeking of dead meat. She is a siren, like in the Greek myths. Or the evil mer-folk of Celtic legend. Melusine. The death goddess of the lake.

And she is hungry.

Her voice fills my head with subliminal enchantment. Out of the corner of my eye, I can see my brother Howie approaching the gunwale, shuffling like a wind-up doll, his eyes blank and staring. He's planning to jump overboard, just like Taylor Dylan, and swim to the shoal, and very likely get dragged underwater to drown. Melusine probably has a whole refrigerator down there, filled with the corpses of tourists and Cymri sailors. Her voice is lovely, compelling, more delightful than any birdsong. Howie leans over the gunwale, ensorcelled by the beautiful music.

Clutching both hands on his shoulders, I haul my brother backward with all of my strength. He whirls around, his face twisted in fury. Howie has never looked angrier, not even when Geoffrey fell asleep on watch. He raises one fist to smack me across the face.

"I will set them free," purrs Melusine's voice in my head. "I will let them all go, if you will come to me, Silkie Llewellyn."

My claws dig into my brother's shoulder muscles, drawing blood. His fist strikes the side of my head, a glancing blow, but it still smarts. It hurts my feelings even worse. Howie is usually pretty nice, but now he does not seem like himself. He resembles the methamphetamine addicts uptown. When they are in need of their drug, they look depraved. It pains me to see my brother acting like that.

Then I spot an abandoned tool, lying on the deck where a crewman had dropped it. It was as though the Goddess Morgana had given me a wonderful idea. I scoop up the caulking gun in one hand, and hold onto Howie with the other. I jam the business end of the caulk tube into his left ear. Hoping that I am not causing permanent damage, not deafening my poor brother, I squeeze the caulking gun's trigger.

Howie's ear fills up with thick, brown, sticky goo. I push the end of the caulk tube into his other ear. He smacks me another good one on my cheekbone. It hurts something fierce. Once again, I pull the caulking gun's trigger, filling my brother's right ear with caulk. He can no longer hear Melusine's siren song. Howie looks rather stunned, like he has just awakened from an unpleasant dream to find himself in a strange location. His mouth moves. "What are you doing?" he asks, his expression as puzzled as if he'd discovered me juggling cannon balls.

I have no time to answer. Another sailor, a guy named Marvin Starkweather, has jumped into the water and is flailing away toward the shoal. Instantly, Melusine slithers over the rocks and slips into the lake. She jerks Marvin under the surface, like a snapping turtle does with a baby duckling. And I'm certain that his fate is similar.

"A siren," says Howie in astonishment. "*Y morwen ddhu.*" I nod vigorously and show him the caulk gun. My fingers spell out "plug" and I point to the side of my head, where my ears would be, if I had any. My brother understands. Plug their ears. Fill the crew's ear canals with caulk, so they cannot hear the siren song.

Howie grabs our own father first, wrestling Da away from the railing. I quickly fill up my father's ears with the gooey caulk. Then we catch the other two crewmen, and deafen them each in the same way. It's nearly a miss with the last guy. Da snags his belt, just as he is plunging over the side. It takes some effort to heave him back onto the deck, he wants so badly to go to Melusine.

Yet the siren has another weapon. She can create mind-pictures inside my head. Just like my biological mother used to show me lovely stories about fairies and water pixies and shining, magickal seas. And my dear Mam, Mildred Llewellyn, who is a priestess, uses her mental power to warn me about danger by flashing an image of fire, or a moving car, or anything else that might cause me harm. Of course, Mam's mental pictures are somewhat weak, when compared to the capabilities of a Selchie. My bio-mother's visual images were much stronger, more vivid. But Melusine is a supernatural being, and her mental projections are stunning in their cruel beauty.

I see myself standing proudly at the wheel of a fair bonny tall ship. I am the captain. The crew rushes to do my bidding. Jacky is there. He smells manly, and his face is chiseled and handsome, like an Aztec warrior. Jacky embraces me, caressing my hair, proclaiming his eternal love . . .

I am in a huge mansion overlooking the lake. There are many kitties and doggies. They are all mine. They are well-fed and happy. Somebody else has to clean up after them, for I will be going for a long, slippery ride down the toboggan run . . .

The lake is warm, and the lithe, furry bodies of other seal people brush against me. We propel ourselves through the clear water with our muscular tailfins. We are swimming in pursuit of a big school of trout. I chew the fresh, delicious fish. We will eat our fill, and then we will land on the beach and curl up together in the warm sand, under the bright August sun . . .

"Whatever your heart desires," Melusine promises. "Come to me."

"You cannot have the crewmen of the *Annie*," I retort.

"I do not need any more of them," the siren laughs. She is picking at her long, sharp canine teeth with a white sliver. With a shock of nausea, I realize that her toothpick is made of bone. Very likely a human bone, which recently belonged to Marvin Starkweather or Taylor Dylan. Marvin just got married this past June. And Taylor had four children to support. He was somebody's Da, and his children would never see him again.

This makes me really mad.

"Okay, Melusine, sure, I will be happy to come to you," I project to the siren. I begin stripping off my trousers. Out of modesty, I'm still wearing my orange bikini. "Just a moment. I will be right there."

My father looks frightened, dismayed. He can tell, probably by my expression, that I am intending to go start some trouble. "Silkie, NO!" says his mouth, but it is too late. His grasping hands close on empty air as I dive overboard. Rapidly, I swim through the turbulent, gravelly waters toward the shoal where the morwen, the *demon*, awaits me.

I do not transform into my seal-body. Even in human form, I can swim faster than anybody else in my tribe. I ease through the water like a fish. Melusine sits on her deadly island, her eely tail wrapped around a boulder, mocking me. She believes that I'll try to kill her, and she is aware that I carry no weapon. No cutlass, no harpoon, no arrow. Not even a bread knife. And she knows that I cannot speak, let alone sing any magickal spell.

The island stinks of carrion. Bloated fish and lumps of unidentifiable flesh litter the rocky beach. Melusine laughs at me. She is great and mighty, and it does not occur to her to be afraid. All she sees before her is a teenage girl with webbed fingers, smaller and weaker than she. She probably thinks that I will be a tasty snack.

"Here I am, Melusine," I say in her mind, and rip off the top of my orange bikini. The pentagram is still attached to the strings, the iron talisman sparkling brightly with power. I thrust the Witches' Shield into the ugly face of the morwen. My fingers rapidly form the signs for the magick words:

I banish you be gone.

The siren recoils. Her muddy eyes register confusion. She slithers backward. I pursue her, brandishing my sacred charm like a pirate's lethal sword. Energy throbs down my arm. The pentagram sigil blazes, a fiery star of brilliant cleansing magick.

Lashing her snaky tail in vehement fury, Melusine plunges into the dark water of Lake Michigan, disappearing as if she had never been.

18th October

We sailed all around Beaver Island. There were not any seal people anywhere. I jumped out of the ship and swam up and down the coastline, looking and sniffing for them. There was no sign that the Selchie folk had ever visited these beaches. No tracks, no fish bones, no traces of them at all. If my first family was ever there, now they are gone away again.

25th October

I let Ms. Vonda read my Diary, about the voyage to find my people and the battle with Melusine. Ms. Vonda is not only my best friend's mother, but she's my good friend, too. Most people outside our tribe don't believe in magick. They think it's not real. But Ms. Vonda believes.

After she finished reading my Diary, Ms. Vonda the librarian sat quietly for a long time, as if she was meditating. Her features looked sad. "I'm sorry that you didn't find your family," she told me.

"That's okay," I signed in reply. "Will see them again someday. Maybe in the waters of the Otherworld."

"I hope that you reunite with them long before then."

"Still have my Cymri family, the Llewellyn," I signed. "And so I am blessed."

"Yes, you are," Ms. Vonda agreed. "Tell me, Silkie. Weren't you terribly frightened when you fought that monster?"

"No," I responded truthfully. "I was too mad."

"I would've needed to change my drawers," she confided, and we both laughed. "You know why Melusine wanted you, right?"

"Yeah, for dessert."

Ms. Vonda looked serious. "I think that she intended to capture your soul."

"My soul?" I was astounded. Didn't she know? "I don't have a soul."

"Oh, honey, of course you do!" Ms. Vonda put her soft, motherly arms around me. "You have the most precious, beautiful soul."

"But I don't cry real tears. I transform into a seal, like a werewolf or something. And I eat live fish. Sukie Dylan says that anyone who eats the bait while it's still squirming must not have a soul."

Ms. Vonda stood up and began to rummage through the library books on the shelves. She pulled out the volume of Celtic fairy tales, the ancient legends of our people. "Read this, right here," she pointed.

So I read about the evil *morwen ddhu*, and how they lured sailing ships onto the rocks with their sweet, treacherous music. And how they devoured human flesh, and sustained their magickal powers by consuming the souls of their victims.

"Silkie, you have a truly beautiful soul," Ms. Vonda assured me again. "So many people love you. And you love so deeply. How could you feel such profound love for others if you didn't have a soul?"

"What about Jacky?" I countered. "He doesn't love me, not anymore."

"I think Jacky missed the boat," Ms. Vonda said, handing my Diary back to me. "Now I have a suggestion. You really should write one more list."

People Whose Lives I Have Enriched (with help from Ms. Vonda):
- Mam and Da, the Lady Mildred Llewellyn, and Captain Howard Morgan
- Ms. Vonda Washington
- All of my brothers and sisters, nieces and nephews. Even Howie, though he is still kinda mad at me because he can't get the caulk out of his ears.
- Denita Washington, my Best Friend Forever!
- My kitty cats
- All of the kitties and doggies at the animal shelter
- The nine sailors that I rescued from drowning
- Jacky Hernandez, whom I rescued, too
- All of the people who didn't get captured by the pirates that I beat up
- The crewmen of the *Annie*, whom I saved from being eaten by the Siren
- And all of their children and grandchildren

April was born in Hawaii in 1967, and in her childhood wrote stories about good witches and goddesses. Always she knew she wanted to be a writer. She discovered Wicca some time between 8:00 and 8:30 p.m. on October 31, 1981, while reading a newspaper article about the religion. Subsequent study made her certain that this was her spiritual path. She was initiated in 1990, and chose her pen-and spirit-name based on the month of her birth. In 1992 she moved to Arizona, and became active in the Tucson Area Wiccan-Pagan Network (TAWN). She is the author of various articles and poems in Witchvox, Tapestry *(TAWN's newsletter), and other publications. "A Valkyrie Among Jews" is her first published work of fiction.*

A Valkyrie Among Jews

BY April

"Hi, Mrs. Katz!" Laura Fox said with a smile, steering her housekeeping cart around the old woman. "Going to services?" It was a Saturday late in April 1996, at the Handmaker Jewish Home for the Aged.

Ruth Katz answered in a bland but high-pitched tone. "I'm going to services. You're working today?"

"Yes, I'm being a *Shabbos goy* today!" Laura joked. She couldn't help liking Mrs. Katz, despite the resident's irritability. There was a certain resolve about her, a firmness underlying her feebleness. At each step, she planted her walker before her with rigid determination, and soon arrived at the carpeted chapel.

One end of the chapel served as a church for the Christian residents on Sundays (for the institution welcomed Jews and non-Jews alike). But today—at the other end, where the eternal light shone beside the Ark of the Torah—it was in use as a synagogue.

So pious was Ruth Katz, with the white circle of Sabbath lace on her head. No doubt, Laura reflected, she would despise me—maybe recoil in horror—if she knew what I really am.

Then Laura saw her boss, Gladys Thompson, affectionately staring at her. "So, Laura, tell us Gentiles: exactly what is a *Shabbos goy?*"

"A Gentile servant who works around the house for a Jewish family, when they are celebrating the Sabbath."

"Ah!" exclaimed Ms. Thompson in delight. Then she left Laura at the doors of the main dining room, just across a hallway from the chapel.

It was a relief when the doors had closed behind her, shutting out the synagogue.

This dining room—large enough to seat a Wagnerian orchestra—was lit only by sunlight from the high windows, the electric lights having been turned off after breakfast, and yet somehow Laura preferred to work in this dimness. She drove her wide dust-mop before her, gathering up crumbs, bits of egg, and blobs of gelatin or fruit. Then she wrung out her wet mop to remove every spot from the floor . . . attempting to distract her troubled mind by reveling in the freedom this job had bestowed.

Why, everyone had asked, would a young woman with a master's degree in English, who had left her home state of Hawaii to pursue doctoral study in medieval English at the University of Arizona, suddenly leave her program to take a job mopping floors and cleaning toilets?

Why indeed! The PhD program had been a stifling nightmare, keeping her from the reading and writing she truly wanted to do. Her nights had become sleepless, her days tearful; the silent screams of an approaching nervous breakdown rang louder and louder in her head. And so, at twenty-nine, she gathered up all her education, stuffed it into her background like so many extra rolls of toilet paper in her housekeeping cart, and took a job where the workings of her feverish mind could run their merry course, balanced out by the Zen-like meditation of simple physical labor.

There were also hidden gems: stories in this institution, which was a world unto itself. Laura had been employed here nearly two months; and each day, as she drew her cleaning rag around a hundred shelves of memorabilia, she felt like an archeologist removing layers of dust in the newly discovered temple of some ancient culture.

Jacob Horowitz was the most fascinating resident. She tended to postpone entering his room, for poor Mr. Horowitz was quite mad. Once he'd nearly hurt her, flailing his arms from where he sat in his reclining chair, and shouting in obvious terror and anger, "Get out of here, you son of a bitch!" On other days, however, the ninety-five-year-old man could be very docile, sad, and even sweet-tempered. And in his disturbed mutterings, he often appeared to recall the story the nurses had told Laura: of his boyhood flight, at his grandmother's side, from pogroms in Eastern Europe.

This was where epic poetry lay. Here, and no longer in the familiar halls of academia.

The Passover Seder she had recently attended, at her friend Nell Steiner's house, had been the most meaningful in her life, but also the most painful. More than ever, the traditional foods—bitter herbs symbolizing the Israelites' affliction in Egypt, salt water of slavery's tears, and sweet *haroset* symbolizing freedom—had had personal significance, of her own escape from bondage. Yet they had also been a tie of bondage: to a people, a religion, a heritage from which she had long been estranged, but which kept pulling her back, like a rope around her waist that could not be loosened.

Even now, as she heard the voices in the synagogue, it tugged at her. She knew she would plan her rounds so as to be back in the vicinity at the end of the service, when the congregants sang "Ain Kelohenu." Just at the thought of it, she began to sing softly as she mopped:

Ain kelohenu, ain kadonenu,
Ain k'malkenu, ain k'moshi'enu.

"There is none like our God; there is none like our Lord; there is none like our King; there is none like our Deliverer." The words came back to her, as if the Hebrew school she had attended from age seven to age twelve had been just the day before.

But since then, she had heeded the call of a different song.

· · ·

It was the song of the breezes, the oceans, the moon; it was the echo of ancient poetry, calling her back to the days when an inno-cent, lusty God played his reed-pipe through the forest, and a Great Mother Goddess stood at the cradle of an infant humanity. It was old—older than the Torah, older even than Stonehenge—yet also new: as modern as feminism, as the computer age, as the Pagan revival that Laura had joined. At eighteen, she formed a Witchcraft coven with a few friends. And at twenty-two, she stood bound and blindfolded in a magic circle consecrated with salt water and burn-ing incense, where a high priest led her through a symbolic ordeal, anointed her with fragrant oil, then removed the bonds and blind-fold, and gave her the title of "Priestess and Witch."

She was now a first-degree initiate in the religion called Wicca—an Old English word for a magic-worker.

Her Old English dictionary contained another word for "witch": *wælcyrie*. In some Norse-Germanic stories, these warrior-maidens were mortals who practiced magic; in others they were immortals who rode airborne horses and carried off slain heroes to resurrect in Valhalla. In Richard Wagner's operatic tetralogy *The Ring of the Nibelung*, Valkyries were daughters of Wotan, ruler of the Gods; and if any man saw one of them on the battlefield, he knew he was destined to die.

Laura had spent four evenings, in her Tucson apartment, transported to the realms of myth and heroism by videotapes of the *Ring*. At her side was her boyfriend, Tom Reilly, whom she had met in the Pagan club at the university.

Tom was the handsomest young man she had ever dated: he had light brown hair, blue eyes, an eager smile, and a cute, hooked nose that might have looked Jewish—although his Irish-English family was not. In addition to Paganism, he shared her interest in Humanism.

Actually, he boasted membership in a dizzying number of religions and creeds—five major ones and at least seventeen minor ones. "My five major religions are Wicca, Discordianism, the Church of the SubGenius, *Star Trek*, and Monty Python." He had introduced her, on their second date, to Discordianism—the worship of Eris, goddess of chaos and confusion—and to the Church of the SubGenius, which promised its adherents "eternal salvation or triple your money back."

"Let's see," Laura replied, "if I were to name my five, they would be Wicca, Discordianism, Humanism, Mozart, and Wagner."

After watching the *Ring*, Tom would often whistle its most famous piece, "The Ride of the Valkyries." And the couple sometimes called each other "Brünnhilde" and "Siegfried," after the Valkyrie-heroine and the dauntless hero who marries her.

Tom also went with Laura to Nell Steiner's house for Passover, his first Seder. With delight he donned a *kippah*—the little skullcap, which suited him well!—and read portions of the liturgical Haggadah with all his characteristic vivacity, as if it were one of his favorite Monty Python routines. Afterward he raved, "I've had a wonderful time! I'm adding Judaism to my religions!"

His real reason, Laura suspected, was apparent the next time they went to the supermarket. Tom went straight to the kosher foods section.

"Oh, Thomas!" Laura lamented. "After all the wonderfully rebellious, anti-monotheistic things we've been through together—the Pagan club, the Humanist club, *The Ring of the Nibelung*—you go *Jewish* on me!"

"That's right, I'm Jewish now!" said Siegfried the Fearless, as he loaded two jars of gefilte fish into the shopping cart.

He did not comprehend her pain; he could not. He had never been raised in any religion save a vague, nominal version of Christianity. He did not know what it meant to leave a tribe.

. . .

She dunked her mop into the bucket on her cart, to scrub the next lane of the dining room. *It was a rape*, she thought, *being raised in Judaism. Or in any religion where you're taught you must never stray from the fold.*

At first it was a seduction. Her memories of Hebrew school were a soft tapestry in which lessons in the language and history entwined with the glittering threads of songs and dances, of jam-filled cookies and apples dipped in honey. Family and friends remarked on what a religious child she was.

Her teachers portrayed Judaism as the fount of all wisdom and kindness . . . in contrast to the lawless ancient religions with their baby-burning rituals. The word *pagan*, when her teachers uttered it, was spat out, like a piece of worm-infested pork.

But here and there she had a question the instructors had trouble answering.

"Why was it justifiable to kill people for working on the Sabbath in Moses's days, when we don't kill people for that today?"

"Well . . . *back then* it was necessary to take harsh measures in order to keep the new religion going, and to keep people from falling back into idol worship."

As an adult, Laura knew that the stories about "pagan" evil—especially infant sacrifice—were fabricated, or at least exaggerated. Pagan peoples had certainly committed their share of wrongs, but no more than the ancient Hebrews.

Humanist literature had revealed the sordid details of the Bible. She recalled how, in Numbers 31:17–18, Moses told the Israelites to treat their enemies: "Now therefore kill every male among the little ones, and kill every woman that hath known man by lying with him. But all the women children who have not known a man by lying with him, keep alive for yourselves." In other words, rape the virgins. Her Hebrew classes hadn't even mentioned *that* passage.

In reality, their god was never the only deity she had worshipped.

In her small private school, the fourth-grade teacher, a white man devoted to ancient Hawaiian religion, brought to life the majesty of nature and of nature's gods. "When I go fishing," he told the class, "I always do what the Hawaiians did: I throw one fish back into the ocean, as an offering to the sea god."

He led his pupils along the Oahu beach, to observe the birds, the crabs, the sand turtles; he took them to black lava-rock tidepools, filled by pounding breakers, to see colorful starfish and reddish sea cucumbers. And he told tales of the one who, countless aeons ago, had created those black rocks: Madame Pele, the volcano goddess.

There were no active volcanoes on Oahu, only on the Big Island, and from there came the lore of how Pele was slain by a wicked sister. But then her family's grief turned to awe, and the murderess fled in defeat, when they all beheld Pele's indomitable spirit above a fountain of flame.

Laura then wrote her own story: of how villains throw several children into the volcano, and Pele builds a soft bed of ashes to catch and rescue them. The little writer had begun to believe in Madame Pele: to believe there really was some spirit, or deity, who inhabited and ruled the lava-filled mountains.

But one day, when she was nine years old, she was standing at the big window in her living room, gazing out over the ocean, contemplating Hawaiian mythology . . . when, into the midst of her reverie, there crept the teachings from Hebrew school.

Thereupon the question struck her: if there is only one God, *who is Pele?*

It was uncomfortable, even frightening. For the first time, a cloud of condemnation—for worshipping "other gods"—began to loom on the horizon.

At first, she made up a story to explain it: Pele was God's little sister! Yes, they were related spirits, related beings. But that didn't make her comfortable for long. How could a singular God have a "little sister"? Laura was constructing a pantheon!

"Hear O Israel, the Lord is our God, the Lord is One." She said this holiest of Hebrew prayers at bedtime every night, to feel peaceful and keep bad dreams away. But that one Lord allowed no room for a Lady.

That was when monotheism first oppressed her. It happened years before the Goddess—who first appeared to her as Pele—reappeared as the Wiccan Goddess. The oppression began when Laura's Jewish self and her Pagan-fantasist self finally met . . . and a stern, biblical God said "no" to her imagination.

. . .

Rubbing a stubborn smudge on the dining room floor, she felt grateful she hadn't turned on the lights. The dimness was comforting, a safe haven for her sorrow. All the cruelties, all the lies she had been told . . . it all came upon her again. And just a few feet away, a rabbi was carrying around, for his congregants to touch and kiss, the book that contained all that rape and murder.

"Judaism is an *evolving* religion," her liberal, feminist mother had said. "It is not like it was in biblical times."

An eloquent argument; but for Laura, the religion had not evolved enough. "Show me the day, Mother," she now said bitterly, almost aloud, "when an updated book is kept in the Ark—*then* maybe I'll consider rejoining the tribe!"

In reality, though, she knew she wouldn't—not even then. There was simply no substitute for Wicca. This she had learned from experiences with Nell Steiner.

. . .

They met at a discussion of the University Religious Council. The subject was "The Meaning of Spirituality," and among the panelists were a few Christians of different denominations, a Baha'i, a

44

Muslim, an atheist, a Sikh, Laura Fox representing Paganism, and Nell Steiner representing Judaism.

"I believe in the importance of the feminine," said Nell. "One of the things I teach is the mystical, feminine consciousness in Judaism."

She did not just say it: she glowed with it. She radiated maternal love, like a goddess incarnate.

I've got to get to know this woman! Laura thought.

After the main discussion, when people were mingling, Nell and Laura approached each other. With her long chestnut-red hair and blue-green eyes, the Pagan looked Irish; no one could have guessed her actual origin. For some reason—perhaps self-punitive— she told Nell she was from a Jewish family.

The expected result: a shade of sadness came over the middle-aged woman's face. "So many young Jews are seeking spirituality elsewhere," she wistfully commented. "I am trying to bring them back: to show them there is spirituality, and meditation, and women's mysteries in Judaism."

The words stung; it seemed that Nell stood as Laura's conscience, materialized before her. And yet, Laura began to wonder whether this softly radiant woman might help her heal inner discords, to connect with her Jewish heritage in a new way.

A psychic rapport developed between them. Nell was one to whom Laura could confide anything. Always open-minded, understanding, and blessed with a subtle, quiet, but brilliant sense of humor, she became a second mother to the struggling young writer.

But never did Laura attend any of Nell's rituals without a knot in her stomach.

Nell's adoration of "the feminine" had a feel of artificiality: it seemed *grafted on* to a religion that was, in essence, patriarchal. This was evident in her favorite song at the Seder: "A Web of Women." It rhapsodized about the women who had preserved Moses's life: his mother, his sister, the two midwives who delivered him, even the Pharaoh's daughter who adopted him. Yes, Laura thought with

45

a pang, these women saved the Hebrews . . . but only by saving the savior of the Hebrews, who was a man.

She knew a story about a woman and a man who *both* became saviors of the world. But oh!—a Seder was no place to be thinking about Brünnhilde and Siegfried.

The greatest problem was Nell's anxious insistence upon monotheism. Whenever she spoke of the *Shekhinah*, the feminine aspect of divinity, she repeatedly emphasized that the Shekhinah is "one" with "God," not separate. It was as if she had some terror of suggesting the Wiccan concept of a God and a Goddess! Consequently, in Nell's meditative Sabbath rites, the feminine presence was subordinated, mentioned not nearly as many times as the masculine "God." As congregants sat in a circle in an unconventional synagogue, their eyes closed, Nell told them to visualize the four Hebrew letters in the Holy Name—then "absorb" them one by one into their bodies.

Absent was the richness of Paganism, with its unashamed personification of Nature's aspects. The goddess Demeter, in wintry grieving for her daughter Persephone, abducted to the Underworld. The merry, goat-footed Pan, innocently flaunting his erect penis in the woods. The storm gods and earth goddesses of the North. All of this had to be homogenized, blended into a dull gray, dovetailed toward the worship of a formless abstraction.

She loved Nell no less, and the disappointment was heartbreaking. The rites, though mystical, still left her feeling like an outsider: a heretic, a Witch, a *wælcyrie* among Jews.

•　•　•

She was finished cleaning the dining room. As she gathered her "Caution: Wet Floor" signs, another voice intruded into her thoughts. It was Wagner's voice in the conclusion of "Judaism in Music," an essay first published under the mysterious name of K. Freigedank, or "Freethought":

> To become, communally with us, a human being, the
> Jew is enjoined firstly thus much: to cease to be a Jew . . .
> You Jews: take part, without looking back, upon this
> rebirthing work of redemption through self-destruction;
> then we are united and indivisible! But think, that only
> one thing can be your redemption from the curse weigh-
> ing upon you: the redemption of . . . *going under!*

"*Curse?* Oh, Ricky, *really!*" she scolded, with an insolent squeeze of
her mop-wringer.

Richard Wagner was a Satan in the worldview her parents had
presented. They didn't exclude him from her music education, but
they impressed upon her his consummate arrogance and vile per-
sonality. And in Israel . . .

There probably wasn't a single child in Hebrew school who did
not dream of making a pilgrimage to that country. Laura's mother
had been there, and told her exciting stories about hiking in the
desert mountains and beholding the majesty of Jerusalem. And
what was the one thing forbidden in Israel? Who was the poison-
ous serpent cast out of that Garden of Eden? Richard Wagner and
his operas!

At twelve, Laura had seen only *The Flying Dutchman* from among
his works. When the heroine sang her first notes . . . slow, tender,
descending, then rising again, with soft luminescence . . . it was the
Voice of Love itself. "It shouldn't be banned from Israel," she protested to her mother, "just because the Nazis used it! The music is
still beautiful! And Wagner lived long before the Nazis."

"Oooh, but he had the same kind of German patriotism!" Mrs.
Fox replied, with a shudder. She went on a bit about the compos-
er's proto-Nazism.

The girl felt as if she were standing at the window again, looking out over the sea. Again, a rumbling stormcloud loomed on
the horizon. How could any person of conscience love music so
accursed—created by an anti-Semite, relished by the Nazis, and out-
lawed in the Holy Land?

A few years later, her father saw a television production of *The Ring of the Nibelung,* of which his teenage daughter saw only snatches. "I'm revolted by its glorification of battle," he said, "of conquering people for the sake of conquest!" Then he told her part of the story.

"Brünnhilde disobeys an order given by Wotan, her father. So the god decrees she must become a mortal woman, and fall into a magic sleep, and the man who wakes her will be her husband. Then she says, 'If that must be, then make sure a coward won't wake me, but a hero.' So Wotan places her sleeping body on a mountain, and surrounds the mountain with flames."

Laura was electrified. "I *like* that!" she exclaimed. But she felt naïve, as if she were falling for a romance that contained some subtle, insidious message. She wanted to ask, "So, how is this Sleeping Beauty story a glorification of conquest?"—but the question got stuck in her throat.

Years later she went forth alone, determined to confront the demon, determined to meet him herself in the pages of books. And from there, an extraordinary Christian Humanist stepped forward, whom some authors called a "neo-Pagan."

The alleged glorifier-of-conquest had encouraged vegetarianism—in the belief that it made people peaceful. The basis of his philosophy he called *tätiges Mitleid*: "active compassion."

Laura often remembered that phrase on the job. Whenever a demented elderly resident railed at her, she would remind herself, "*Tätiges Mitleid*, Laura. Remember, *tätiges Mitleid.*"

She had met the devil at the crossroads . . . where three ways meet, on a stormy heath, at an ancient, crooked tree . . . and, as legend had it, in some ways he had proved a charming gentleman.

Continuing her morning rounds, she skipped Jacob Horowitz's room; for although his mutterings were quiet, she suspected he was in one of his volatile moods. She parked her cart outside each of the adjacent rooms, and went emptying the wastebaskets, scrubbing the toilets, and spot-mopping the floors. The goings-on in the synagogue were barely audible at this distance. And she wondered: what would Wagner have thought of her?

A vision came. He was walking toward her on the heath, wearing the dark coat and cap he wore in a famous photograph. He smiled, as if holding her up as a shining example, a Jew who was "ceasing to be a Jew"!

The vision faded. Indeed . . . had he encountered her at the crossroads, where three ways meet, beside the ageless, gnarled tree . . . perhaps he would have doffed his cap to her.

The last word of his essay—*Untergang*, "going under"—was wondrous, with many meanings. It could denote the sinking of a ship—as in *The Flying Dutchman*, when the terrible ghost-ship goes down, and the captain and his beloved both die to their former, trapped lives, to rise up over the wreckage in newfound freedom. It could mean the fall of a kingdom—as in *Götterdämmerung*, the fourth *Ring*-opera, when Brünnhilde bids Wotan, "Rest now; this is the end you dread and long for," and the gods perish in flame so that the world might be reborn. It was, Laura discovered, a powerful theme in Wagner's works: the need for "redemption through self-destruction."

A Wiccan initiation was very much an *Untergang*. It was a re-enactment of the Goddess's descent into the Underworld.

Laura could still smell the hyssop, the scent of holiness, in the warm herbal bath where her priest-friend had left her, while he dedicated the circle in his living room. She lay in tranquil meditation, feeling the presence of the God and Goddess, looking back over her life, and knowing, with greater assurance than ever, that Wicca was her path. She remembered the excitement—even the thrill of fear!—when her friend led her through the passage between the worlds of matter and spirit, and through her own death. From there she emerged transformed.

She drew a breath of peace, remembering that night—but could hardly believe what she was thinking. "Judaism in Music" was Richard Wagner's infamous anti-Semitic essay: she resented him for it, she despised him for it . . . yet within it she had glimpsed beauty.

The last sentences reiterated his most uplifting musical leitmotifs, reminding her of the renewal she had *undergone*.

Prior to that ritual, the God of her childhood had taken after her with lightning bolts. She saw herself an outcast on the heath: pelted with rain and hail, and utterly alone. She was damned: for although Judaism had taught of no eternal perdition, no lake of fire, she was damned in a worse way than even an apostate Christian could be damned . . .

Once, during her adolescence, her father had said to her, "So many of our ancestors, throughout the ages, fought and suffered and died in order to keep the faith alive. Don't you think you owe it to *them* to remain in it?"

Thus the apostate Christian might fear for his own soul; however, it was only for his own soul. The ex-Jew might feel the weight of an entire people resting on his shoulders.

Her Wiccan *Untergang* had delivered her from the biblical God's wrath; never again would she be struck by lightning bolts of self-hate. But the sky was still gray with guilt and sadness, for her initiation had not silenced the distant, haunting cries—the wails of mourning for a lost daughter—of the pale ancestral shades.

One of them, their white-haired earthly representative, was Jacob Horowitz.

He had known persecution; yet on many days he defiantly cried out, "I'm Jacob Horowitz! I'm a Jew! I'm a Jew!" Faith had sustained him, enabling him to become a successful American businessman, a husband and father, a philanthropist, a pillar of the Jewish community in Tucson. Now, in his delirium, he still needed to surround himself with his culture's artifacts, such as his collection of record albums, including *Fiddler on the Roof*. Judaism was his only solace, his last link with reality. A devastating stroke had robbed him of everything—home, business, family life, coherence—but not his Jewish soul.

The very embodiment of her people's tenacity, he was her manifest accuser.

She peeked in his door. He was awake in his recliner. She pushed the cart into the opposite hallway.

Continuing her work, she had to contemplate how other Pagans, born Jews, had attempted to combine the religions. A leading Pagan journal published a long, fascinating "Judeo-Pagan forum." Some buttons for sale in occult catalogues said "Jew-Witch"; there was at least one newsletter for "Judeo-Pagans" . . .

Laura sensed, however, that such things might not be for her, tempting as they were. The older she got, the more she wanted a clean break with her first religion—with no loose ends left hanging; no lingering, nagging attachments. *"Take part, without looking back!"*—Wagner's obnoxious and inspiring words reverberated through her mind. Judaism was an ex-husband with whom she had once been in love, but who had since abused her: beat her, shouted at her, threatened to kill her if she left him . . . and ever since the divorce he kept coming back to court her again. Sometimes he was angry and threatening, but more often pathetic and pleading; and the sight of him brought back worlds of painful memories, of love and hate.

"Get that guy out of your life!" would have been any feminist friend's advice. And the Pied Piper—whose pipe was a 120-player orchestra—stood beckoning, with his conceited smile, as she mopped . . . all too ready to show her the way.

He stood beside her on a mountaintop, overlooking many peaks and valleys, his patronizing arm around her shoulders; and with his other hand, he gestured toward the world. A golden beam of dawn pierced the clouds of guilt and sadness, as he told her how to rise above them. *"Behold, maiden,"* the Tempter whispered, *"the Ride to freedom. Cease to be a Jewess, and I will make thee a Valkyrie."*

· · ·

She was approaching the chapel again, and "Ain Kelohenu" rang forth. Its melody suggested renewal: each verse rising in pitch, opening like a flower, soaring up to the sun like a great bird, then gracefully finding its way back to its note of origin, where the next verse began. Laura busied herself cleaning the two nearest rooms, so she could listen.

After the service, the rabbi sent her with a plate of sliced cinnamon cake to put in the nurses' station, a traditional courtesy to the staff. He was a short, rotund man with a New York accent who always looked as though he were about to crack a joke. When she returned, he happily plied her with her own small plate of refreshment: a little pickled herring; a morsel of *challah*, the braided white bread; a slice of cinnamon cake; and a tiny plastic cup of kosher wine. She and Tom loved kosher wines.

At moments like this her burning anger against Judaism abated, and she found herself in the grips of a baffling incredulity at that anger. How could something be evil when it brought such comfort and enjoyment? These elderly congregants, the relatives and children with them, and this adorable, pudgy little rabbi—they felt they were drinking from a well of spiritual refreshment! To them it was not about lies, or conquests, or cruelties; it was all about goodness, guiding them in the way of goodness. The people had channeled their thinking—caused a new world of philosophy and literature to arise out of monotheistic confinement—developed humor, ethnic food, music—created, over the ages, a vibrant culture in their wanderings—and Ricky you damn fool, you bat-blind bigot, how could you not see this!

She sensed him step up behind her, placing his hand upon her shoulder again. At first she did not turn, but in her mind's eye she could see the handsome ghost frowning, shaking his head in disapproval.

She glanced at him once, empathically, and also with reproach. He faded away.

She secured her cart and headed to the employee dining room, very hungry. She took her tub of vegetable stew from the refrigerator and put it into the microwave, then went to the cafeteria for a glass of water.

The kosher meat dishes looked tempting and smelled good, but Laura had noticed a heavy, clogged feeling in her body whenever she ate meat. And that was not her only inspiration for vegetarian cooking . . . .

She had another motive—or rather, a *leitmotiv*. The flavors of sweet potatoes, squash, carrots, mushrooms, peas, and delicate spices blended into a glowing Wagnerian chord.

It was difficult leaving the dining room. An afternoon sleepiness made her head and limbs hard to lift. She was growing weary in body and mind.

Her next job was to clean up the synagogue. She had to bring the engraved silver wine chalice and the wooden board with challah crumbs to the dishwashing area, and the white tablecloth to the laundry.

Alone, in the quiet of the chapel, she contemplated the religious implements, sensing affinity with them; yet they felt foreign. *I don't belong here.* She glanced up: the Ark and eternal light whispered gently, "Won't you come back?"

No, this is not my spiritual path; and the worlds of anguish seemed endless.

Recently her mother had reassured her on the phone, "I release you willingly!"—from Judaism. And her father had sent her a lovely letter about her Pagan religiosity, saying, "I feel as if the wall between our two fields has come down, and I can wish you 'Good harvest!'"

They never said a Mourner's Kaddish for her, as if she were dead to their people. But she almost wished they had.

It would have satisfied her need to be punished; and at the same time, it would have clinched her dislike of Judaism. It would have hurt more, yet it would have toughened her more; it would have made the clean break cleaner. But now—despite her deep gratitude—their acceptance increased her guilt. Such loving parents deserved a child more loyal to their faith!

Resisting the weight of weariness, she entered Anna Rosenberg's room. Rosenberg, who lay completely incapacitated, always had the radio on her end table tuned to the classical music station. An announcer was speaking on the radio, and immediately Laura recognized that he was summarizing Act III of *Die Walküre*—the second opera of the *Ring*.

Her heart jumped into her throat. Her first thought was, "This is a Jewish nursing home! Don't they have a rule against playing this stuff around here?" Then she hurried out to clean a neighboring room, so as to be back when "The Ride of the Valkyries" began.

A *whoosh* on the strings—and her foot was in the stirrup. Another *whoosh*—her other foot was in the stirrup. Her lifeless quarry secured to the saddle behind her, she gave her horse the spurs . . . and they were galloping up a mountain . . . bounding, bounding, toward a cliff. The strings and piccolo were shrieking gusts through her long chestnut-red hair, which streamed out from beneath her helmet—and then, borne on trumpets and horns, with a graceful leap they were over the cliff, soaring into the air.

Her blood had turned to white fire. Her hands were moving rhythmically, with preternatural efficiency—feeling hardly any sensation, as if no longer part of her—and the objects in the room appeared spectral, not real. Only a half-conscious body was doing the housekeeping, while her soul was thirty-five thousand feet up in the sky, clasping the rein.

The work in that room was done—or was it? Did the mirror need one more squirt? Well, yes, it did have some spots—any excuse to keep working there. No, now, it's time to get out! You're here to clean, not to . . . horse around. *Damn it, lady, turn it down! I can't leave while you Wagnerize me.*

With a dizzying jolt, she yanked herself out of the room—heart still palpitating and the cool headwind still in her lungs. She went to clean a small lounge, where several residents sat listlessly in their wheelchairs.

Suddenly, her ears were jarred. Somebody was playing Scott Joplin's "The Entertainer" on a portable tape player. Cringing, she spot-mopped the floor, trying to screen the tune out, much as she liked it. She went to clean Mary McDougall's room.

Things went from bad to worse. McDougall's radio was loudly tuned to some trite "golden oldie" song. Between that piece, "The Entertainer," and "The Ride of the Valkyries," the area was starting to fill with an interesting conglomeration of sounds.

She pushed her cart to the last room in the unit, belonging to Jacob Horowitz. It was quieter there, in the corner of the wing. And it looked safe to enter, for he appeared to be sleeping.

Setting down her tray of detergents, she turned on the light at the sink, which made the rest of the room seem darker. Then Horowitz stirred in his bed.

"Please . . . please," he stammered. "Just give me a little more time."

There was something unusual about the way he said it. It was calmer than his usual utterances, which tended to be either frightened, or weak and sad. There was a note of gratitude in his voice: he seemed glad to see her, but wanted her to wait a moment . . . for something.

A strange feeling came over her. "What, sir?" she asked, turning toward him.

"Please," he stammered again. "May I rest?"

The strangeness began to feel chilly. "You can take a nap if you want." Surely, she told herself, that was all he meant. She went about scrubbing the sink.

"May I rest?" This time he seemed more in earnest.

Cold waves pulsated through her body. She could not deny it: she sensed what he meant. She felt her eyes grow wide with awe. Had he recognized her?

She tiptoed over to the bed. His gaze fell upon her: a calm gaze, a gaze of recognition. What sort of spectre did she present before him? She could not know; yet he looked upon her as if she were a visitor from another world—comforting, but unearthly.

"Please," he said, softly and without fear, "please, wait. Just a little more time." A moment later, however, he repeated his request, "Please, please, may I rest?"

The room was quiet; all the cacophony had ceased. She looked around, and they were alone. All was deserted in the dim light where these two met. The entire universe seemed to have fallen away and vanished, leaving only them.

There was no question about it: he knew what she really was. She had left Valhalla, gone into the world of mortals, disguised herself as a housekeeper, her true identity invisible to all . . . except those who were halfway into the spirit-world. For madness here is sanity there, and his madness had given him the second sight. Now he was torn between wanting to go with her, and wanting to stay.

She leaned over him. She smiled with love. "Yes, Mr. Horowitz, you may rest. It's all right. You can have the rest you long for." She gave him a nod of permission.

The remainder of the afternoon went by as a blur, a dream. The next wing was filled with hollering Alzheimer's patients, but she hardly saw or heard them. Some mysterious transformation was happening within her; her hands moved rhythmically, her heart pounding to hoof-beats.

With the day's work complete, Brünnhilde removed the full trash bag from her cart, tossed it into the bin, and replaced it with a new bag for the next day. She spilled out the last bucket of dirty mop water, locked up her cart in the closet, and stepped out the main door into the warm air of a Tucson parking lot.

To the north were the bare majesties of the Catalina mountains: blue-gray in the afternoon haze, a vast rock dotted with sparse desert plants. The sight filled her with exuberance. Those great peaks, this clear sky, looked like the perfect place to ride.

Siegfried came to pick her up, in his pretty blue Integra. She got in and threw her arms around him. "Hel-*lo!*" he said, putting his arms around her. How wonderful to hug Siegfried again. They drove off to the grocery store.

On the way, she told him about the encounter with Horowitz. "Ah, he recognized you!" said her boyfriend, with his usual, teasing smile. "I've got to fix my car horn so it'll sound like the horn notes in the opera"—for Siegfried always blew a hunting horn wherever he went. "Won't it be fun to honk at everybody with Siegfried's horn blast!"

They really *were* like Siegfried and Brünnhilde, she reflected. The *Ring*'s protagonists were, from one angle, an oddly mismatched couple: a lighthearted comic hero and a much more serious, even tragic, heroine. Yet they were also well suited, being complementary.

"Sieg," she said after a moment's silence, as they were pulling into the parking lot at the store, "do you remember, when I first took this job at Handmaker, you said to me on the phone, 'My Brünnhilde is becoming a housekeeper by day and a Valkyrie by night'?"

"Yes."

"Well, isn't that like . . . getting the cart before the horse?"

They both laughed. The laughter spiralled outward into the universe, a laughter of healing.

.   .   .

After that day, Jacob Horowitz never ceased to regard her as a harbinger of death.

Sometimes it was with great terror. One time he started screaming, "You're here to kill me! You're here to kill me!"

But usually the sight of her elicited a frenzied longing. "Take me away! Take me away!" he begged, on more than one occasion.

"Where do you want me to take you?" she would ask each time. She didn't expect a coherent answer, but it would do no harm to ask; it might even tell her something. Sometimes he appeared to be trying to name a place, but the place remained nameless.

Once he wanted to go off by air. She found him, oddly enough, in a wheelchair beside one of the back doors to the wing, seemingly abandoned. He was staring out the glass door. Then he turned to her and said, "Is this the way to the airport?"

"No, it isn't."

"Which way, then?"

"There's no way to the airport from here, sir. You are in a nursing home."

He got a little frantic. "Give me a ride! Give me a ride! Give me a ride!"

This time she was explicit. "I'm sorry, right now I'm on my day job; I can't give any hero a ride. Except back to your room. Do you want me to take you back to your room?"

He must have given some feeble assent, because she ended up placing her hands firmly on his wheelchair and bringing him to his room. Thankfully, his attendant met him there, and the disguised Brünnhilde went on her way.

Then there were times he regarded her with grief. One day he watched from his chair, forlorn, as she cleaned the sink. Then he began to stammer, almost sobbing, "Please, please . . ."—as if pleading to be spared, and also pleading to be taken.

She sensed he was in one of his quieter moods, so she approached and placed her hand upon his thin, gnarled one. He appeared slightly calmed, relieved at her touch.

She began to sing, "*Ain kelohenu, ain kadonenu, ain k'malkenu . . .*"

"*Ain k'moshi'enu,*" he weakly recited, completing the verse.

His expression was still sad, but a touch of light had come over him. It was the exhilaration of one stumbling at night through the strange, tangled forest of dementia, who suddenly beholds a glimmer of memory.

She went back to the sink, leaned over it, and prayed silently. *Goddess, please, take him—take him gently! Let there be no pain, or sorrow, or fear at all! Let it be effortless, in perfect happiness, perfect peace . . . Please, dear Goddess, as soon as he is ready, release his spirit.*

She was nearly weeping.

• • •

Her battle was not over. Every time she entered Handmaker through the front door, she walked past a glass case filled with Jewish artifacts, including a miniature woman in a Sabbath veil, her hands spread over some candles on a table. A label beneath her said, "Woman Blessing Sabbath Candles." Sometimes Laura wanted to smash the glass, and set that little woman free.

Yet she also observed the reverence with which she prepared the synagogue every Friday. She drew her dusting rag over the wooden Stars of David, the small lectern, the stained-glass window with its Old Testament image, and other surfaces. She vacuumed the carpet, brushed the magnificent golden cloth on the main lectern, dusted around the prayer books, and moved the rack of fringed shawls to a more accessible place. Sometimes this work gave her a mysterious kind of pleasure: the whole area, and the things in her hands, would seem to smile, exuding sacredness.

Was there a place—within the confines of her head, or out in the farthest reaches of space and time—where all the cacophonous pieces of music might converge? Was there some fifth, or sixth, or seventh dimension . . . or perhaps a gnarled, ancient tree on a windswept heath, where three ways meet—nay, where many ways meet—where even "Ain Kelohenu" might merge in a new, as yet unheard-of harmony with the wild strains of the "Ride"?

For one moment, she had glimpsed such a place; now the vision had to be pursued, for it was not easily won. The thrill of quest brought a smile to her lips. So, resolute, she set off along the rough, winding, mist-shrouded road, where many souls—the living and the ghosts—called out their imperfect guidance.

One ghost watched her with insulted pride. He had wanted to be her only mentor, her only redeemer. Now he glared like Wotan, seeing that his favorite daughter had defied him. He had taught her lessons in beauty, and in a deeper sense of compassion; he had helped lift her into the saddle. But in the end, he too had been an oppressor. So now he would have to step back and take his place among all the other spirits.

She would experience many initiations, many goings-under, on her journey; and, somewhere beneath her armor, there would beat the troubled heart of a Jewess who had wandered from her people. Yet now she knew that whenever she wept the bitterest tears, and passed through the darkest night of the soul . . . eventually there would come a warm breeze, a breath of the Goddess; the vision of parted clouds before a fiery mountain; a peal of laughter or a leitmotif of Redemption—to lift her up again.

She had glimpsed the meeting place of harmony; it was a beginning. And it was the strangest, most unfathomable of beginnings—because it had not begun with progressive feminist services or a Judeo-Pagan forum.

It began on the day she alighted before an aged Jewish warrior, bravely fighting his last battle, and asking her to take him gently up upon her steed.

Alex Bledsoe grew up in West Tennessee, an hour north of Grace-land and twenty minutes from Nutbush. He now lives between two big lakes in Wisconsin, writes before six in the morning, and tries to teach his two sons to act like they've been to town before. He has been on a Bardic Pagan path since the early nineties. He wrote the Lady Firefly short stories originally published in Pan-Gaia *magazine. His first novel,* The Sword-Edged Blonde, *was published in 2007; Charles de Lint called it "easily one of the better books I've had the pleasure of reading this year," and* Publisher's Weekly *gave it a starred review. Alex's next two novels,* Blood Groove *and* Burn Me Deadly, *will come out in 2009.*

Draw Down

BY Alex Bledsoe

Arizona Territory, 1874

Sheriff Matt Klaren looked at the woman his deputy brought before him. She was middle-aged, heavyset, and dressed in an outfit sewn together from pieces of other, better clothes. She had feathers woven into strands of her red hair—not in the Indian way, but in her own unique fashion. She looked like she might've crawled from the feverish dream of one of the Chinatown opium smokers Klaren had encountered when he visited San Francisco after the Civil War, except her expression was one of clear-eyed, mundane outrage.

"Ma'am," Klaren said as he stood. To his deputy he added, "Silas, take off your hat, you're indoors now. And take the shackles off the lady, please."

"Yes, sir," Silas said. He was ten years older than Klaren, with white hair and gaps in his teeth. Klaren was the third sheriff he'd served in Rollins Creek, and he liked this young, even-tempered lawman better than either of his predecessors. He unlocked the wrist shackles and hung them back on their wall hook.

Klaren sat on the front edge of his desk. Out the open door, he saw a few horses already tied at the saloon across the street. Farmers and ranchers from the outlying spreads would soon arrive for their regular Saturday sojourns to the railroad depot, dry goods store, and telegraph office. He wanted to clear this up quickly. "Now, run that past me again, Silas. You say this lady is a *what*?"

"A witch," Silas repeated. "A handmaiden of Satan. And it ain't me saying it, it's according to the Reverend Studdard."

Klaren sighed and rubbed the bridge of his nose. "I reckon I heard you right, then. Was kinda hoping I hadn't."

He looked at the woman, who met his gaze with her own calm, confident one. Here in the territory, women tended to be as hard-edged as the men, if not harder. She did not seem the least bit concerned with her predicament. Instead, she appeared mostly annoyed by the inconvenience. "So, Miss O'Hara, is that true?"

"Do you not think Satan would prefer a young, pretty handmaiden?" Iona O'Hara said. She had an Irish lilt, flattened a little by her years in America, and all the fire her red hair promised.

"Ma'am, I'm not too qualified to state the preferences of either God *or* the devil. I just keep the peace."

"Oh, do you now? And I was peacefully minding my own business when your deputy here showed up to arrest me, I'll have you know."

"She was working in her garden, ah . . . nekkid," Silas said, looking down. "Just like the reverend's complaint says."

"Aye, on my own land," she said unrepentantly. "Which, for someone else to see, would've meant they were trespassing, despite all the signs I've put up. That *is* against the law here in this territory, isn't it? I could've shot him if I'd wanted and been well within my rights, could I not?"

"There's that," Klaren agreed. "But this ain't the first time I've heard strange stories about you, Miss O'Hara. They say you stand outside waving a knife around every full moon. They say you've got a bunch of strange statues in your garden, naked women and goat-men and such."

"And who would be 'they'?"

"The good citizens of Rollins Creek. Or at least a fair percentage of them."

"And doin' what you want on your own property in private became against the law when?"

Klaren chuckled nervously. "There's the law, and there's the law. I grant you a person, even a woman, ought to be able to do what she wants on her own land. That's why most of us came west in the first place. But your neighbors also got a right not to worry you're loco and might start slittin' throats in the middle of the night, should the mood strike you."

She scowled knowingly. "You mean that Reverend Studdard has a right to get rid of anyone who doesn't agree with him."

"He's protecting his congregation."

"He's protecting his own behind."

Silas made a coughing sound that Klaren recognized as a stifled laugh. He glared at his deputy, then returned his attention to the woman. "Well, *I'm* protecting the people of Rollins Creek. Most of us would prefer it if you'd just move on before there's any real trouble. There's plenty of open land between here and California, and you don't seem to have a problem taking care of yourself. I'm sure you could find a spot with more amenable neighbors."

She balled her fists. "Oh, so because most of the people want something, that makes it the right thing?" she snapped.

"Ain't sayin' that. It's a free country, and if you want to find a nice fella to marry, turn that homestead of yours into a working farm, and start being more neighborly, I'm pretty sure nobody would mind."

"But if I want to keep to myself, do whatever I want, and be answerable to no man, then I'm likely to get lynched, is that what you're saying?"

"Ma'am, people don't get lynched in Rollins Creek."

"You mean until now," Silas said.

Two dozen townspeople had gathered in the dusty street outside the jail, squinting against the sun. Reverend Thaddeus Studdard stood at the front of the mob, his severe black silhouette sharp in the sunlight.

"Well, look who's showing his face," Iona said as she glared out the open door. "The grand inquisitor himself."

Beside Studdard stood Zess Lloyd, former gunfighter and current convert to Christianity. Short, thin, and leathery, he was also the only man who'd ever out-drawn Klaren in a fair gunfight.

"Damnation," the sheriff muttered. "Silas, keep Miss O'Hara in here. I'll see what they want."

"My hide," Iona said. Klaren ignored her.

He stepped onto the jail's porch and faced the mob. They grew silent under his gaze and averted their eyes. Only Reverend Studdard and Zess Lloyd did not look away.

"Morning," Klaren said. "Looks like another hot day. And to what do I owe this pleasure?"

"Thank you for arresting that woman," Studdard said, pointing his long finger at Iona. She stood defiantly in the jail's doorway, hands on her hips and feet spread. "She's a witch and a sorceress, and she must be brought to justice."

"If she's a sorceress, then she's not a very good one," Klaren pointed out. "She didn't know I was sending Silas to arrest her. Maybe you're giving her a bit more credit than she deserves."

"She *deserves* the Lord's justice," Zess Lloyd said.

"Zess, I'll speak for the congregation," Studdard said. He clasped his hands before him and spoke with the same rolling, dramatic voice he used in his pulpit. "Sheriff Klaren, Rollins Creek is a new town in a new territory. We're not yet even a state. And we won't be if we allow her kind of godless conduct to continue."

He smiled and changed to a more casual tone. "You're a young man, Sheriff. The devil has many snares, one of which is over-confidence, the scourge of the young. That's why the Lord admonishes us to honor our fathers."

"And mothers, you arrogant toad," Iona snapped.

Silas eased past Iona and leaned against the wall beside the doorway. Silas was the best kind of deputy, one who thoroughly understood his job and had no desire to be sheriff. He'd have a scattergun ready should things turn violent, and the first man to go down would be Zess Lloyd.

Klaren glanced at Zess. The former hired gun had plenty of blood on his hands from his past, but he was two years into a change that seemed genuine, and Klaren didn't want a true Christian convert's death on his conscience. For that matter, he didn't want *anyone's* death if he could help it. This would require finesse, not lead.

"So what do you figure we should do about the situation, then, Reverend?" Klaren asked Studdard.

"Test her."

"Test her?"

"Yes, the way the Catholic Inquisition did to identify witches. The Papists may be apostates, but in their time they knew how to root out Satan's evil. If she passes the test, I will have no further complaint, because God will have spoken."

"Ask him about these tests, Sheriff," Iona said as she emerged from the jail to stand beside him. About half the crowd took a step back. "Ask him how I'd have to win his little challenge."

Keeping his tone casual, Klaren said, "Seems a fair question. What have you got in mind?"

"The dunking stool is most efficient, given the presence of Lake Rollins," Studdard said.

"And what exactly is that?"

"The accused is tied to a chair affixed to a long pole and placed over something used as a fulcrum. She is then dunked underwater for progressively longer periods until she confesses."

"Or drowns," Iona added.

"That don't sound like too good a test to me," Klaren said. "Sounds like if you pass, you still fail."

"Possibly," Studdard said. "But her spirit would be with the Lord."

"And my body would be feeding the catfish at the bottom of the lake," Iona shot back. "Call me a heathen, but I'm rather fond of it, old and fat as it is."

"You *are* a heathen," Zess said. He had one of those tight, emotionless voices that made everything sound like an indisputable fact.

"Zess!" Studdard said sharply, but the crowd muttered their agreement. "You can see, Sheriff, that feelings run high on this. I've counseled patience and prayer, but I might not be able to control these folks much longer."

This presumptive superiority made Klaren angry, although it barely showed. "So all that's standing between them and this woman is you?"

"And the Lord," Studdard said with simple, utter certainty.

Klaren looked at the crowd—at their sour, dusty faces all filled with righteous hatred—and said firmly, "Y'all better understand one thing. What's standing between you and this lady ain't the Lord, and it ain't the good reverend here. It's *me*. And I don't mean just a man with a gun, but the sworn upholder of the law of this country. That's what this star on my chest stands for. You want to take her for rough justice, you got to go through me first."

"Fine," Zess said. Immediately everyone stepped away from him. He moved easily into his gunfighter slouch, his fingertips dangling near the pistol strapped to his thigh.

A boy broke away from his parents and dashed down the street, yelling, "The sheriff and Zess Lloyd are gonna draw down on each other!" Instantly people emerged from the livery stable, dry goods store, and saloon.

"I thought you didn't wear a gun no more, Zess," Silas said. Like Klaren, his tone was light and casual, belying the tension that now filled the air.

"The reverend said it might be needed," Zess said. "Looks like he was right."

Klaren felt the throb of the old wound in his side where Zess Lloyd had beat him to the draw three years previously. Another inch toward his navel and he would've died in slow gut-shot agony, a thought that snapped him awake in a cold sweat many a night.

He folded his arms, deliberately not readying for a fight. "Zess, you beat me once, that's a fact. But you and me both know it was a near thing. You ought to consider that it's been two years since you drew on somebody. I've stayed in practice. That might tip things my way."

"Might," Zess said. "'Cept the Lord's on *my* side."

"Zess!" Studdard said, appalled. "The Lord does not condone violence!"

"Must've read a different Bible than the one I did," Iona muttered.

"The Lord gave me a talent," Zess said simply. "My sin was not using it for Him. This time I will."

"I'd stand back, Reverend," Silas said. "Things could turn messy real soon."

Klaren slowly unfolded his arms and lowered his gun hand to his side. His spurs rattled in the silence as he stepped down into the street to stand ten feet away from Zess. Neither man moved, or looked away from the other's eyes.

"By the moon and sun!" Iona bellowed angrily. She clomped down the wooden steps and stood in the dusty street between the two men. "Is this how your Jesus would've settled this?" she demanded. "Did he tell Pilate, 'Meet me in the street at noon?' Well, it sure isn't what my Brigid would've done, I can tell you that."

She faced the crowd of church folk, now augmented by additional onlookers. "I've done no harm to you people, and it wouldn't break my heart to never see any of you again. But I won't be chased away, and I won't be bullied." Then she turned to Zess. "You claim to be doing your God's work. As I recall, he says, 'Love thy neighbor.' Mine, she says, 'Harm none.' Now tell me, does that sound like they wouldn't get along?"

Zess cut his eyes briefly at her before snapping them back to Klaren. "My God is the one true God."

"Good for you. Then shouldn't you be doing as he commands? I'm your neighbor—literally, since your spread bumps up against mine. Is this how you show neighborly love?"

There was a long moment of silence. Zess tried to keep his attention on Klaren, but the big Irish woman before him could not be ignored. He met her eyes for a long, tense moment. Then he sighed and said, "Ma'am," touched the brim of his hat to her, and walked away. The crowd parted to let him pass. He crossed the street toward the saloon.

Iona turned to Studdard. "And you. You've been calling me names and preaching against me in that pulpit of yours for months now. Don't think I don't hear about it just because I don't polish your pews with my behind. Well, here I am. Say it to my face."

Studdard said nothing, and scowled because he knew he had no graceful way out.

Suddenly a woman in the mob shouted, "You're a witch, that's what!"

"That's right!" someone else added.

The air filled with cries of assent. Simultaneously, another man rushed from the crowd and pointed a gun at Iona from point-blank range. He screamed, "*Die*, witch!" She had no time to react.

Two shots simultaneously rang out. The man's unfired pistol flew into the air, and he fell to the ground, bleeding from holes in his shoulder and gun hand.

Klaren, pistol still smoking, stared at the fallen man. He'd only fired once. Then he saw Zess across the street, gun also in his hand.

"Which one's yours?" Silas asked quietly.

"Shoulder," Klaren answered as he slipped his gun back into its holster. That meant Zess had shot through the crowd without hitting anyone and struck the man in his hand at a distance of fifteen yards. With, Klaren noted, the sun in his eyes.

"Well, this is just great!" Iona bellowed in exasperation. "Now someone's gotten hurt." She knelt beside the man writhing in pain. "Hold still, you big fool," she said as she tore a strip from the hem of her dress and tied it around his hand.

"No, witch, don't touch me!" he hissed through his teeth. He tried to squirm away and resist, but the pain was too severe. Ignoring his protests, she tore away his shirt and examined the wound in his shoulder.

She looked up at Klaren. "Now *this* is a problem. That bullet of yours is still in there, Sheriff."

Klaren turned to Silas. "Ride over to Fire Lick and get Doc Chumley."

"There's no time for that," Iona said as she got to her feet. She pointed to two men in the crowd. "You, and you. Bring him into the sheriff's office. Sheriff, clean off your desk and put a pot of hot water on the stove. I'll need me a good, sharp knife as well."

"That man tried to kill you," Klaren pointed out.

She smiled for the first time since her arrival. "Sheriff, you of all people should understand. That star you wear says you had to protect me, and I can appreciate that." She pulled a necklace from her dress. "The one *I* wear, the oath I took to my goddess as a young lass in Ireland, says to harm none. If I *can* help someone and don't, that counts as doing harm. So we're two of a kind."

She suddenly realized no one had moved. She bellowed, "*Git!*" and the designated lifters carried the wounded man past Klaren and Silas. Iona followed, snatching the knife from Silas's belt as she passed.

The speechless crowd stared after them. Klaren said loudly, "Reckon that's the end of the show for today. Reverend Studdard, you either disperse your flock or I'll shepherd them all into my jail, where it'll be a might cramped."

"This doesn't change what that woman is," Studdard said defiantly.

Klaren almost laughed. "No, sir, it sure doesn't. It don't change that she's willing to help someone who tried to kill her, which looks a lot more like Christian charity than anything y'all have done today."

From inside the jail, Iona's voice rang out. "By the spirits of earth, air, fire, and water; by the strength of the Lord and love of the Lady; I ask for your guidance in healing this man's—oh, for crying out loud, have you never seen a little blood before? Go sit down and get out of my way, then!"

"That is pagan idolatry!" Studdard said. "She is calling on the devil for help!"

Klaren stepped right up to Studdard. "Reverend," he said quietly, letting the anger show in his eyes. "You may mean well, but I think you've stirred up enough trouble here today. One more word out of you and I will lock you up, and gag you to boot."

Studdard opened his mouth to reply, then thought better of it. He swallowed, nodded, and looked away.

Klaren turned his back on Studdard and went back up onto the porch. The crowd slowly dispersed, muttering among themselves.

"Guess time off hasn't slowed ol' Zess down too much," Silas said.

"That's a fact." Klaren looked down at his gun hand, still trembling as the adrenaline burned off. "Glad we didn't have to find out."

"'We?' He wasn't mad at me."

Klaren grinned. "He might've been after you filled him up with buckshot."

"And," Silas added admiringly, "that Miss O'Hara is one firebrand of a woman."

Klaren nodded toward Zess, still watching from across the street. "I expect you ain't the only one who thinks so." He touched the brim of his hat in salute to the ex-gunfighter, then followed Silas into the jail.

Eugie Foster calls home a mildly haunted, fey-infested house in metro Atlanta that she shares with her husband, Matthew, and her pet skunk (and sometime muse), Hobkin. She received the Phobos Award and has been nominated for the British Fantasy, Bram Stoker, and Pushcart awards. Her fiction has been translated into Greek, Hungarian, Polish, and French, and her publication credits number over one hundred and include stories in Realms of Fantasy, Interzone, Cricket, Cicada, Orson Scott Card's Inter-Galactic Medicine Show, Jim Baen's Universe, *and anthologies* Best New Fantasy *(Prime Books),* Heroes in Training *(DAW Books),* Magic in the Mirrorstone *(Mirrorstone Books), and* Best New Romantic Fantasy 2 *(Juno Books). Her short-story collection,* Returning My Sister's Face and Other Far Eastern Tales of Whimsy and Malice, *will debut in 2009 from Norilana Books. Visit her online at www.eugiefoster.com.*

A Nose for Magic

By Eugie Foster

I thought I was just being a normal guy when the first thing that dazzled me about Lauren was her fragrance. I would discover it was about as normal as metal-noise-grindcore-ambient music. But working in the computer lab that day, I was transfixed by her scent. It was a floral blend—hibiscus, wild tulip, and honeysuckle—nice, but standard. But as she explained how her pet had mauled a semester's worth of research papers, all stored on the CD she brandished, I caught a trace of dark chocolate and balsam, and, like a memory of sweetness, honey. The combination was so unusual, I barely heard her. I only realized she'd finished talking when she handed me her disc.

Obvious teeth marks stippled and scraped along it. Cat, perhaps? Or maybe a toy poodle?

"I don't know if I can salvage anything," I said. "In the future, there's this thing you can do to prevent losing data—"

"Make backups?" I scented cayenne pepper and cardamom. It matched her tone, arch and rueful. "I assure you, that lesson has been seared into my psyche."

I grinned. "Maybe we'll get lucky."

Ginger and white pepper.

I spritzed the CD with fix-it solution. I had my doubts, but this stuff was the closest thing to a miracle I had. The acrid smell blotted out her perfume, clearing my sinuses like a sluice of ice water.

When I finished wiping the disc, the scarring was gone. "This doesn't look so bad." I stuck it in my drive.

Vanilla and fig.

Was she carrying a spice rack? My nose is quirky sensitive, which has its drawbacks when I'm in classes filled with techie geeks who can hack any software program but can't figure out the proper application of soap. Now it had me good and truly confounded.

"What perfume are you wearing?" I blurted.

"I'm not. Can't stand the stuff."

"Huh." The drive whirred like a trooper, giving its all. It could've been singing Gilbert and Sullivan for the life of me. "Do you use a special shampoo?"

She tugged at her hair, auburn and wavy. "Nope. Just some drugstore brand; I think it's supposed to smell like blueberries. That affects my CD how?"

"Oh, sorry." My face heated several degrees. "I just wondered."

"That makes two of us."

"Huh?"

She tapped my monitor. "Is it working?"

"Uh. I mean, yeah. I'm reading your files."

"Thank God!" She leaned over the desk and kissed my cheek. "And thank *you*."

I lost sensation in my toes and fingers as all the blood vacated my extremities. "N-no problem. Want me to burn you a backup?"

"A thousand yeses."

I fumbled a blank disc out and stuck it in the burn tray. While the computer hummed to itself, a heady bouquet of wild sage and red wine permeated the air.

"You've just saved two lives, y'know," she said. "I was ready to skin Koushee and then throw myself off the roof of the astronomy building."

Circulation dribbled back to my brain piecemeal. "Koushee's your cat?"

"Skunk, actually."

"You have a *pet skunk?*"

She laughed. "Sometimes animals choose you instead of the other way around. Don't worry, he's de-scented."

The computer flashed triumphantly.

I ejected both discs. "My name's Derek, in case you have any more skunk-damaged CDs."

"I'm Lauren. And I won't, or if I do, I'll be too busy having an aneurism to make it to the lab."

"In that case, my shift ends in ten minutes. You want to get some coffee or something?" I couldn't believe how cool that came out. Usually with members of the XX set, I hem and stutter, an unfortunate shortcoming that becomes more pathetic and tragic the prettier they are. And Lauren was a hottie by anyone's standards.

"Sure," she said, "except I'm not a coffee person. Want to meet my skunk and have some tea instead?"

"Yes!" was out before she was done asking.

Lauren lived off campus, a short stroll from the computer lab. When she opened her door, a strange smell wafted through—burnt cinnamon or allspice. It wasn't unpleasant, certainly better than eau de overflowing cat box, the prevailing aroma in my ex-girlfriend's place.

I trailed along, sniffing. "Is that incense?" I asked.

In her cramped kitchen, Lauren set a dinged kettle on the stove. "What is it with you and smells?"

Before I could answer, a pair of glowing green orbs peeped around the corner.

"Cripes!"

The green eyes resolved into a pudgy animal. It was tawny buff with stumpy legs, a huge bush of a tail, and entirely non-scary brown eyes. It waddled over, and the kitchen's overhead revealed a pair of cream stripes down its back.

"That's Koushee." Lauren swept the animal into her arms. "Say hello to Derek, you brat. He's the reason you're not a stole."

Koushee's wedge-shaped head swiveled to follow me, nose snuffling.

"This is the little guy who chewed up your disc?"

"The stinker snagged it from the coffee table when I wasn't looking. By the time I caught him, he'd gotten a couple of good chomps in." She ruffled the fur behind his ears. "Fuzzbutt here likes shiny things."

"I've never seen a skunk this color before." Or this close.

"He's an apricot chip. Most people don't realize they come in more than black and white."

"Can I pet him?"

"Fine by me. He'll let you know if he's not keen about it."

He didn't bite when I reached out, which I took as consent. His fur was lush and silky. Skunks were soft. Who knew?

The kettle gave a plaintive wail from the stove, and Lauren dumped Koushee to the linoleum. She spooned tea leaves from a tin into a cast-iron teapot that bore a striking resemblance to the critter at our feet, having two eyes at the base of the spout and a pair of round ears near the handle. Four stubs at the bottom could've been legs, and an off-center bulge a tail.

"Is that a skunk teapot?"

"Now what sort of whacko would come up with a skunk tea-pot?" She winked. "It's a tanuki, a Japanese raccoon dog. There's a long history of tanuki teakettles. They're supposed to be magical."

She held out the tin. "Sniff?"

Pretty girl says sniff, I sniff. I got a noseful of juicy guava, delicate marigold, and violets.

"What is it?"

"A blend I special order. Wait 'til you taste it."

She poured boiling water into the tanuki kettle. I half-expected it to yelp and scamper off, but it sat like a good teakettle while aromatic steam drifted from its spout. If the dry leaves had smelled good, the addition of hot water made them phenomenal. Without asking, Lauren spooned dark honey into my mug. She also filled a shallow saucer with tea, blowing it cool before setting it down.

"For Koushee?"

"If I don't give him any, he sulks."

Leaving the skunk to his tea, we took ours into a crowded living room. Along one wall was a floor-to-ceiling bookshelf filled with tomes in various stages of worn. They were stacked vertically and horizontally, leaning, listing, and separated by the odd knickknack. A plush fox was wedged between a stack of tattered paperbacks, a plastic gargoyle crouched in the arch formed by two hardcovers, and a jagged, black rock propped up a tower of mismatched spines.

Lauren lounged on a brown futon couch—the only seating—and I perched beside her to sip my tea. I burned my tongue.

"Good, huh?"

"Mmm." I puffed at the steam whorls, stifling a pained whimper.

"Want a cookie?" From beneath the futon, Lauren retrieved a box featuring a picture of Beatrix Potter's Peter Rabbit. "Amaretto biscotti, actually."

I doubted my scalded tongue was up for biscotti. "That's a strange place to keep food."

"Koushee stuck them there." Lauren bit the ears off a bunny.

"Your skunk seems to get into a lot of stuff." I risked another sip. No burn this time, and yes, it *was* good.

"He's high maintenance, but I like that he's clever. Plus, most witches don't think to cast hexes against skunks."

I remembered to swallow my mouthful of tea. "What?"

"Cats are common; everyone has a cat. Dogs and ferrets too, these days. I'm as surprised as the next gal to have ended up with a skunk as a familiar, but really, skunks are ideal: curious, intelligent, sensitive. He's also a great lap warmer in winter."

The strangest thing was happening. My thoughts kept leap-frogging away from coherent sentences. While Lauren spoke, I submerged deeper and deeper into a boggy, green-tea morass. A stream of headlines about drugged drinks and black market kidney harvesting spooled through my head, but they spooled right out again.

While I blinked in a tea daze, Koushee trundled in.

"Skunks also have impeccable timing." Lauren set aside her mug so she could hoist him into her lap.

She petted him—long, languid strokes. His eyes glowed that disturbing green, but this time it didn't faze me. After all, Lauren's eyes were glowing too.

Although I knew something queer was happening, I sat blissfully frozen, at peace with the world. A quiet grunting, between an oink and a purr, thrummed through the room. Koushee, of course.

Lauren thumped my chest, and her hand sank in wrist-deep. I didn't stir, although a part of me was hollering and having hysterics. It didn't hurt, more like a warm tingle. She yanked, and there was a squirming shape, all claws and teeth, gripped in her fist. The creature (lizard?) spread a pair of fleshy wings (bat?) and sank its fangs (snake?) into her thumb.

Lauren yelped, which shook off some of my paralysis, and flung the thing away. The lizard/bat/snake slithered into her kitchen. Koushee sprang after it.

"Dammit!" She chased after both, and sounds of breaking dishware crashed out.

The hysterical me was building up momentum.

"Derek!"

Still, a pretty girl in distress trumped hysterics.

In the kitchen, Lauren crouched over Koushee. The skunk was backed in a corner, tail fluffed to its full spread. He clamped the lizard-thing's thrashing wing in his jaws and clutched the rest between his front paws.

"No bite! Drop it!"

Koushee hissed.

Lauren held out her hand. "Give it."

The skunk eyed her.

"Give the nasty to Mommy. Do you want a cookie? Nice cookie?"

It seemed Koushee thought the proposed trade equitable; he let Lauren have his prize. She had a Tupperware container in her other hand—a long, skinny one, the right size for uncooked spaghetti. She shoved the lizard-thing in and snapped the lid shut.

"Derek, get me the duct tape. In there, above Foxy."

I charged to the other room. On the shelf over the toy fox, a roll of gray tape had been jammed between a pair of tattered paperbacks. I snagged it, starting a waterfall of books, and dashed back.

Muttering to herself, Lauren unwound a length of tape. Still clutching the spaghetti container, she used a steak knife to cut the strip free. Some of it doubled over, sticking to itself and twisting into a messy ribbon. I steadied the Tupperware for her while she sealed it shut.

Close up, the lizard/bat/snake turned out to be none of the above. Aside from having wings, it scrabbled at the plastic of its prison with six sets of wicked claws on the ends of its six spiny legs—which Biology 101 informed me was scientifically improbable for either mammal or herp.

I felt a nudge at my ankle. Koushee wobbled on his hind legs, his front paws waving in the air.

"Could you get him a treat?" Lauren asked. "Skunk cookies are in the drawer by the sink."

Uncooked spaghetti and shards of porcelain ground underfoot as I offered Koushee a bone-shaped biscuit from the drawer. He snatched it and trotted into the living room. Lauren tailed him, and I followed her.

The skunk disappeared beneath the futon and crunching sounds ensued.

"So, who did you piss off?" Lauren plopped down.

I sat beside her, mostly because otherwise, my knees would've folded where I stood.

"I saw you'd been marked at the computer lab," she continued, "but didn't realize it was a curse until Koushee told me."

"Koushee *talks to you?*"

She squinted. "You seriously have no clue, do you? Derek, sweetie, I'm a witch. Magic's for real."

"Nuh-uh. I'm a Protestant."

"Oh dear. Okay, look." She hopped up and grabbed the plush fox from the bookshelf. "Here." She plunked it in my lap.

The fox had two shiny, black button eyes, and a fuzzy crimson coat that had seen better days.

"Thanks?" It smelled like my grandmother's attic: lavender and dust.

"*Oracle fox,*" Lauren said, "*fox so bright, share your voice, share your sight.*"

"Excuse me?"

She blushed. "I was eight when I wrote that spell. At the time, it seemed like a good idea to imbue Foxy with the oracle voice, and I thought rhyming couplets were the height of sophistication."

The fox wiggled and opened its soft muzzle. "*A curse reveals a nose for magic,*" it said.

I almost chucked it across the room, but Lauren leaned in to hear the fox-spouted doggerel, giving me a straight-on view of her cleavage.

"*Avert with charm a fate most tragic,*" the fox chanted. Its voice was high-pitched and nasal, with a smug, lisping quality. "*Bring the curse to its maker; break the spell to forsake her.*"

I turned the fox upside down, looking for a battery hatch or a pull string, or better yet, an off switch.

"*Avert a witch's hex, don't kill her.*"

It kept talking, even upside down. No off switch either.

"*A life mundane or so familiar.*"

Nope, I couldn't deal. "I need to go." I stood.

"Don't be silly. Sit down and finish your tea."

For a whole half-second, I considered going against my hard-wired, guy conditioning. But Lauren remained a pretty girl, albeit one with a prophesying stuffed animal. I sat, lifted the half-empty, lukewarm mug of tea from the futon's arm, and downed it.

Even tepid, the stuff was good. I swallowed, and sunflower petals with a hint of cocoa beans lingered on my tongue. The skip-hop of my heart mellowed, and adrenaline-knotted muscles unkinked.

Lauren set the spaghetti container on the floor and stepped to her bookshelf. As soon as her hand passed over the black stone, I smelled ginseng and menthol.

"What's that rock?"

"Smoky quartz. Why?"

"Did you douse it in some Chinese herbal concoction?"

Her eyes widened. "Is that what you smell?"

"Don't you?"

She glanced at the plush fox. "*A curse reveals a nose for magic.* I was going to ask if you see things other people don't—"

"Nothing comes to mind."

"But now I want to know how long you've been sniffing the unusual."

"Define 'unusual.'"

"Strange, heady scents that other people don't notice."

"That's not magic. That's having a good sense of smell."

"Foxy says no."

"If a stuffed fox says so, it must be true."

Lauren grinned. "I *said* I was eight. C'mon, work with me. When was the last time your nose got overwhelmed by something extraordinary or distinctive?"

"Aside from you?"

"Aside from me."

Megan's cat box came to mind, but it seemed unchivalrous to bring up my ex's housecleaning shortcomings.

Koushee emerged from the recesses of the futon, biscuit crumbs clinging to his whiskers. He stuck his paw on my ankle, and I was immersed in scent memory: rancid fat and decaying flesh steeped in ambergris and ammonia. I gagged. Koushee removed his paw, and the smell was gone.

"What is it?" Lauren asked. "You've turned green."

"Megan's apartment. It was disgusting and . . . and *wrong*."

"Who's Megan?"

"My ex. When we started going out, she smelled like peaches and cloves."

"And then?"

"Last week I was staying over at her place, and, well, 'overwhelmed by something extraordinary or distinctive' sums it up, but not in a good way."

"Did you eat or drink anything there? A curse needs to be imbibed."

"She cooked dinner. Mac and cheese."

Lauren nodded. "Then what?"

"A *stink* woke me in the morning, so bad I almost puked. I thought it was her cat box. I grabbed my pants and bolted. Ended up calling her later and breaking it off over the phone. Not my finest hour, but the thought of meeting up with her in person started my eyes watering."

"Yep, Megan cursed you, all right. Don't feel too bad. It's common for noobs to try to explain the magical with the mundane."

"She cursed me because of the breakup?"

"Actually, no, she cursed you before that—although dumping someone over the phone is way up there on the curse-worthy front. But it seems you are what we call a *feral*. See, magic is mostly genetic—our crowd is way inbred—but sometimes folks dripping with power pop onto the scene, ones who don't have a sage or seer anywhere in their bloodline. I'm thinking Megan triggered a feral defense mechanism because a magic schnozzle is near unheard of, so she wouldn't have prepped for it. It probably saved you from being thralled to her."

"Thralled? What's *thralled?*"

"Thrall is a nice word for 'slave.' If a witch binds another's magic, she controls them. So runs traditional witch society."

"All your base are belong to us," I muttered.

Lauren raised an eyebrow. "I guess. Although it's more like a high school clique than Zero Wing. A feral thrall equals big-time popularity points."

"Lucky me," I said.

She frowned. "I'm betting her familiar tagged you. You said she has a cat?" Lauren rolled her eyes. "It's probably black and has some unoriginal name like Greymalkin."

"Isis."

"Uh-huh. So yeah, straightforward spell, straightforward counterspell. You have to confront her, like Foxy said."

"Why?"

"Because that," Lauren pointed at the trapped curse, "is a psychic parasite. Uninspired but nasty—fangs for rending thoughts, claws for tearing resolve, blah blah blah. It eats the thinking part of your brain, then it propels you to its maker. Voila, one thrall. You have to send it back to its summoner to be rid of it."

I shuddered. "I'm opposed to brain eating, so explain this confronting thing."

"Easy smeasy. Well, maybe less on the easy and more on the smeasy, but essentially, all you have to do is take the curse to Megan. If she wants you back, and she will, she'll ask you to obey her three times. Don't."

"That's it?"

"She won't make it easy for you to say no." She handed me the spaghetti container. "I've imbued the duct tape with virtue. It's sealed against malice and mayhem, but you can open it, Luke."

At my uncomprehending expression, Lauren winked. "'It has a light side and a dark side, and it binds the universe together.'"

I chortled. Weird curse and witchcraft aside, this girl was wicked geeky, a trait I admired.

"Pay attention, genius. You have to tell her three times you deny her and she has no power over you. Then release the curse. It should go for her—your cue to run away, quick as a bunny."

"Confront, deny, run away. Check."

She scooped up Koushee. "Now kiss him on the nose."

"Uh." I'd have preferred kissing Lauren.

"So he knows to watch out for you, because I like you."

Oh hell. I kissed the skunk.

· · ·

Megan's apartment was only a few blocks from the bus stop, but by the time I trudged to it, my backpack with the spaghetti container felt heavier than a semester's worth of textbooks.

I didn't notice anything on the stairs, but outside her door I smelled mold and an undercurrent of ammonia.

I knocked.

When the door opened, all traces of ammonia whisked away, replaced by peaches and cloves.

Megan looked as luscious as she smelled. The tight, low-ride jeans hugged the curve of her hips, and the white, button-down blouse clung to her breasts. Her golden hair curled around her shoulders with a playful bounce that made me think of other pieces of jiggling anatomy.

"Derek."

"May I come in?"

Megan stepped aside, brushing past me to lounge on her sofa. "Have a seat," she said.

She smelled so good—like ripe, spiced fruit—I wanted to bury my face in her hair. It took all my willpower to stay upright.

"I'm not sticking around," I said.

She pouted, her big, cornflower-blue eyes winsome. The delicate aroma of bruised aloe drifted up, tugging me to her side. At least I kept on my feet.

"What's your hurry?" She smiled, flashing cherubic dimples. "Hasty words were said, unfortunate words."

Her fingers drifted to the top button of her blouse. Red musk and freshly turned earth. "Didn't we have fun?" The button parted to reveal the shelf of her bra.

I swallowed. "Yeah."

I let her take my hand and lift it to the next button. It unfastened at my touch.

"Undress me, Derek."

I was going for her bra hook when I realized what was happening. *Undress me*, she'd said, and here I was, obeying her like I was already thralled.

I recoiled. "I-I'm just here to return something." Trying to rein in the shakes, I jerked open my backpack and grabbed the spaghetti container. The curse hissed through the plastic.

Megan gasped. The gasp turned into a squawk, and she fell over, writhing and twitching.

"Derek." Her voice was strangled, like she was forcing words through a constricting throat. "Call 911."

My pretty-girl-in-distress reflex activated, and I raced for the phone. I had it off the cradle and my finger on the 9 when the stink enveloped me. Fresh skunk. I've never been sprayed, only experienced it in passing from skunk-dog confrontations or the occasional skunk-car meet up. This was worse. Much worse. My eyes streamed with tears.

"Derek, hurry!"

What was a skunk doing in Megan's apartment? I hit the 1. Had Koushee followed me? But Lauren said he was de-scented.

I was a fingertip away from hitting the last 1 when I caught on. *Call 911* was a command as much as *undress me* had been. I slammed the phone down and swiveled around.

"You'll survive." I inhaled, and the skunk stench was gone.

Megan's transformation was sudden and scary. She glared, all pretense of medical crisis abandoned. "You little prick! This time I won't be so nice. I'll have you cleaning my toilet with your tongue. Isis!"

Megan's black Persian materialized and bounded into her mistress's waiting arms.

"*Exaudite maledictum meam!*" Megan intoned.

Isis's eyes glowed amber. The reek of burning tar and smoldering ashes hit me.

"Crap, crap, crap." I fumbled with the Tupperware container. The tape resisted, twisting and stretching.

"*Sisters of darkness, heed me.*" Megan's eyes were taking on the same color and illumination as her cat's.

"I deny you, Megan," I said. "You have no power over me."

"*Vindico juvenem—*"

"I deny you, Megan," I babbled, the words tumbling out. "You have no power over me."

My fingernails caught an edge of folded tape. I ripped, and the top came off with a sound like an imploding vacuum.

"*I call upon blight and desolation—*"

I threw the spaghetti container at her, curse and all, and bolted for the door. "I deny you, Megan," I shouted over my shoulder. "Youhavenopoweroverme!"

I spilled into the hall.

Behind me, Megan shrieked. There was a liquid noise, wet paper tearing. My mouth filled with the stench of sulfur. I lunged for the stairwell. A tendril of hot copper curled down my throat, but as I charged down the stairs, it dissipated as fast as the skunk musk had.

When I burst outside, all I could smell was sunshine and sky. I staggered away, quick as a gimpy bunny, and hoped my heart would quit trying to burst out of my chest. It slowed, eventually, and I headed back to Lauren's.

•   •   •

As soon as I pressed the doorbell, a bouquet of wild berries and juniper hit me. Lauren appeared a moment later and ushered me in.

"How'd it go?" She plopped onto her futon.

"The opposite of easy smeasy. She almost got me with the last one. Except a skunk happened to spray just then, and it shocked my head clear."

"A skunk—?"

Koushee, on cue, popped out from under the futon.

"Oh, he *did* help you!" Lauren scooped him up. "What a good boy," she cooed. "Who's a clever skunk? Koushee is, yes, he is."

I cleared my throat. "Lauren, is there something important about threes?"

"Yepper. It's a whole big mystic foundation."

"When I was here, you asked me to do three things."

"Did I?"

"Get the duct tape, finish my tea, and kiss your skunk on the nose."

"So?"

"And I *imbibed* something you brewed."

Lauren studied me from behind a pair of round skunk ears. "You think I cursed you?"

"Did you?"

She cuddled Koushee. "The thing about familiars, they're faithful and steadfast unto death, the best allies, but they're also all instinct and impulse. Koushee knows I need a bigger magical arsenal in order to maintain my autonomy; however, he can't grasp concepts like term papers and flunking out of school. He hooked us together in his own, simplistic way because he sensed you could be useful to me. But I'm *not* a traditionalist. I don't curse or thrall people. My friends and lovers support me because they want to and because they know they can count on me to do the same."

I flushed when she said *lovers*.

"I did dose your tea with a tranquility spell, but only because I didn't want you to freak when I went prospecting for curses."

Koushee purr-oinked as Lauren rubbed his head.

"So what happens if I deny you three times?"

"Go ahead, if it'll make you feel better."

I did, but my heart wasn't in it. Nothing happened except Koushee's whiskers quivered in what I was betting was the equivalent of a skunk laugh.

"If you want," Lauren said, "you can take off, go your own way, and I'll go mine. No harm, no foul."

"And if I stay?"

"Then I teach you about magic, and we become allies."

"What kind of allies?" My voice ended in a squeak, ruining my attempt at nonchalance.

Lauren set the skunk down. "That depends." Her hair smelled like pomegranates. "What kind do you want to be?" She kissed me, and her lips tasted like magic.

Koushee trotted away, thoughtfully giving us some privacy.

C. S. MacCath is a Celtic/Heathen hybrid whose fiction and poetry have appeared or are forthcoming in PanGaia, newWitch, Strange Horizons, Clockwork Phoenix: Tales of Beauty and Strangeness, Murky Depths, Mythic Delirium, *and* Goblin Fruit, *among others. At present, she is working on the first book in a series of novels entitled* Petals of the Twenty Thousand Blossom *and a short fiction collection entitled* Spirit Boat. *You can find her online at www .csmaccath.com.*

From Our Minds to Yours

BY C. S. MacCatH

I am burning sage, as much as I can stand to breathe. The glassworks is redolent with it, and I can see the Bling beginning to tear up. One woman is clutching a handkerchief she pulled from the black leather handbag that broke Maya's phoenix. The other woman is edging toward the door. Sage is hard to come by anymore unless you grow it yourself; you can't buy it in bulk like you could in my mother's day. So I'm squandering a little of my garden to get rid of them. They don't look like buyers to me, and I don't want them to break anything else.

"Do you make these?" The handkerchief bearer approaches the counter and gestures at the gallery, where clouds of sunlit smoke wreathe a menagerie in glass. Her lips stretch into a Carmine Rose smile, and she tucks a loose strand of Ash Brown #5 behind her ear.

"No, the shop belongs to a friend of mine." I cross my arms under my breasts and inhale, settling into my best "impassive black woman" posture. It's a technique that often works for me in court, given my taller-than-average stature and somewhat masculine features. I'm hoping it will discourage her from making conversation.

The woman hesitates for a second and then says, "Oh. So you just work here."

"Only when she needs a hand."

"Oh. And she lets you burn . . . whatever it is you're burning?"

I grin. "Sage has a cleansing vibration."

"Oh." The handkerchief bearer departs. Her compatriot is actively seeking exodus now. A moment later they're gone, so I open the doors and windows.

They hate to be called Bling. They say it's offensive and old-fashioned, but I think it's accurate. They come out of their corpo-villages smelling of car leather and canned atmosphere, swipe their credit cards a few times, and cart their slum treasure home in shiny electric sedans. To be fair, most are decent people, and I've provided legal representation to more than a few. But they're Inside, where medical care is consistent and superior, where markets still carry almost everything they used to, and where the village Intranet shapes their vision of the world. We're Outside, where many no longer have access to medicine, where we grow or barter for much of our food, and where we have whatever Internet we can afford. I'm lucky: I have a good education and a wealthy family, so I can live and work wherever I want. Most don't have that choice.

The back door opens. "You've had Bling today!" Maya shouts forward.

"How can you tell?" I shout back.

"You smoked them out."

"They broke your phoenix!"

"No! That piece took me hours. Did they pay for it?"

"Of course not."

"Girls, put your sweaters away and go say hello to your Aunt Adande."

There is a rustling of fabric and then a thunder of girl-feet into the gallery. Fran is twelve and young for her age, a black-haired beauty of a child; her younger sister Sammi is quiet and tough, ten going on thirty. I meet them halfway to slow them down, and they fling their arms around me.

"How did it go?" I look up at their mother.

She tosses me the car keys and shakes her head. Salt-and-pepper wisps fall over her brow. "He was good with them. He listened while they told him about their nightmares. He asked what prompted their interest in Peridyne toys and suggested they play with cheaper alternatives. Then he recommended we spend more time together and told us to use our imaginations."

"So he was useless, and he didn't tell you anything you didn't already know."

"He was kind, and he didn't know what to do."

"How much did he charge you for his kindness?"

"Adande, please."

I sigh and release the girls, who go into the back room to play. "I'm sorry. I know this is hard."

"And please don't smoke my customers out anymore."

"They broke your . . . "

"I know; you told me. But were they interested in anything else?"

I think about the question. "Not that I can remember," I tell her, "and I'm sorry for that, too. I'll try to be more . . . approachable when I watch the shop."

Maya laughs aloud, lays a slim, white hand on her midriff, and sits down. When she looks up at me, her gray eyes are merry. "Yes, that's you, my love—approachable."

"You should see me in court."

The girls begin to sing a Peridyne jingle, and Maya sobers.

"Why don't you let me take them back into the village and buy them a few things?" I ask her.

"Because I don't love you for your income, that's why, and because our lives aren't about the things we own."

"But if it will calm them . . . "

She reaches out and draws me toward her. "Teach them to play chess."

"Okay." I wrap my arms around her shoulders, lean down and lay my chin on her head. "But I still feel partly responsible for this. If I hadn't taken them into the village, they wouldn't have known what they were missing."

The girls are loud now, and the jingle is feverish. They burst into the room. Fran tugs at her mother's sweater.

"Will you take us into Peridyne *now*, Mom?"

"First of all, when did 'please' drop out of your vocabulary? And second, there isn't anything to play with in Peridyne that we can't duplicate here. We've already talked about this."

"Yes, we know." Sammi pushes her sister aside and steps forward. "You can't afford Peridyne toys, and the behavioral specialist told us to learn to play with what we have. But we *need* them, Mother."

"Why do you need them, Sammi?" I ask her, kneeling down.

"Because it hurts us not to have them."

I glance up at Maya, who nods her head in the affirmative. "It's what they say every time I ask them."

"How does it hurt you?" I wrap my dark, weathered fingers around their perfect, pale hands and look into their eyes, so like their mother's.

"It just does," Fran answers, and begins to sing again.

·   ·   ·

My car is crowded with people and food, and my trunk is full of witchery. There is a cascade of conversation falling over me: the community garden vis-à-vis the fucked-up weather, the fossil fuel statute. There is magical talk as well: the work of this evening's Moon, Beltane planning, the new rune set Sylph is making for Fran. It's a soothing thing, this friendly babble, and it loosens the knot of worry around my heart.

"How did the doctor's visit go today?" Sylph reaches up and puts her hand on my shoulder.

I glance into the rearview mirror at her freckled face and blue eyes. "He told them to spend more time together and to use their imaginations."

"What a crock." Her nose wrinkles. "How are the girls?"

"They're still having nightmares and singing Peridyne jingles."

"And you think this is happening because you took them to the mall?"

"I don't know. I can't imagine where else they could have seen Peridyne-branded toys. Not even I can find them outside the village or the Intranets, and I've got subscriptions to Peridyne and Microfield at work. The jingles I can understand. There's always some kind of music playing on the login screens, but you have to have a paid account to get into the online stores."

"Weird."

"Speaking of weird, you heard about Levi, right?" Dodge leans forward over his belly, and the beads on his silver beard braids click together.

"No. What happened to him?" Anni leans around to look at Dodge and rests an ancient hand on his knee. Her long, white hair loosens at her nape and falls over the collar of her blouse.

"He was caught in Peridyne two days ago stealing a blender."

My head jerks up. "A blender? What would a fifteen-year-old boy want with a blender? And why didn't Matt call me?"

"I have no idea, and because he can't afford you. Besides, you don't do criminal law." Dodge strokes his braids and grimaces.

"He knows I'll barter with him, and I can defend Levi in a misdemeanor case."

"Tell him that yourself. He'll be there tonight, and so will the boy."

We arrive at Maya's house as the sun is setting. Matt's ethanol conversion is parked out front, and he is sitting on the porch. Dodge plugs my car in, greets Matt with a grip of the forearm, and follows the others inside. I hang behind and sit down on the porch swing.

"I heard," I tell him.

"I thought Dodge would say something."

"Matt, I'll take repair work for payment, you know that."

"I wasn't going to ask."

"You should always ask."

"He's so torn up about this." Matt runs his hands over his close-cropped hair, and the fine lines around his dark eyes deepen as he frowns.

"How did he even get into Peridyne? It's a gated community."

"Well, my garage abuts the woods on one side, and the Peridyne mall abuts them on the other. He and the boys just cut through."

Levi opens the screen door, looks down at me, and offers his hand. I shake it.

"I know you're probably talking to Dad about the blender I stole, and I didn't think he should have to talk to you by himself." He comes outside and sits on the porch railing. "Will you represent me, Ms. King? I can work it off in trade."

"That's very mature of you," I tell him. "I'll take your offer of trade under advisement, but I have already decided to represent you."

"Thank you," he says, and his shoulders sag.

"Why did you steal the blender, Levi?" I look up at him and rest my hands on the seat.

"I don't know." His voice quavers, and his eyes fill with tears. "I honestly don't. Me and Peter and Yarrow never went into Peridyne when we were kids; we just played in the woods behind the garage. And then about two months ago, we decided to check the place out. After that, I started having these awful dreams."

My fingers grip the swing reflexively, but I manage to keep the anxiety out of my voice. "You've had nightmares?"

"Yeah, they're really bad sometimes, too. I'll be happy in them and be buying all kinds of things, and then I'll wake up and be . . . hungry for the stuff I dreamed about."

"You never told me about this." Matt stands up, and his rough hands reach out to his son. Levi allows himself to be embraced, and his long, blond hair falls over his father's shoulder. He sighs, rests there a moment, and then steps back.

"Because it was stupid, Dad. What was I supposed to do, tell you I was craving Peridyne blenders?

Maya peeks around the screen door and smiles. "You guys about ready?"

I stand up and position myself between the men and my beloved, giving them a chance to regain their composure. "We'll be right in."

. . .

Levi's case is easier to resolve than I expect it to be; I am able to negotiate a three-week community service sentence after a single phone call to the Peridyne prosecutor. During the conversation, though, I sense she's almost inclined to dismiss the case—not unusual for a first-offense misdemeanor, but even so her tone strikes me as odd. I resolve to discuss the interaction with Matt, but when I call him I barely have the chance to announce myself and say a few words.

"Levi's dreams are getting worse," he interrupts me, "and he hasn't slept more than a few hours at a time since you saw him on Friday. He won't sleep alone in his room anymore either; he says he's afraid he'll go sleepwalking."

"Matt, that's horrible. Have you taken him to a doctor?"

"And have the doctor tell me the same thing he told Maya? I can't afford that. There's something else," he adds, lowering his voice. "I went into Peridyne yesterday to see the store where Levi stole the blender and ended up spending a week's earnings at the mall. I have no idea why I did it, and you'll never believe the crap I bought. But I haven't felt this good since I was popping disco biscuits, and I can't bring myself to take anything back. I've got it all stuffed into a box at the garage."

"What the hell is going on?" I lean back in my chair, take off my reading glasses, and rub my eyes.

"I don't know, but I'm not sending my son back in there. I don't care what you've negotiated."

"Let me get back to you in a little while, all right? I want to check in on Maya and the girls and see how they're doing."

I dial her number at the shop, but nobody answers, so I dial her cell. By the time I get her voicemail, I am already in the car. I arrive at the glassworks to find it closed and speed on to her house a few blocks away. The police are out front, and Maya is standing on the porch wearing an old sweater and jeans. I don't see Fran and Sammi, but as I get out of the car I can hear them singing somewhere inside the house.

"What's going on?" I ask her as I run to the porch, but a stocky blond officer in a Peridyne uniform intervenes.

"Who are you?" she asks.

"I'm her attorney," I reply, and look down at the woman. "Now I'll ask again, and I expect an answer this time. What's going on?"

"The girls ran away this morning," Maya tells me, wiping her eyes on her sleeve. She has been crying a long time. "The Peridyne police found them outside the mall."

"I'm glad they're safe," I tell her and turn toward the officer. "Thank you for your help. Now, why are you still here, and why haven't you permitted my client the use of her cell phone?"

"My cell phone is inside. I heard it ring . . . "

"The children are being questioned by Child Protective Services. The parent is not permitted to be present."

"Are there police officers inside the house?"

"Yes," Maya answers. "Her partner took the girls in."

"Did you give her partner your specific consent to be there?" I ask her.

"I . . . I don't remember."

I move past her and open the screen door. Fran and Sammi are sitting in the living room with two middle-aged women in expensive business suits and pumps. There is a police officer in the kitchen, opening cabinets.

"You!" I point at the officer. "Do you have a warrant?"

He looks into the living room and walks toward me, a sausage-fingered hand on his holster. "Who are you?" he asks, raising a thick, black eyebrow.

"I am Maya Cleary's attorney, and I asked you if you have a warrant for the search you are currently conducting."

"She invited me in."

"Then why is she outside? No, I think it more likely that these women used their authority as agents of Child Protective Services to bully Maya, and you seized an opportunity to follow them into the house and conduct an unauthorized search."

"We have a legal right to question children we believe are in danger." One of the women walks toward me. I glare at her, and she stops.

"Their mother has a legal right to have her attorney present during that questioning." I answer. "So after this officer has shown me his search warrant, I will sit down with you."

"I apologize for the misunderstanding, ma'am. If you'll excuse me." The policeman slides past me and walks out of the house.

"Now," I turn my attention to the women, "you'll begin by telling me exactly what you've asked these children. After that, they'll be given the opportunity to tell me what has happened in their own words. When they've finished, you may proceed with your questions."

"I think we've satisfied ourselves that Fran and Sammi aren't in any *immediate* danger." The second woman lifts her head and frowns.

"Excellent. Then you'll be going now." I follow them out and stand on the porch with Maya while her guests depart in their respective vehicles. When they have gone, she lays her head on my shoulder, and I wrap her in my arms.

"Thank you," she says simply, and then draws in a deep breath. "Let's go talk to the girls."

"I need to call Matt first," I tell her. "And you should speak with him before you go inside."

．　．　．

Levi is in the basement, reading to Fran and Sammi out of a book of fairy tales he brought from home. I can hear his voice rising above the drone of the dishwasher, strong and sure despite his weariness. Maya is pouring tea out of a Japanese pot and slicing hot bread. Even under stress, she soothes and comforts the people around her, a magic I'm certain I'll never master. Matt takes a plate and cup from her, smiling his gratitude.

"I've been thinking about this," he says to Maya, "and I've made a list of things your family and mine have in common." He takes a bite of bread, opens a folded sheet of paper, and invites us to follow his notes.

"Okay. We both have businesses near Peridyne, which means we both get village customers pretty regularly. The children were fine until they went into Peridyne; then they started to crave village products and have bad dreams. I went into Peridyne and felt like I'd taken Ecstasy while I was shopping there." He looks at Maya. "Have you ever been to the village?"

"I went in once a couple of years ago to get nutmeg for a recipe, but I found it at the food co-op after that. I'm not comfortable in Peridyne," she adds. "But what about Adande? She goes in and out of there all the time."

"She also has the money to buy whatever she wants when she wants it, just like the people who live there." He turns to me. "Have you ever craved anything from Peridyne?"

"Well, as much as I like to complain about the place, you're right. I have the money to buy whatever I want, and I do shop there from time to time. But I wouldn't say there's anything in Peridyne I can't do without. What are you getting at?"

Matt sips his tea and puts his mug down. "This is going to sound crazy, but hear me out. I think Peridyne residents are being infected with something that makes them brand-loyal, something they shed. I think Maya and I have been exposed to it because we have shops near the village, and that's where the kids picked it up. I also think you've been exposed, but probably not to the same extent, and whatever cravings you might get are satisfied when you shop there."

"You mean like a virus?" I ask him. "What kind of virus would make you crave things only after you've seen them up close, drug you if you satisfy the craving, and give you nightmares if you don't?"

"I don't know," he answers. "I'm not a doctor; I just know machines."

"Nanobots could do it. I've read about how they treat diseases and stuff." Levi is standing at the basement door, listening to us. "Can we have some bread? We can smell it all the way downstairs."

Maya tells Levi to get plates out of the kitchen cabinet, and I pause to consider what Matt has said. Suddenly, I begin to see connections between events: the prosecutor's eagerness to resolve Levi's case, the behavior of the Peridyne police, and the visit from Child Protective Services.

"They don't know what's happening either," I murmur thoughtfully. "They've had more visitors from the Outside and an increase in crime, but they don't know why."

"How do we find out if Matt is right?" Maya asks.

I turn to Matt and say, "My sister is a nurse practitioner at the Microfield College clinic. Let me see if she has any ideas." Then I pull my cell phone from my handbag and dial Halla's number. When she answers, I give her the situation in brief.

"Adande, I know you don't approve of our lifestyle, but I can't believe you think Peridyne is deliberately addicting people to its products. That's just paranoid."

"I'm not prepared to argue with you about this. These children need medical attention their parents can't afford. If I bring them into the clinic and pay for their visits myself, will you examine them and do blood tests?"

"Of course I will. I have emergency walk-in hours tomorrow morning; you can bring them in then." She pauses. "And I'm sorry

I said you were paranoid. If my friends' children were behaving as you've described, I'm not sure what I'd think."

"Thank you for saying so," I tell her, and end the call.

Microfield is a four-hour drive from Peridyne, so Matt and Levi stay at Maya's house overnight, and I collect the children early in the morning for the trip north. The girls are subdued; they're old enough to realize their behavior is hurting Maya but too young to fight their cravings and deal with their nightmares alone. So Levi reads to them all morning with the same weary courage he showed the night before, and I am moved once again by the quality of his character.

When we arrive, Halla's assistant ushers the children into separate examination rooms and asks me to wait outside. Halla is my younger sister by almost a decade—a polished, gracious woman like most of her neighbors, and with many of the same attitudes. She is compassionate with me and with the children, though, examining each of them separately and listening to their concerns.

"Physically, they're fine," she tells me after she finishes. "But they're under quite a bit of stress. Whatever it is they're dealing with, it's upsetting them. Tell you what," she offers, "I have a colleague and friend in the Physical Sciences department who might have a microscope capable of seeing nanoparticles. If you like, I'll ask him to look at their blood samples. At least then we can rule out your concerns and move forward with diagnosis and treatment."

"Thank you, Halla. I really appreciate this."

"It's good of you to be so kind to them," she tells me, and there is an undertone in her compliment I choose to ignore.

The children and I do not stop for lunch in Microfield as we might otherwise have done. Instead, we wait until we are well outside of town and picnic in a public park while Levi finishes reading from his book.

"You're growing into a good man," I tell him afterward, while the girls are taking turns on a nearby swing set.

"Thank you, Ms. King." He offers me a half-smile and looks over at Fran and Sammi. "But my dad was right about what's happening to us, and I think I'm right about what's causing it."

"What makes you think so?" I ask him.

"Nothing else makes sense, and I just feel it." He shrugs. "You won't be able to fix this, and neither will Dad or Maya."

"Don't give up on us yet," I tell him, and squeeze his arm.

He pulls away and stands up. "Some problems can't be solved, Ms. King," he tells me, and then goes to play with the girls.

. . .

I am awakened at four o'clock the following morning by a hammering at my apartment door, and I open it to find Halla there. She is still wearing the same skirt and blouse she had on the morning before, and she looks tired and disheveled.

"Yusef looked at their blood," she tells me as I usher her into the kitchen and heat water for coffee. "Then he looked at his own. Then he called me, and we looked at mine. Then we looked at all the samples again under a different microscope. We wanted to be sure." She sits down at the table and puts her head in her hands. "He says we all have a significant number of nanoparticles in our blood."

"So Microfield is doing it as well." The kettle whistles, and I grind the beans for coffee. "I would imagine it's a widespread practice then. There are at least, what? Four corpo-communities per state on average? Two per province in Canada?"

"And several abroad. If that's Peridyne coffee, I don't want it," she tells me as I put a mug in front of her.

"Free Trade. I get it through the food co-op."

She wraps her fingers around the mug and takes a sip. "You should probably throw this mug out, scrub everything I've touched, and toss your cleaning rags after I leave."

"What do you know about these nanoparticles?"

"Yusef told me they can only communicate over short distances, no more than a few meters."

"Which would explain why Matt and the children didn't have any symptoms until they first went into the mall."

"Perhaps. Your friend's euphoria might also be symptomatic; nanotreatment is often used in lieu of antidepressants. I prescribe it all the time."

"So they have the ability to regulate brain chemistry?"

"We think these are programmed to communicate interest in corpo-products and interfere with serotonin levels. The nightmares might be the result of a lack of exposure to fresh nanoparticles. They don't run forever; they're machines, but the brain can come to rely on them for neurochemical support." She slides her cup over to me, and I refill it.

"Either that, or they're operating on a reward-and-punishment system."

Halla looks at me over her upraised mug. "We talked about that, too. When I left Yusef at the college, he told me he was going home to wake his family and pack. I doubt he'll ever go back to work."

"Levi was right, then."

"How so?"

"He said some problems were unsolvable, and this was one of them." I fold my hands on the table and lean forward. "In the last week, I've interacted with a number of middle-level Peridyne officials, and they don't appear to know what's happening to them. Upper-level officials are part of the corporate infrastructure, so if they know about this, they're facilitating it. And since corpo-villages are privatized, our only recourse would be to contact the state and federal governments."

"Would they believe us?"

"Would it matter? The corpo-villages are mini-states; they have their own, inviolate legal systems and they contribute heavily to election campaigns."

"Unsolvable," she says, and shakes her head.

I lean back and gaze over Halla's shoulder into my study. The desk lamp is on and turned toward my altar, where I had been praying before bed. My wooden statues of Ochosi and Yemaya are illuminated there beside green and blue pillar candles, and a bouquet of spring wildflowers rests between them in a crystal vase.

"Maybe," I answer, "and maybe not."

· · ·

We are burning sage. It wafts upward through the open casement windows, carrying our prayers to heaven. Wreathed as it is in holy smoke, Maya's basement is a place out of dream. Glass dragons and other beasts hang on fishing twine from a powder-blue ceiling. The walls are painted with murals, mandalas, and little-girl musings. Hand-thrown candleholders rise in twisting columns to various heights, illuminating the room in the flickering hues of flame and glass.

My chosen family is here: Maya, Fran, Sammi, Matt, Levi, Dodge, Anni, and Sylph. Halla is here too, looking uncomfortable but interested, and I am proud of her for reaching out. There is also a woman I have never met, Sylph's High Priestess from her coven back home, who has come to escort Anni, Maya, Matt, and the children to Sunwise Sanctuary at the end of the ritual.

"Please change your mind." Maya's fingers are threaded through mine, and she is looking up at me with wide, haunted eyes. "Come with us."

I put my free hand on her cheek. "I can't. Halla can't do this by herself; she's already addicted, and who knows what else might happen once we expose this?"

Halla is standing behind me, and she circles around to speak to Maya. "I'm sorry we haven't met before, and I'm sorry Adande is involved in this." She wrings her hands. "But I will take care of her and return her to you as soon as I can, I promise."

"Let's get started." Anni moves to the edge of the circle. We link up, and she leads us in a grounding meditation until we are tapped in like the root of an old tree and breathing with the earth beneath our feet. We unlink. She fetches a candle from the altar and walks to the center of the circle.

"The most sacred words a witch can say are 'As I do will, so mote it be'," she begins. "When we say them, we promise to tell the truth always; how can we will anything with mouths that lie? When we say them, we promise to keep our promises; how can we will anything with honor that wavers?"

Halla nods in agreement and relaxes a little. Dodge squeezes her shoulder and smiles encouragement.

Anni continues. "This thing we've discovered is damaging to our will. It makes us want things we don't want. It makes us do things we wouldn't do otherwise. It takes away our most sacred power." She walks clockwise around the circle and looks at each of us in turn. "Tonight we take it back, and tomorrow we start returning it to everyone else."

Sylph joins her in the center of the circle, and together they cleanse it, cast it, and bless it. When they're done, Sylph takes the candle from Anni and speaks.

"When you feel ready, come and speak your will to the group."

A moment passes in silence while we all gather our thoughts, pray to our gods, and string the right words together in our minds. Dodge takes the candle first.

"I'm not going anywhere," he says. "I promise to stay right here and watch out for everybody's places while you're gone. It's gonna take more than a bunch of little robots to take *me* down." He stops, strokes his beard, and thinks. Then he approaches the children. "I am a son of the Wolf, and I am your friend. I will walk in your dreams from now until you feel better, and I will guard you. Don't worry if you don't see me; wolves know how to guard from the shadows." He opens his arms and gathers Levi, Fran, and Sammi into his embrace. "As I do will, so mote it be."

"So mote it be!" We echo his words, and he passes the candle to me.

"By Libra I come to you," I say as I walk into the circle, "by the Justice card and the balance of scales. I am a woman of Law. I am here to tell you that I will protect your rights and your freedoms, and I will fight until this ugly thing is gone and the people who have done it are punished. By Ochosi and Yemaya I do so swear, and as I do will, so mote it be."

"Yes!" Dodge shouts, clapping his hands.

"So mote it be!" The response is loud and firm; the energy is rising now. Halla reaches for the candle. My eyes widen, but she nods, so I hand it over.

"My name is Halla King-Crichton. I am a nurse practitioner in Microfield," she says, and steps forward a few paces. "I help people to heal, and I promise to keep doing my job, even if it gets hard. I also promised Maya I would take care of my sister." She looks at me and whispers, "So mote it be?"

"So mote it be!" I say, and grin.

"So mote it be!" The group shouts, and there is more clapping and cheering. Levi walks over to her and asks for the candle. She gives it to him.

"I told Ms. King a couple of days ago that some problems can't be solved." He looks at me and lifts his head. "I'm sorry I said that now. I promise to try and be more hopeful and to help find whatever answers there are."

"I hope that boy marries one of my daughters someday," Maya says, and adds, "I hope his best friend marries the other."

The rite continues. Sylph promises to galvanize her old coven when she gets home. Her High Priestess, an iron-eyed Queen of Swords, promises to network with other sanctuaries and groups so that Pagan refugees have places to go, people to turn to for help. Anni promises to e-mail every warm body in Congress and keep e-mailing them until they start intervening in the matter. Fran and Sammi promise to be good and to help in whatever way they are able.

Matt and Maya take the candle together, and for a moment I wonder if time and separation will turn my beloved's heart in his direction. I feel a spike of jealousy, and then I promise myself that I will love her no matter whom she chooses, that I will respect and bless whatever decisions she makes. They approach their children.

"We are your parents," Matt says, his voice shaking, his hands flat against his legs, "and though we don't entirely understand what's happening to you, we *will* find a way to make things better. So don't worry, okay?"

Maya opens her mouth to speak but begins to cry and falls silent instead. I move forward to put my hands on her waist, and the rest of the circle moves with me. We surround the two families, touch their arms, their heads, and take their hands. We offer solace, compassion, and whatever strength our wills can muster.

"So mote it be," Anni says, and puts the candle out.

The coals burn down. We close the circle and file upstairs for food and conversation, passing suitcases, bags, and boxes along the way. We don't know when we'll see each other again, so we try a little too hard, laugh a little too loud, and hold our farewells in check until the last possible moment.

"She won't leave you, Aunt Adande." Sammi finds me alone on the porch, struggling to compose myself so that I can go back to the party. She reaches up, takes my hand, and pulls me down to eye level. Her gray eyes are clear and deep, and her long hair is pulled back into two tight braids.

"You don't think so?" I ask her, and wonder how old her soul is.

"She loves you, and so do we. We don't leave the people we love just because we're apart for a while."

Old, I decide. Very old indeed. I stand up, and we go back into the house together.

Sophie Mouette is the pseudonym for two widely published writers of speculative fiction, romance, and erotica. The two halves of Sophie—Dayle A. Dermatis and Teresa Noelle Roberts—met more than a decade ago at a writers' conference. Although they've always lived on opposite sides of the country (and for a few years on opposite sides of the Atlantic), they've remained close friends and critique partners, and it was only natural that they should write together as well. Teresa describes herself as an eclectic Pagan and Dayle is a rigidly anti-dogmatic Pagan, but both see strong ties between sex and spirituality, and that theme often features in their work. For more information about Sophie and her multiple personalities, see www.cyvarwydd.com and www .teresanoelleroberts.blogspot.com.

Under a Double Rainbow

BY SOPHIE MOUETTE

Andrea: Alpha

Andrea Eisley took a deep breath, preparing to do the invocation that would open GoddessFest 2008. She surveyed the gathered circle, fighting past her first impression of corn-fed housewives. There had to be more to them than she could see on the surface. They'd come to GoddessFest, which meant at the very least they were curious and open to unconventional ideas. For all she knew, any of them might know more about women's spirituality than she did, or be a mathematical genius, an FBI agent, a professional wrestler, or any number of colorful possibilities. But they looked about like any randomly chosen group of Kansas women might. Mostly white—Andrea, whose ancestry included Chinese, Cuban, and Anglo-Irish, felt very conspicuous—and mostly conservatively dressed, except for a few students. Mostly boring-looking. She couldn't help comparing them to the women in the New England college town where she'd last taught. A random selection of women from Northampton would have more ethnic variety, but more importantly, more women with presence.

Or maybe she was being unfair simply because it didn't appear to be a date-rich environment. *Lady, I didn't volunteer to help with this conference just to meet a partner, but would it have been too much to ask to have a few single fortyish dykes in this group? We've got couples, baby dykes, and a whole lot of straight women.*

She supposed it was a good thing that she got tapped for a tenure-track position at Kansas State right around the time the coven in Northampton went out of control and Cecily dumped her. It was time to get out of town, and art history positions weren't that easy to find. But why couldn't it have been at Cornell or Berkeley or anywhere more exciting than this?

Her eyes were drawn again to an older woman in a black jersey skirt and slightly asymmetrical jacket. A familiar face that Andrea couldn't place, she was quirkily attractive with her short salt-and-pepper hair, her big earrings—she'd be irresistible if she didn't seem so sad. Andrea kept looking at her surreptitiously.

And every time, the older woman was still wearing the damn wedding ring. Just her luck. The only really intriguing woman in the place was straight.

Well, best to get on with the ritual, even if she was uninspired. At least the rain had died to a warm drizzle and everyone was willing to move out to the hotel terrace. It wasn't exactly a glorious setting, with its view of the campus in one direction and what, to her eastern eyes, looked like endless flatness in the other, but it was less sterile than the conference center. She thought sadly, looking at the view, of the hills around Northampton. Of her friends there. Of chocolate-brown Cecily with her carpenter's hands, who didn't love her anymore.

It was small wonder Andrea was distracted. She meant to say Isis, the mother-protector of Egyptian myth. But what came out of her mouth was Iris.

Iris? She ran through her mental database. Iris was the Greek divine messenger and goddess of the rainbow. That would work on this drizzly day, and a messenger goddess seemed appropriate where people had come to learn. Besides, she didn't want to correct herself in front of so many women who were looking to her as the expert. Better to ad-lib. "Iris," she intoned, "Lady of the rainbow, goddess of communication, give us the power to listen and speak clearly, so we may receive what messages we need to learn at this gathering."

There was a collective gasp.

Andrea opened her eyes, alarmed. Her ad-lib hadn't been *that* awe-inspiring!

A double rainbow was forming in the eastern sky.

Sometimes, Andrea tried to tell herself, something that looks like a sign is just a coincidence. But she didn't really believe it. For the first time in her life, Andrea—and everyone in the circle—could *see* the results of a ritual, not just feel the warmth and energy that could arguably be good group dynamics or self-delusion.

And for this to happen at a time when her heart and faith were equally dried up . . . she didn't know whether to be ecstatic or terrified.

From across the room, a short, curvy black woman in a loud rainbow Pride T-shirt winked at her and grinned broadly.

That pushed Andrea toward panic. The rainbow-clad woman, with her cocoa skin and short, reddish hair, looked like a slightly softer version of Cecily—and she hadn't been there when the ritual started.

• • •

Meghan and Trish

Meghan wrapped her towel more securely beneath her armpits—for the third or fourth time—took a deep breath, and pushed open the door that led from the women's dressing room to the pool area.

A gust of moist, heavy air clogged with the scent of chlorine hit her. At the same time, so did the noise. She'd made sure the dressing room was echoing-empty before she changed. It was a stark contrast to the cacophony of women's voices, calling and laughing, and the splashes as they dove into the pools. Over it all, the sound system was playing Meredith Brooks's "Bitch."

Meghan stepped to one side, not wanting to be framed in the doorway. Nobody seemed to be paying a whit of attention to her. Still, she automatically did the Fat Chick check: *Am I the fattest person in the room?*

She was never sure if she should be relieved or guilty when she saw that the answer was no. In fact, at that moment, a large, stunning woman walked by, turning her head to flash a brilliant smile at Meghan. She had, Meghan thought, a perfect hourglass figure—and yet she had to weigh at least two hundred pounds. She didn't try to hide it, either: She wore a skinny spandex racing suit of diagonal rainbow stripes, which contrasted nicely with the black French braid that reached to her waist.

Meghan felt vaguely embarrassed by the dark blue suit she had hidden under the towel, with its carefully placed ruffles and little skirt. But it was the only one she'd brought, and something about the confident way the other woman walked made Meghan not want to retreat to the dressing room.

A moment later, she saw Trish.

Her former lover was sitting in one of the sunken hot tubs, her arms up along the sides, her eyes closed.

Emboldened in a way she'd never felt before, Meghan went to the hot tub and sat on the yellow-tiled edge, slipping her legs into the water. The four other women in the tub said hello, then went back to their conversation. Their greeting caused Trish to look to see who had arrived. Meghan couldn't read the expression that flickered across Trish's blue eyes.

"Hi," Trish said softly. "I . . . I guess I wasn't sure if you were still going to come."

They'd planned the conference as a vacation, before they'd split up.

"It was easy enough to get another room," Meghan said. "People needed a fourth for their quad room so it would be cheaper. I still wanted to hear the speakers."

Trish hesitated, then placed one hand on Meghan's foot, under the water. To Meghan's surprise, she reacted to the touch. Her immediate response to Trish had always been nothing short of magical to her. She could feel each of Trish's fingers, individually placed on her arch. How could the top of her foot be so sensitive?

She deliberately distracted herself by asking, "Did you find another roommate?" She didn't want to know the answer, hated the pain that made Trish close her eyes for a moment.

"No," Trish said. "I left it as a single. I'm glad you're here, Megs. I've missed you."

"Have you?" Meghan didn't intend to be harsh, but the pain dragged the question from her.

"Yes." Trish spoke the simple word with clarity, strength. "I've missed you, and I was hoping you'd be here, because I wanted to see you and talk to you."

One of the other women in the tub said goodbye to her companions and stepped out of the water. Meghan noticed that she was short, with small breasts and large thighs. The woman draped her towel around her shoulders as she walked away, not trying to cover up.

Meghan took advantage of the distraction, and dropped her own towel and slid into the hot tub as quickly as she could. Over the chlorine haze she could smell Trish's lavender-scented hair. It lanced through her, right down to her clit. How could she be reacting so strongly, when the rest of the emotion wasn't there for her?

She wanted to sit closer to Trish—her body wanted to, almost desperately—and feel their thighs brush together. But her heart sheered away, her mind latching onto the fact that they were in a public place and wasn't everybody going to laugh at beautiful slim blond Trish and her fat mousy old girlfriend?

The large woman in the brilliant rainbow bathing suit walked by the tub to the edge of the pool. Barely pausing, she dove in, the movement more graceful than Meghan would have imagined. She glanced at Trish.

"Do you think she's pretty?" she asked.

Trish pursed her lips. "In some ways, yes. She has an aura of confidence, which is very sexy. I'd say she's prettier than the woman over there, who's obviously trying to suck in her stomach, or the one over there, who's got a lovely body but looks entirely uncomfortable in that bikini. But honey," she said, shifting so that she was facing Meghan (and her foot sliding across Meghan's calf in a way that made Meghan shiver), "none of them can hold a candle to you. I just wish there were some way I could get you to believe that."

Meghan closed her eyes, feeling tears prick behind her eyelids. "It just seemed like anywhere we went, people were watching us, trying to figure out what you were doing with someone ten years older and a hundred pounds heavier."

"I don't care what people think!" Trish exclaimed, smacking the side of the tub with her hand.

"Blessed be, sister!" a woman, walking by, called out.

"But you wanted me to lose weight," Meghan said.

"Only because you seemed so unhappy with it, and also because of your health," Trish said softly, cupping Meghan's face. "Your beauty has nothing to do with the size of your thighs, Megs. I fell in love with you because of your passion, your laugh, your spirituality, your compassion. But the fact is, on top of that, I do think you're gorgeous. If I didn't love you so much, I'd hate you for the fact that your skin is so soft and perfect that you never have to wear makeup. I think every inch of you is sexy, especially the dimples at the backs of your knees, because otherwise, why would I be so obsessed with licking them?"

Trish's voice got huskier and lower as she talked, until the last line was breathed in Meghan's ear. "And the way you react to that . . . ooh, honey, it just drives me up between your thighs, because you are never so beautiful as when you come all over me."

The steaming water wasn't what was making Meghan flush, and it couldn't counteract the stiffening of her nipples or the ache growing in her clit.

"I'm not sure I believe you," she said. Then, quickly, as Trish's face began to fall, she grinned and added, "I think we need to experiment and see if it's really true."

They were in the elevator before Meghan realized she'd completely forgotten her towel.

And she didn't care.

Ash and Calliope

Calliope Moonlight had the most luscious ass that Ash Stormwind had ever seen.

Right now that ass was clad in a screaming purple thong ("the same color as my hair in the eighties," Calliope always said), and Calliope's hips swayed provocatively as she headed toward the bed where Ash was lying.

Only to plop down, followed by Calliope opening a bottle of black glitter nail polish with which to adorn her toes.

Ash rolled over and suppressed a sigh. They'd had hot, hot, hot sex when they arrived at the hotel, before going down to participate in the opening ritual. Then they'd had a few drinks at the bar and met some of the other women before coming up to their room to crash. They'd attempted some halfhearted fumbling, but they were both too tipsy to get down to any serious business.

Now it was the next morning, and Ash just didn't feel . . . settled. She'd tried grounding and centering, but that didn't seem to work. She didn't think she could meditate with the scent of nail polish scoring the air. And she was far too restless to just sit here on the scratchy hotel bedspread.

"I'm going to get some ice," she announced, rolling off the bed and reaching for her "Get a Taste of Religion: Lick a Witch" T-shirt.

Calliope looked up, a lascivious grin curving her full, kissable lips. "Excellent idea."

Ash grinned back. Surprisingly, she hadn't been thinking about ice like that . . . not that it wasn't a good idea.

·   ·   ·

As she shifted from foot to foot, waiting for the groaning machine to spew more ice into the bucket, she watched a truly steamy babe walk by. The woman wore a tiny black dress and high heels with straps that wound around her calves. Her hair was dyed into a rainbow of colors and part of it reached to the curve of her butt. The rest of it was pulled up and twisted around, so that the ends stuck out in a rainbow halo.

Ash selected a piece of ice with the intent of lasciviously sucking on it. Instead, she found herself crunching down on it, and simply nodding a hello when the woman caught her eye.

What was that all about? she wondered. Normally she would have been sidling up and asking if the woman were available. Ash and Calliope didn't have a truly exclusive relationship, although neither of them had dated anyone else since they'd started dating each other three months ago. There just hadn't been time . . .

Ash swallowed the remaining ice chips so quickly that she got a cold headache. *Sweet Mother*, she thought. *I'm not hot for that woman's butt because I'm in love with Calliope Moonlight.*

·   ·   ·

Calliope was sprawled on her stomach, reading the program information packet, when Ash returned. Ash put the bucket on the desk and sat gingerly on the edge of the bed.

"Hey . . . " she said.

Calliope looked up. "Hey."

"What's your name?"

Her lover blinked. "It's Calliope, sweetheart."

"No, I mean your real name?"

"That is my real name." Calliope rolled over until her head was on Ash's lap. Her hair tickled the sensitive skin on Ash's thighs. "I picked it all by myself. Mmm, no panties," she said, nuzzling up under Ash's miniskirt. "Why do you ask?"

Ash took a deep breath. "I was just thinking about our relationship." It was hard to think, though, with Calliope's tongue tracing circles maddeningly closer and closer to her crotch. "I guess I was . . . wondering . . . if there was more to it than . . . sex." The last word came out as a gasp as Calliope reached her pussy lips and thrust the tip of her tongue in and out. Not enough to make Ash come, but enough to make her blindingly close. She spread her legs, hoping Calliope would take the hint.

"Not right now," Calliope mumbled. For a moment, Ash couldn't remember what the question was. Even when she did, she decided she couldn't care. Couldn't even focus. She fell back on the bed and pushed up her T-shirt, pinching her own nipples as Calliope licked her, coaxing out her juices. She had such a way of bringing Ash so close to the edge . . .

Calliope slipped a teasing finger inside of Ash, slowly. Ash tried to squirm on it, but the finger left as carefully as it had entered. Then Calliope slid the finger into Ash's ass, just as she flicked her tongue across Ash's clit.

For an interminable second, nothing. Then Ash's body imploded, her hips raising off the bed as everything inside her turned to fiery liquid.

When she came back to herself, Calliope was at her side, face glistening. "I love it when you come so hard," she purred.

Ash responded by flipping over and crawling on top of her. She straddled Calliope's thigh, gently rubbing her tingling clit against her lover's flesh. She was too sensitive to come right away, but soon . . . Calliope wriggled, trying to press her own cunt against Ash's knee, but Ash smiled and shook her head, and pinned Calliope's arms above her with one hand. Calliope moaned. Ash dipped her head and nipped at Calliope's breast, scraping the nails of her other hand against her lover's other nipple. Ash rocked her hips back and forth, still amazed at how sensitive Calliope's breasts were; sometimes she could come just from them being played with.

But Ash wasn't in the mood for long, drawn-out sex. Suckling Calliope's nipple, she reached down and, pausing to ensure Calliope was suitably drenched, plunged three fingers into her. Her cunt clenched hard around Ash's hand as she came, and Calliope screamed loud enough to no doubt startle the people in neighboring rooms. Spurred on by her lover's orgasm, Ash's body reacted in kind, her clit shivering, trembling, as she came.

Afterward, Calliope nestled in the crook of Ash's shoulder, her hand curved around Ash's hipbone. Inexplicably, Ash felt tears come to her eyes. This felt so right, not just on a playful level, but on a deeper, emotional one.

"Look," she said. "This is a really stupid time to bring it up, but I feel like our relationship has gone beyond just mind-numbing, bed-breaking sex. I think there's more here, and I want to explore that. If you don't, well, I guess that's cool too, because we didn't go into this with any expectations." She was amazed at how she was chattering on, but Calliope wasn't saying anything, and she was afraid if she stopped, she'd hear something she didn't want to.

"Mary Beth Watkins."

"What?" Ash asked, confused.

"I want to take this further, too," Calliope said. "My parents named me Mary Beth Watkins." She held out her hand. "Pleased to meet you."

"Ashley Jazcoviak," Ash said, twining her fingers around Calliope's rather than shaking her hand. She swallowed against the lump in her throat. "So, tell me, what brought you to GoddessFest 2008?"

Miriam, Alone

Sex toys? Miriam stopped in her tracks outside the vendors' room. Unlike the other vendors at GoddessFest, Aphrodite's Toybox, "Run by Women for Women," had set up in a private room, not the main hall. There was a steady stream of traffic going into the room, almost all young to Miriam's fifty-something perspective, giggling and cooing as they headed in. She almost followed the herd, but stopped just outside the door. *I should head for the dealers' room and look for that book vendor instead. That part of my life is past. It's not as though I have any sex life to use sex toys in.*

This seemed to make her unique at the conference. The couple whose room was on one side had fooled around several times during the night and again in the morning—loudly. The ladies on the other side tried to be more circumspect, but their headboard and hers shared a wall, and whatever they'd been enjoying sometime around dawn had gotten the bed moving violently. Everywhere she looked, women were kissing, holding hands, whispering obviously naughty things to each other. And it wasn't just the lesbians. There might be no men at the conference, but every straight woman she started chatting with seemed to bring the conversation around to sex. Or so it seemed.

Miriam looked down at her wedding ring. Fifteen months ago, she would have smiled to herself at all the juicy young things enjoying themselves. And at the end of the weekend, she would have gone home to David wet with anticipation as she did at the end of any time they were apart—to be screwed senseless while she spun tall tales for him based on the people she'd met and the erotic hints she'd overheard during her travels, and he in turn would invent fantasies of his own. They'd never acted on these fantasies once they'd found each other, but they'd come of age in an era of freedom and experimentation, so each had had plenty of past experiences to draw on for their bedtime stories. It had been a remarkably good and lustful marriage for almost thirty years.

But fifteen months ago, David had collapsed in the kitchen while making dinner. He'd been dead by the time she got there from the computer room—dead, the doctor said, probably before he hit the floor, from a massive heart attack.

And Miriam had buried her heart and her libido with him—or so she'd thought until this weekend. Her heart was still in mourning—might, she figured, always be. But her libido seemed to be active again. *It's just a weird hormone thing,* she told herself firmly. She'd been experiencing plenty of those lately.

Or maybe it was the memories conjured by the notion of sex toys. She and David had had a few favorites that they'd picked out together from one of those discreet catalogs. She'd thrown them all away after the funeral, along with her pretty lingerie. They had been a shared pleasure, and she no longer had anyone to share it with.

She was about to move on when Andrea Eisley from the college walked by. She was talking with someone else, but she smiled at Miriam, and Miriam felt herself flush. *Yup, it's a hormone thing,* she thought, *but it's nothing to do with menopause.* She seemed to be developing a ridiculous crush on Andrea, who not only was at least ten years younger than she was but who also taught at the same school she did, in the same department David had been in. David would have laughed.

David would have thought she was hot, too.

A sudden visual: Andrea sprawled on Miriam's favorite black sheets, legs parted, a ripe plum of a pussy just waiting for her tongue. It was like riding a bicycle, right? She hadn't done anything like that since her undergraduate days, but she bet she still remembered how to make a woman scream.

Maybe she didn't need a sex life to enjoy sex toys. She could get one just for her, one that didn't have any memories attached to it. But she and David always chose them together, and always at home, curled up in bed with a catalog, not going into a store. This was different, scarier. *And it's one more thing I'll be doing on my own, without him. It was hard enough learning to go to the movies by myself. Can I really do this?*

Just then, a woman came out of the Aphrodite suite, a large lavender shopping bag in each hand and a huge grin on her face. She was about Miriam's age, broad-hipped and handsome, her graying blond hair in a French twist, her calf-length denim skirt and navy cotton sweater brightened by a colorful rainbow-print silk scarf. "Don't be shy!" she exclaimed. "It's amazing what they're doing with silicone these days!"

Yes, I can do this! Miriam thought, and entered the room.

Fifteen minutes later, she too came out smiling with a lavender bag in her hand.

•   •   •

Miriam thought she knew her vibrators, but the Rabbit Pearl was something else. It whirred, it quivered, it rotated, it had "ears" to stimulate her clit. The next model up probably brought you coffee in bed. It was intimidating, frankly. She needed an image to get herself going.

Flash to David, stroking his cock and smiling lovingly as he watched her. That one came unbidden—she had tried so hard to avoid thinking of him that way, naked and raunchy and beloved. Her eyes filled with tears, but she also found herself getting wet.

She felt a flash of guilt, and then laughed at herself. How had she gone fifteen months without letting herself think of his beautiful penis? That was part of him, too, as much as his gray eyes or his laugh or his mind or his terrific cooking, all the things she had let herself remember and daydream about. Later she would probably cry, but now . . . now she could almost taste David's cock, almost feel the size and heft and texture of it in her mouth, almost feel it entering her, and the sheer need she felt made her touch the little quivering ears to her clit.

Wow, it was powerful. This could get addictive.

She imagined David, caressing her. She almost felt him teasing her labia with his cock, getting ready to enter her.

Then she pictured Andrea, spread for her as she had imagined before, waiting for Miriam to tease her with the Rabbit Pearl. She tried to focus her thoughts on her husband again, but the mental images kept flashing through her head: the younger woman arching and squirming, spreading her legs, eager for more.

Wouldn't it be wonderful to fuck Andrea with this beast? As she thought that, she teased apart her lips and slipped it inside. Oh yeah, this was going to be good. Almost too good. She wanted to dwell on her fantasies a little longer, to dream of David and imagine Andrea, but the pictures blurred in her head to a kaleidoscope of impressions and sensations. The rotating beads stimulated her sensitive lips, the ears were still flicking her clit, and, hell, it was over a year since her last orgasm.

Her body decided to make up for lost time by giving her a series of them.

She'd never screamed in pleasure while masturbating. She did that time.

Calming down, she patted the vibrator fondly. Maybe someday she'd have sex with another person again, but meanwhile . . . "Looks like the beginning of a beautiful relationship, Rabbit—as long as I don't run out of batteries."

Shelley and Jann

Shelley hadn't realized how much she missed men until there weren't any around. The final Saturday workshop had let out, and as she viewed the participants mingling and talking in the hotel atrium, she noticed a distinct lack of testosterone.

Except for the guy sitting in the nubbly blue overstuffed chair that mirrored the one she was sitting in. The main difference was that he had a woman on his lap, who was wearing a flowing, gauze, rainbow-printed dress. They were necking, seemingly oblivious to the conference attendees milling around them. His hand had slid up her thigh, dragging her dress with it, dangerously close to exposing her panties—or to answering the question of whether she was wearing any.

Shelley squirmed in her seat, eyeing his large hand with its dusting of dark hair. It had been a long time since she'd felt a man's hand on her. Since before she'd been with Jann. Being bi didn't always mean being poly, and she and Jann were married according to everything but the state of Kansas.

"Have you noticed the dearth of men around here?" she asked Jann.

Jann tucked one side of her blond pageboy behind her ear. "Of course," she said. "This is a GoddessFest, after all."

"But lots of men are pagan," Shelley protested.

"True." Jann's eyes slid to focus on what Shelley was watching. One eyebrow raised. "I imagine if this was called PaganFest, it would have attracted more men." She tapped the schedule of events. "They've billed this as a women's thing, and that's what all the topics are about."

Typical of Jann, a magazine editor, to get into semantics, Shelley thought with a smile.

"Speaking of the schedule," Jann continued, "we've got two hours before the banquet. Let's go to our room and sample some of that Robert Mondavi '97 Reserve Cabernet that we brought."

In the elevator, Jann pressed Shelley against the wall, snaking her hand up under Shelley's short linen skirt and finding her panties damp.

"Watching that couple turned you on." Jann's breath was hot against her ear. "Were you thinking about what it's like to be fucked by a man?"

"Yes—no—maybe—" Shelley wasn't sure how to respond, and the maddening stroking of Jann's fingers wasn't helping her concentration.

"It's okay, love," Jann breathed. "I'm not offended. We're both unashamedly bi. I want you to tell me about your fantasies . . . "

The elevator door opened, but Jann took her own sweet time pulling away. Shelley blushed, wondering how much the waiting people had seen.

Her thighs trembled, and she had to sit down when they got to their room. Jann laughed, low and sultry, as her fingers plucked at the buttons of Shelley's burgundy silk blouse. She flicked open the front clasp of Shelley's bra and slid both garments off her shoulders, then pressed her back onto the bed.

"Tell me," she said. "Tell me about being fucked with a real cock."

She leaned down and nipped at Shelley's lower lip, at her neck. Shelley squirmed, the sudden bright sensations adding to her arousal.

"Men are stronger than women—bigger," she said. "Their skin is rougher—the hair tickles, no, scratches." It was hard to form coherent sentences. Jann straddled her and drew the silk blouse over her breasts, her stomach; the soft fabric whispered against her skin. Through the silk, she pinched Shelley's nipples, gently but mercilessly.

Shelley tried to open her eyes, but they fluttered shut. "Cocks . . . they're warm, and pliable, even when they're hard. Like velvet-wrapped steel. And there's something about a man's thighs when they spread you open."

"Like this?" Jann purred, sliding down and parting Shelley's legs. Shelley felt a breath of cool air as her panties were pushed aside, then felt something nudge against the entrance to her cunt, slipping in her juices. *When had Jann put on the harness?* she wondered. It didn't matter. She just needed, desperately, to be filled.

"Like this?" Jann persisted.

Shelley moaned, and Jann's hips twitched, just a little. Not enough to drive the dildo home.

"Kind of," Shelley managed. "Different. Oh gods, please fuck me!"

"Imagine," Jann said. "Imagine it's a real cock." She lifted Shelley's legs over her shoulders, and thrust hard.

Shelley grabbed Jann's hips, urging her faster. "Yes—please. Yes!" An orgasm tore through her, then another. She imagined Jann tweaking her nipples while a faceless man relentlessly fucked her, and she exploded again. Dimly, she heard Jann cry out as the other end of the dildo did its work.

When she recovered, she snaked a hand down and caressed Jann. "That turned you on, too," Shelley said, amazed. She brought her hand up and let Jann taste her own juices.

"Well," Jann mumbled around Shelley's fingers, "I'm still bi. I can appreciate a hot, hard cock in my pussy." She grinned as Shelley caressed her face. "I have a confession to make. I saw the same couple earlier, and had the same thoughts. That's why I had the harness ready."

"Evil woman," Shelley said fondly. "Care to join me in the shower?"

"You go ahead," Jann said. "That bottle of wine is calling to me."

But when Shelley emerged from the steamy bathroom, Jann didn't have the bottle open.

"The little corkscrew on my Swiss Army knife isn't working," she said. "The cork's too hard. I've called room service for someone to bring us a better one." She'd adjusted her blue knit dress and chunky silver jewelry, again looking every inch the cool professional. Shelley unwrapped the towel from her head and let her curly dark hair start to air dry; the satin robe she was wearing was enough cover for a maid to see.

Only it wasn't a maid who brought what they needed. It was Corkscrew Boy.

He wasn't a boy, really, despite his bleached, spiky hair and goatee; Shelley guessed him to be in his mid-twenties. He nonetheless seemed kind of stunned when Jann opened the door—which was when Shelley realized the room smelled like sex, and the harness wasn't entirely hidden under the pillow.

Jann smiled and handed him the bottle, asking if he would do the honors. Then she dragged Shelley into the far corner of the room.

"So, what do you think?" she asked. "Kind of cute, isn't he?"

Shelley stared at her. "Are you serious?"

"I wasn't sure until I opened the door," Jann said. "I didn't expect them to send a guy. But once I saw him, it clicked."

"What about protection," Shelley hissed, keeping one eye on Corkscrew Boy, who was gamely struggling with the bottle.

Jann smiled that lascivious smile again, and Shelley's legs wobbled. "I told you I'd been thinking about this," she said. "All of the ladies' rooms downstairs have condom dispensers, so I bought a couple, just in case."

An image flashed before Shelley's eyes, of Jann on her hands and knees, being soundly fucked by the cute bellboy. Howling with pleasure as Shelley reached under and fondled her nipples.

She kissed Jann hard, one hand cupping her breast. "It can't hurt to ask," she said.

Andrea: Omega

Andrea drowsily snuggled against Cecily, enjoying the short body, muscular yet soft, that fit so well in her arms. Still mostly asleep, she reached to cup her lover's breast—then sprang from the bed, poised to scream.

Cecily was in Massachusetts. Andrea was in Kansas, and that comfortable body in the bed was a stranger . . . was, in fact, the woman who'd seemed to materialize in the circle on Friday night.

The stranger sat up, nonchalantly naked. She was almost a body double for Cecily, Andrea couldn't help noting, only with better-defined muscles; fuller, higher breasts; and glossy skin that looked airbrushed.

And before Andrea could say or do anything, she began to glow. A shimmering rainbow took shape behind her, and her impossibly perfect dark skin reflected all its colors.

"You're—you're Iris!" Andrea said with a gasp. The rough texture of hotel carpet, the whir of the air conditioner, the bland cream-on-beige striped wallpaper told her it wasn't a dream—her dreams were never that precise with mundane details. She still pinched herself. It didn't work. Her heart was racing, in part from shock, but more from awe. She'd thought of the various goddesses for so long as lovely metaphors for female power. But this was no metaphor. This was divine female power in the flesh, and she'd been sleeping next to it! "But what are you doing . . . "

"In your bed? You summoned me, child. You asked me to help you and your people receive the messages they needed." The form might look like Cecily, but the voice was unique, layered as if a thousand women spoke through this one. "Everyone else has been catching on just fine. But you are so busy being a homesick, love-lorn, *insufferable* Yankee snob that subtlety just wasn't working. I figured this form would get your attention."

Andrea's face brightened. "Is the message that there's hope to work things out with Cecily?"

The goddess shook her head. "No. It's that you have to stop thinking of *this*"—gesturing the length of the dark body—"as the beginning and the end of your desire. You have to be open to other possibilities for anything good to happen to you." And Iris began to change. A rainbow of forms, a rainbow of women, all different and all beautiful, passed before Andrea's astonished eyes. In the end, Iris settled into a fair-haired, middle-aged woman of medium build—blue-eyed, with a simple, chin-length haircut and dimples, the type of woman Andrea would have seen on the streets and figured was as dull as boxed mac and cheese. But in that shape, she stalked around the bed to Andrea, moving like a sexy predator—the joy of the erotic hunt transfiguring her unassuming appearance to something that made the human woman gasp.

She bent Andrea down over the bed with the kind of sizzling roughness Cecily could sometimes show, putting her hand between Andrea's legs. "What are you doing?" Andrea gasped. Her reaction wasn't fear—already she was too intrigued and aroused to be scared—but puzzlement. "I thought Iris was a virgin goddess."

"Depends on how you define *virgin*." The hand cupped her mound. "I don't believe you've ever had a man yourself . . . " One finger entered her. "But that hardly makes you an innocent." She punctuated the last word with a slap on Andrea's ass. Not hard, just enough to get her attention.

"What are you doing?"

Another spank, another caress. "I know you crave this sometimes . . . and you were afraid you couldn't find it here. Now look at me. Look at me!" Andrea contorted herself to obey. "Remember this face. Remember this body. This is who is about to spank and fist you. This."

"But you're not some Midwestern housewife. You're a goddess."

"And are you saying your theoretical Midwestern housewife cannot embody the Goddess? Do you understand so little, when you and the women you've gathered here so yearn for the divine feminine that you called me here?" Each word was emphasized by a blow that brought heat and pleasure to Andrea's reddening ass. "You are Goddess. You are all Goddess, even the ones who seem the most ordinary. Goddess is inside everyone."

A pause in the narrative, if not the spanking. Andrea was moving to the rhythm of the blows, arching to meet them. Moisture dripped down her legs. Iris worked another two fingers easily into her dripping cunt. "Though the Goddess is not inside everyone in the way I am going to be inside you. Open your legs."

Patiently, inexorably, blissfully, one finger at a time, the divine hand filled the human pussy.

So full, so beautiful. Nasty and sacred and hot, all together. It was close to cosmic when a human lover did this to her. Now, fisted by a goddess, Andrea felt her soul split open, felt her shell of intellectual superiority melting away and the fears long hidden behind that shell healing. She came, but it was beyond anything she had experienced before: something like exploding, something like reforming, something like finally waking up from a long dream.

She lost consciousness.

When she came around, she was tucked into bed, all physical evidence of the adventure cleaned away except for a slightly tender butt. Iris was still with her, clad now in a chiton made out of a living rainbow. "I am needed elsewhere, my dear. Other women need my mediation. But I will give you another hint before I go: not every woman who marries is strictly heterosexual. And if you can be patient with someone grieving for a loss far harder than yours, it will be worth your while."

"I knew I'd seen her before! She teaches English at the college. Someone pointed her out, because her husband was in my department but passed away the semester before I—" Andrea realized she was alone.

No. Not alone. The Goddess was still inside her heart.

And somewhere in this very hotel was a lovely woman who, at the very least, might become a friend.

An eclectic writer and poet, Melodie Bolt enjoys working with fairy tales and mythology to create haunting characters in contemporary landscapes. Her stories have appeared in PanGaia *and* Kiss Machine, *and she has poetry forthcoming in* Tales of the Unanticipated *and* The Shantytown Anomaly. *Originally a Jersey girl, she now makes her home in Michigan, where she attends graduate school at the University of Michigan-Flint and participates in the Flint Area Writers critique group. She is a member of Broad Universe, a group that promotes women writers of science fiction, fantasy, and horror. When not writing, she spends her time harvesting cat hair from her furniture. To learn more about Melodie, visit her website at www.mcbolt.com.*

Selk River

BY MELODIE BOLT

The white grocery bag tucked under my fleece whipped from the wind like a three-year-old waving a sheet of tinfoil. My hand clutched the plastic with a death grip. That ordinary bag held all that was left of my world: my toddler's favorite stuffed animal, his MuMu. I took it with me everywhere, just as my son would have. Yet I was far from home, riding on the back of a motorcycle, in Iceland, behind a stranger named Oleg.

I longed to dismount, but there were no strip malls or even gas stations this far north of Reykjavik. We kept weaving north on the dark ribbon of asphalt that cut past white and black sheep fenced in fields of green, the occasional farm nestled near a smoky river, and the stretches of black, lichen-covered lava.

My thoughts drifted to my down parka back in my Wisconsin closet. The fleece I'd brought was fine for walking the streets of Reykjavik, but did not provide enough protection on the road. Though the sun shone almost all twenty-four hours, the Icelandic summer wind felt like a winter wraith with frozen fingers. The air crept up my sleeves and pant legs, pulling heat from my body and flinging it across the choppy permafrost ground.

I shifted, restless. Oleg patted my leg with his hand, cupping his palm and fingers over my knee. The cold didn't seem to bother him, perhaps due to his black leathers or maybe his Icelandic heritage. He patted my leg once more, then gripped the handlebar again. I wasn't sure what his touch meant—sympathy at my discomfort or a promise of greater intimacy.

Leaving Reykjavik with him probably hadn't been a bright idea, but at the time it seemed a better option than getting drunk and wandering around the city as a lonely and desperate woman picking up lonely and desperate men.

Fuzzy, gray mounds in the distance sharpened into steep, pine-covered hills. When we entered the fjord valley, the bike slowed. We passed shaggy horses grazing near a barn and then we arrived at the city of Hólar. I'm not sure what I expected when Oleg said we'd drive north to the agricultural college, but it wasn't this.

Our destination consisted of a four-story building that looked like a large house (the college), a church with a moat of gravestones, a scattering of sod homes, and a small, gray, aluminum structure with a sapphire fish painted on a sign. No stores. Not even a gas station. And hardly anything you could even call a street.

We parked. Stiff and cold, I dismounted, pulling the plastic bag out from under my jacket and letting it dangle from my wrist. Oleg grabbed a small duffel bag from under a cargo net, and we entered the college lobby.

When we'd left the city after throwing back a couple of lemon drops, packing a toothbrush hadn't crossed my mind. Nor had the thought that everything else of mine was sitting in a hotel room now several hours away. It was stupid for me to come here. I didn't even have any freaking idea what time it was with the damn White Nights. And my stomach grumbled its complaint about missed meals the instant I smelled onions and fish wafting down the hall.

We entered a small, sunny room that, with its fabric-covered tables, looked more like a restaurant than a college cafeteria.

"Do you want fish?"

I nodded and rubbed my arms. "And coffee if they have it."

He gestured for me to sit. I grabbed his bag and settled at an empty four-seater in the sunshine. I put the duffel on the floor and tucked the MuMu on the chair next to me.

The hair on my neck stood upright from the cold, and I eagerly grabbed the coffee that Oleg brought with the tray of food. My hand reached for the flask in the fleece's inner pocket, but I stopped myself. Maybe later.

I picked up a forkful of fish and chewed, but my grief flavored the food with ash and I struggled to swallow. Every meal challenged me to find a reason why I should nourish my body while my husband and son lay dead.

Oleg unzipped his jacket and hung it on the back of the chair. Unbelievable that he'd worn only a T-shirt and didn't show any signs of being cold.

"My friend is a professor here. He works in the aquarium. He found new shrimp . . . shrump?"

I gave a halfhearted smile. "Shrimp."

"Yes, so I go to see shrimp. You can swim in the pool."

"No." I shook my head. "No swimming."

I pushed some potatoes around as I imagined the panic of the passengers as the plane sank—sparks flying, people screaming, the icy, dark water filling the cabin. But I didn't really know if they drowned or burned or died from the impact. The airline never recovered their bodies. I saw the plastic bag on the seat next to me, but couldn't touch it now. It hurt too much.

He shrugged and ate. "I think water's too hot. It's heated from below." He pointed to the floor and shrugged. "But there are other things here. The church has a very old Bible, and then there are the horses."

I must have looked unenthusiastic.

"I like my horses made of metal," he said, and grinned at me. I caught myself smiling back.

"After here, we go west to Laugarhaull. On the way, in Strandir, is a sorcery museum. If it interests you, we can stop. There are grimoires, runes, and much history about the trials."

I looked up, surprised.

"What happened in Salem did not happen only in Salem," he said.

"How many witches burned?"

"Witches are women, yes?"

I frowned as I thought it through, then nodded slowly.

Oleg leaned back and pushed his empty plate away. "I don't know for sure, a couple maybe. Most who died were men and most of them were hung."

Oleg reached to his neck to adjust a silver chain. A silver pendant popped over the edge of his T-shirt, and I saw etched on it a thick-girthed tree with almost claw-like roots and abundant foliage.

"Do you believe in magic?" he asked.

I snorted. "I don't even believe in God."

In the city, my first vodka impression of him had focused on the scar that ran over his left eye down to his cheek. I didn't care. I just wanted someone to distract me from my pain. Now, I found myself studying his eyes. Specks of white drifted in dark blue like whitecaps on the Atlantic. I wondered what swam underneath the surface.

Was he different? Probably not. He'd want sex. Men were men, weren't they? Always thinking about the same thing. How to get it. When they'd get it. And how long it had been since they got it.

He reached across the table and tentatively stroked the back of my hand. What was the worst? He'd do me whether I participated or not, because he'd justify in his mind that I owed him, for the ride, because I'd left the city with him, because he'd bought me lunch. In the end, it would just make it easier for him to take what he wanted.

I told myself I didn't care. Whatever happened to me didn't matter. My life ended when Aaron's and Dylan's did, but my body shivered.

"You're cold." He stood and unhooked his jacket from the chair. As he came close to me, I thought about his arms restraining me, hands bruising my flesh, making me take what I deserved. I blinked the thoughts away as he handed me the jacket. It was a charcoal color, with wear creases making the leather soft and supple.

I peeled my fleece off to fit my arms through the close-fitted sleeves. The jacket's lining, short, bristly gray and light-black fur, tickled my arms. His hand lingered on my shoulder as I zipped it.

"Don't spill anything on it. It's very old. And special. Okay?"

"What do you do when it rains?"

"Rain gear." He shrugged, trying to look nonchalant, but his eyes hardened, boring into mine to make sure I understood.

We returned the tray with the dishes and then walked to the main staircase. The banister wound up elliptically, worn smooth from generations of palms. The stone steps sagged, thin in the middle. Oleg walked in front carrying the duffel.

"Where are all the students?"

"No school now, only tourists. Some Germans are on the first floor. We have number four, alone."

The realization surprised me that I'd reached that pivotal point so fast. I had to put out for him or see how he would take no for an answer. Swallowing hard, I tried not thinking about my thighs brushing together as I climbed the steps. I looked at the walls to distract myself.

Annual class photos in rectangular frames housed rows of individual headshots. They started in the 1950s . . . now '72 . . . '87. Every few steps took me through a decade. I couldn't help but wonder . . . who's married? Divorced? Who has children? Who's dead?

I stopped climbing for one moment and studied the faces. My husband looked liked this boy, second row, third one from the left. Memories of meeting Aaron in Minneapolis came to mind. He'd come from Iceland for graduate school, and that's where we met before marrying and settling in Wisconsin.

And what of my son? How would his face have changed as a man? The pudgy three-year-old cheeks would have slimmed down. Would they have bristled with stubble? Been clean-shaven? I'd never know, but surely the dimples would have remained. The dimples that bloomed whenever he clutched his Mu. I fought tears away.

We reached the fourth floor, the college apex. The wooden ceiling slanted down sharply to the left, with chairs tucked snugly underneath. Rooms were on the right. Each door had a plaque with a different Icelandic word. We went to the end of the hall and he pulled a key from his pants pocket.

"What does that say?"

"Temptation." He slid the key into the lock and twisted.

I was glad I couldn't look into his eyes—no need to see the anticipation glinting there. I braced myself for a king-sized bed with a mirrored ceiling, and wondered, if I called out Aaron's name, would he slap me?

As he strode into the room, I saw two twin beds pushed against opposite white walls. Between them stood a large desk under a dormer with a crank-style window—a typical college room. He dropped the duffel on the left bed and pulled out a wool sweater.

"Okay, I go now to see shrimp." He walked over, grasped the doorknob, and paused. "The shower is across the hall. I'll be back later." Quietly, he closed the door.

Screw you, I thought, I'm not going to clean up just because you say so. You'll have to take it dirty or not at all.

The right-side bed sagged as I sat down. I tossed the fleece on the end of the bed and ran my fingers through my hair, then lay back, warm in Oleg's jacket. Unhooking the plastic bag from my wrist, I pulled out Dylan's Shamu whale. A small smear of chocolate stained a patch of white, matted fur. I touched that spot, knowing my son's lips had brushed there. Pressing his favorite toy close to my heart, I stared at the ceiling as tears slipped from my eyes into my ears and hair.

A short while later I woke, still alone. I needed more sleep, but my nerves danced. I sat upright and grabbed my fleece. The flask slipped out and I opened the top and took a swig. My stomach contracted as the Stoli hit. The room smelled intensely sour, almost with a stench of decay, and a pulse of fluid surged up my throat. Concentrating, I willed it back down.

I needed some fresh air, and I climbed onto the desk and sat down crosslegged. I placed the flask next to me and then pushed aside the filmy curtain and cranked open the window. Breathing in deeply, I savored the chill breeze on my face, my body cozy in Oleg's jacket. My stomach settled and my heart slowed.

A storm front was gathering, and I thought back to the day I arrived in Iceland; it had rained then, too. Grief had kept me from leaving the States sooner but, like me, Sigrid had no blood relations once Aaron and Dylan were dead. I felt obligated to ease Aaron's grandmother from this world to the next. On the flight over, I had prayed she'd take a message to my husband and son when she died. Wouldn't she tell them how much I missed them? How much I loved them? And especially tell Dylan how sorry I was? But as I stood on Sigrid's porch, rain soaking my fleece, Sigrid's neighbor's daughter (already moved into the apartment) told me Sigrid was dead. She'd been laid to rest by friends. The rain washed my tears away, but not the bitterness that burned my heart.

Dark clouds rolled down the fjord, and thunder sounded distantly. I so desperately wanted to ask for forgiveness, but there was no one left but me and I couldn't forgive myself. The guilt of living crushed the very life out of me. Anger and remorse for what I hadn't done and hadn't said shredded my heart. I looked at the whale on the bed. Nothing mattered.

Tears rolled down my face. I wiped my cheeks with the back of my hand and moved to retrieve a tissue. There was a clatter, then vodka spilled across the desk and pattered onto the floor.

"Shit." As I scooted off the desk and squatted to reach for the flask, two tears dripped and splashed onto the leather.

A bolt of electricity seemed to jolt my spine. I jerked upright. The room spun. A heaviness weighed on my chest and I struggled to breathe. My back and butt slipped flat onto the desktop, my legs dangling over the edge. The booze soaked through my jeans while my mouth dried and my tongue swelled. My brain could not tolerate movement.

The curtain whipped in the air. My hair brushed my eyes. I tried to wipe my face, but my fingers felt stuck together, my elbow unbending. The raspy exhalations from my breathing were blotted by the crack of lightning and thunder's boom. Rain blew in, soaking the desk, the floor, and me. It seemed to sharpen my sense of smell, sprinkling me with horses and hay, sweet damp sod, tantalizing wafts of seawater.

The door thumped against the wall. Oleg swore in Icelandic and rushed to me. He caressed my face, his hand brushing against something rigid that felt attached to my nose. As the lightning cracked, I clearly saw whiskers. Disbelief barked out of me, a ragged cough. My God, I'm hallucinating.

Gripping me under my arms, Oleg dragged me off the desk, my head propped against his chest. I smelled sweat, damp wool, coffee, and something else, something that didn't make sense but felt unthinkingly, naturally right; he smelled like the sea.

Down the hallway and stairs we went. Fear darted through my mind. Had he planned a gang-bang for the Germans? I could do nothing. The vertigo kept me immobilized. I wondered what he had slipped into my coffee.

He surprised me with his gentleness as he lowered my head to the floor. Then he straightened and knocked. A door opened and I heard Oleg say, "Magnus." My eyes closed and I faded away to quiet darkness, the only sound—blood spinning in my head.

• • •

Gears shifted and I smelled exhaust. Oleg watched me from the passenger seat in front. He frowned. I wondered if I had disappointed him. Maybe the sex sucked. The unseen driver, probably Magnus, snapped at Oleg, who turned around and fumbled with the zipper at his waist. With his feet braced and his back pressed against the seat, he raised his butt and tugged his leather pants down, peeling them off, revealing a pair of jeans. My heart skipped a beat, then skittered wildly as I realized the sex was yet to come. I tried to plead with them but again, only a barking cough passed my lips. Oleg turned and stroked my cheek, and I tried but couldn't pull away.

The car skidded to a stop, and when the men got out a rush of air filled my head with tides and fish. A terrible, unfilled need surged in me. My body tightened with urgency, like tensing for an orgasm.

Both back passenger doors opened. The driver grabbed my arms and pinned me, though I still couldn't move. Oleg pulled at my pants. I shook with fear and a horrible longing for freedom. I desperately wanted them to hurry up and be done with it so I could feel the ocean lick my skin.

Then I realized Oleg was tugging his leather pants up my legs; he wasn't raping me. Relief swept through me, flooding my heart with the closest thing to happiness I'd felt since the day before my family died.

The driver dragged me out. Oleg ran around the jeep and grabbed my ankles. He and Magnus carried me toward the water, swung me at the rocky edge, and then released me. I flew through the air with the trajectory of cement. I tried to scream, but the water engulfed my cry.

The paralysis and vertigo evaporated with a sharp prickling, like a bad case of pins and needles. As I tried to get my arms to reach and legs to kick, I panicked and thrashed. They were still melted together.

I realized I was ready to die. Acceptance spread through me, and I quit moving and waited for my breath to give out. Then, with a splash, Oleg jumped in next to me and pulled my head above the water.

As I exhaled, I felt my nostrils open. Sea droplets sprayed his face. He laughed and started walking toward the shore with his arm tucked around me. I struggled against him, not wanting to leave the water's comfort and the promise of an end to my suffering. I fought to submerge. My legs, which refused to split apart, moved well in a butterfly-like kick. I tried to loosen his grip, but I was exhausted. His strength overpowered me. I closed my eyes for whatever came next.

In the back seat, Oleg's friend dried me with a blanket. As he rubbed, my skin prickled and twitched. Then my fingers, though numb with cold, flexed and curled. My knees bent and separated. Oleg reached for me and unzipped his jacket. His friend quit toweling me off and got in the driver's seat. We started back to Hólar. No one said anything.

We ended up in Magnus's second-floor apartment drinking coffee. Both Oleg and I wore Magnus's clothes (jeans and woolen sweaters), while ours tossed and bumped in a dryer. The leather jacket and pants hung over a chair.

"What happened to me? Why did you throw me in the water?"

"American?" Magnus asked as he stirred his coffee, clanking the spoon around the mug.

I nodded.

"How do you feel?" He drew the spoon out and licked it.

I frowned. Confused. A little wound-up, but fine.

"Okay, I guess."

"Good. Our local folk remedy worked."

Oleg snorted and smiled.

Magnus shot him a face full of lava.

"Go back to Reykjavik," he said, pointing the way with his spoon, and I wasn't sure if he meant me or both of us.

Oleg said something in Icelandic and motioned to the leather set draped on the chair.

His friend's face flushed and he threw his spoon on the table. Magnus stood and went to the dryer, muttering under his breath.

I looked at Oleg, but his gaze intently stared at some ghost I couldn't see. I watched sadness gather in his eyes and weigh his lips. Not knowing what to say, I pulled my clothes from the warm pile in Magnus's arms and went into the bathroom and changed. We left soon after that and headed west, blowing down the road on the motorcycle like one of the devil's own.

When we passed the exit for Strandir, I thought back to what Oleg had said about the witchcraft museum. I doubted the grimoires had what I wanted. And what did I want? To bring them back? A chance to die with them? Those spells seemed too grandiose for a novice. I'd settle for something simpler—a do-over. Every day I longed to relive that last moment with them to change the past. All I wanted was to fix what I had done wrong.

A few hours later, as we neared Laugarhaull, we climbed a two-track dirt road to cross into the next fjord; it was slow going on the bike. We stopped at the peak to stretch our legs. Cairns dotted the top ridge. Across the fjord to the left of us, a waterfall cascaded near a valley, hazy in the distance. The road wound down the hill to the right and crossed a river that glittered toward the sea. No roads or buildings were situated to the left. Only the wild land.

Oleg pointed toward the direction of the waterfall and said, "That is the Valley of the Gods. Legend says that the old gods went there when Christianity swept the island. All of the springs and wells were blessed by the church, but not there. They left that place as a haven for the Old Ones."

Unlike the pine-covered hills of Hólar, this valley was rocky and steep. The hills reminded me of a woman's legs, with the river, like a burst of amniotic fluid, running to the sea.

He touched my arm and said, "That is Selk River. Do you know what selk are?"

"Oh yes, from fairy tales. They change into seals." I frowned. "They have a special ring or something, right?"

"Yeah, not ring, but clothes. Seal skin." He crossed his arms, the leather creaking just a little.

"I remember," I said, and smiled. Memories flooded my mind of reading fairy tale picture books at bedtime. Then I remembered Shamu, and my smile vanished.

Oleg studied my face.

"Let's go," he said.

. . .

Laugarhaull, a tiny hotel, boasted geothermally heated healing water blessed by Gudmundur the Good and excellent French cooking. After I showered and dressed, I returned to our room, which featured another set of twin beds, and I sat down on mine. Oleg waited for me in the dining room. I reached for the plastic bag, to take it with me, but my heart felt oddly light. So it stayed on the bed and I went to join him.

An array of potted plants and herbs decorated the sill of a huge bay window. Oleg stood when he saw me. We were the only guests. I could hear the chef working in the kitchen, and my stomach grumbled at the smell of garlic and vinegar.

I practically inhaled two warm slices of homemade bread. My tongue savored the melted butter, salty and slick.

By the end of our meal, Oleg appeared restless; his fingers drummed the table and he stared at the river.

"Let's go for a walk," he said.

We wandered down the hotel's drive in silence and headed toward a sheep farm. Oleg climbed over the fence and looked at the gray, weather-beaten barn that loomed next to the river. He turned back to me and extended his hand.

"Won't the farmer mind?"

"No, he's like a brother." An odd half-smile flashed across his face.

I sighed, then gripped his hand and climbed over. The ground, heaved apart by frost, made walking difficult. Oleg wrapped his arm around my waist to keep me from twisting my ankle. His touch felt comforting, almost brotherly.

We entered the warm, dusty barn and made our way toward the back. Oleg moved a couple bales of hay, then tugged on a handle in the floor. He raised a hinged door upwards to reveal a storage space and pulled out a box big enough to hold a wedding dress. A thick layer of dust and dirt covered it, and he put the box at my feet. We sat down on the hay. His mouth compressed as he brushed his hand over the dirty top, scraping thin, arching lines with his fingertips.

"My wife," he said and looked away.

My face drained. I didn't want to know about his life; mine was already too much.

"She died in a car accident." He reached to touch his scar, but let his hand drop. "Two years ago. All this time I never go in the water. For you I go . . . " He paused. " . . . to save you. You would have died without both parts on."

I stared at him, not comprehending.

"From the first time I saw you, I felt something." Oleg touched his chest. "Like a memory. I know you, what you can be." He looked at me, searching my eyes.

What I can be? Not what I am, nor what I was. But the future. Hope. He believed my life had some purpose. But it wasn't true. He didn't know me. He didn't know what I had done.

"No! My husband and son are dead. Without me." My hands clenched. "Too busy. Deadlines and work. My Dylan, my beautiful boy, dead. And Aaron, too. It's all my fault. I should have gone with them."

"Slow down, slow down. I don't understand."

I took a deep breath, the pain curling around my heart, and began again. "The day they died. I had work to finish. For weeks I had been trying to get a promotion. I told Aaron I'd join them in Iceland later. When I drove them to the airport, there was so much traffic. All I thought about was, 'Why didn't Aaron take a cab?' I had to get back. I had to meet my deadline. I rushed them out of the car and what I didn't see . . . " I breathed in deeply, remembering that last moment, that last chance. "What I didn't see was my son's favorite toy. He took it everywhere and slept with it. It had fallen next to his car seat, and I didn't take a couple of seconds to check, to make sure he had everything." I covered my face with my hands. "He died without me. And he died without his MuMu because of me. He was only three."

Oleg tried to take my hands, but I pulled away. "Don't you see what kind of mother I am? None, now. And I can't forgive myself for the mother I was."

And there it was, in the enormity of my loss the forgotten Mu tore out my heart every day. I scanned his face for reproach or disgust, but saw only sadness. He reached for me again and this time I clung to him, burying my face against his shoulder, sobbing.

"Shhh," he said and stroked my hair. We sat like that while I cried myself out. When my sobs slowed, I pulled away from him.

"I have to go," he said.

"Go? Back to the hotel?"

"My time here is over. I have to leave." He leaned close and looked into my eyes.

"What! You're leaving me too? Here?"

He opened the box on the floor and pulled out a gray, spotted jacket and pants, similar to his but smaller.

"These were my wife's. In the past when one of our kind died, we would find a mortal to wear the skin. But humans don't recognize magic now. Everything is technology and pollution and the planet, well, She is struggling to survive. Many, like Magnus, think we no longer have a place here, and they burn the skins because loose magic causes trouble. But I want you to have these. You should . . . you belong." He shook his head, shrugged, and stood.

What the hell was he talking about? He picked up the gray set and grabbed my hand, squeezing my fingers. We left the barn and walked to the river's edge. The ground jutted a few feet over the rippling current. He placed the leathers in the grass and adjusted his jacket, pulling up the zipper. It seemed to melt away, the jacket appearing seamless.

He trailed his fingers down my cheek, then winked at me. In a blur, he turned and dove into the water. I caught my breath and ran forward, looking for him.

He didn't resurface. I sank down onto my knees, stunned and silent. Had he even existed? Did I dream these past days? Was I going mad?

A black, shiny head popped out of the water. A seal, with a scar over its left eye. It blew a fine spray out of its nose and looked around until our eyes met. Then it winked at me.

In my surprise, I reached my hand down to steady myself. The soft suppleness of the gray jacket startled me. Then I smiled as my heart rose from grief's ashes, suffused with the magic of hope.

Linda Steele was born in Wisconsin, but she grew up just about everywhere else. She's especially fond of mountains and would love to return someday to the Andes, where an Aymara shaman showed her how to invoke Pacha Mama's blessing when building a house. A mother of three, Linda has been a Jill-of-all-trades, having been a respiratory therapist, garden designer, creative-writing instructor, legislative assistant, and a public relations coordinator for a major airport. Linda has published a science fiction novel, Ibis, and is currently writing a novel about the Khelds and their world. She lives with her husband in Philadelphia. Her website is http://lindalsteele.com.

The Rune Hag's Daughter

BY Linda steele

Words spoken in the spring pressed like a thorn into Rusa's thoughts. Aunt Edda stood over her, a basket filled with early apples hanging on one arm, telling her she was a bad daughter.

"Summer ends, and you have not taken a man." Wind rustled in the trees that ringed the glade, underscoring the accusation in Edda's voice.

"I told you, I do not want one," Rusa said. She did not look at her aunt, instead attending to a long, lead-lined tray. Using stained tongs, she turned thumb-sized stones in the cooling, heavy liquid.

"Our mothers have held this land and nursed its gifts since Alm claimed it for our people. Will you slay all our generations with your refusal?"

139

Rusa gripped the feet of another diminutive Mother figure and flipped it over. The figure's tiny breasts glistened in silver dots above the dark surface. She did not answer her aunt's charge, and Edda resorted to another path.

"Surely this batch is finished?"

"The sheen must be thick and sure. You've seen the stones of careless crafters, that barely last a year and often read false. Our stones are prized for good reason."

"Our stones show true because our land is true."

To that, Rusa had nothing to say—or add. All Kheld folk knew the best rune rock was quarried from Rappeleye land. A single vein of blue-green stone ran through the hill at her back, stone so precious and true women came from all corners of the land hoping to acquire runes made from the few pounds of it quarried each year. More than that, they prized the nurse stones Rusa so diligently fashioned. Creating nurse stones required skill and deep knowledge of earth elements, for it was through earth that the Mother infused the power of truth. *Rune hags*, people called the women of her family, and rune hags they were, spending more time working stones than their fields.

Having turned every figure, Rusa set aside her tongs and reached for a long-handled ladle carved from a single branch of holly. She dipped it in a nearby pail, scooped precisely the right amount of vapor bath. She tested the liquid with her fingertips, then poured. The golden liquid, steeped from willow root, flowed into the dark, shimmering tray. As clouds of steam engulfed the open area around her, Rusa closed the damper over the pit of coals.

Edda placed her basket of apples several paces away, beside the steps leading into Rusa's cottage. "Mother Rappeleye wishes to see you."

"I cannot leave until these have cooled."

"That's what you said last week." Edda removed her shawl and rolled up her sleeves, revealing ample, well-muscled arms. Much of her life, she had been a stone-shaper, the runes she crafted prized by the priestesses and students of Aurdollen. "I will see to the cooling, and I will put them away. You, go see the mothers."

She felt like a girl again. Edda had that way about her, matronly but stern, reminding Rusa that her lapses had long since passed the point of censure.

The house of the old mothers lifted sturdy stone walls at the edge of a sprawling oak grove. Clumps of grave flowers, benign and starlike, brightened the ground under the trees. Beneath the grove's sparse grass rested the bones of twenty-five Rappeleye generations. To the back of the house, a hedge of hollyhocks, still throwing up spires of flowers, stood watch over a well-tended kitchen garden. Inside the house, Rusa knew, five elderly women would be baking, spinning, and weaving. The old mothers might have more years between them than amaranth had seeds, but they kept busy.

When she reached the packed, swept earth at the front of the house, she spied the eldest of her family seated in a quilt-laden chair, waiting for her. Mother Rappeleye, she was called, for being oldest. She had given birth to seven sons and five daughters, of whom Rusa's mother had been the youngest. Two girls dead of fever before they were two, another drowned with her husband and babe in the great flood. Rusa's mother had died giving birth to her third child, a sickly boy. A shawl covered the old woman's knees, and a soft leather bag of runestones, such as every Kheld woman carried, waited on her lap. Memory vines wove on the pergola, dangling chains of sweet-scented bellflowers.

One for Alm, Rusa recalled, old lessons revived. *Two for Bess . . . Three for Tueri . . .*

"Daughter, we have missed you!" Her grandmother's voice was soft and slight, with the memory of song.

Rusa kissed the wrinkled cheek. Pulling back, she reached into the pouch of her work apron and drew out two vials she had retrieved before leaving her house.

"What is this?" Mother Rappeleye asked.

"Tincture of antimony to quiet the pains in your joints, and tincture of runestone to clear your eye."

"Ah, our maker of potions!" The vial of brown glass gleamed, held up to the lively blue of Mother's good eye. "Thank you, child." She touched Rusa's arm with a frail, bony hand. A lifetime spent crafting stone runes showed in the arthritic fingers.

"I wanted to be sure you enjoyed the colors of this year's leaving."

"This will be the last year I watch the grove shed its leaves."

"I'll make sure it's not!"

"You, child," Mother Rappeleye said, "cannot reverse the years. How quickly they fly! I was a young girl just this morning, it seems, and a young mother just this afternoon, my sons and daughters at my knee." She sighed and looked toward the river and the geese gathering there. "You will be the last of all of us."

Rusa ducked her head. She had known her foot-dragging would lead to this hour. "Would it be so bad to let some other family's daughters settle upon our land, for their sons and daughters to work its fields? The bottom land is rich and fruitful. If they would let me stay in the cottage, work the hill—there would still be runes enough." She touched the gleaming nurse stone upon her breast, hung from a cord of hair. Her mother's hair, brown and lustrous, the hair of a woman who had died young.

"And so they might, should the Cruihcil make an exception in our case. They would, I think, for the sake of your gift. But after you, who would speak to the stones and know which can be trusted? Would you trust runes made by the low-schooled witches of Eastmeary Brenna? Would you trust a water-wise Darm woman to listen to stone?"

She shook her head. There would be no one, and she knew it. They knew it, too, the other women of her clan, who held their tongues around her but pleaded with their eyes. Even now, Mother Dillys wandered around the corner of the house, ostensibly shooing away one of the cats while casting glances in their direction.

"I honor the Mother."

"You know better than that. You deny Her."

Rusa lifted her head. "You know why." For the first time in years, the anger returned. It clamped about her heart, squeezing reason aside.

"Do you think we've forgotten? Every day for sixteen years, our kin have cursed that man for what he did to you."

"To no avail. He was never found, never punished."

He had come to their farm, seeking work, maybe a wife. A man could make a good living for himself as a Rappeleye husband. Although the land itself must pass to a daughter, a hardworking husband might accumulate a herd or master a craft that would pass to a son, who would take that son-portion to support a wife elsewhere. If the Rappeleyes had few cattle and sheep, it was because they'd had too many sons, who year by year had left to settle their new wives' land. Just this year, the oldest of Edda's three sons had wed a neighbor's daughter and moved onto her land, taking his fine herd of swine with him. Only Rusa's youngest brother remained, working the land along with three elderly uncles—Edda's husband and two bachelor sons of Mother Dillys.

Mother Rappeleye sank back into her cushioned chair. "Your attacker has been punished, you may be sure. The Mother visits misfortune upon such men. Make no mistake, She curses their loins and makes their staffs wither. No woman looks upon him with favor. Other men know his weakness and despise him. Only you give him strength, by the power he holds over you still."

She refused to remember that day, had banished it to a place in her mind even she could not find. Or so she'd thought. Every child's laugh, every woman's smile upon naming a man as her love, cracked open the door to a threshold she could not bring herself to cross.

"You want me to have a child," she said, "before I am too old."

"Thirty years is not old, daughter. I am thrice that, plus ten, and I had children into my fiftieth year. You are young enough to have many children."

"To have a child, a woman must couple with a man." In that acrid truth lay the root of her repulsion.

"We had hoped that if enough years passed, you would learn to like one man, at least."

"I like Almar Thornson." She named the red-haired smith who made her grates and tongs. "I like Nobb, the baker."

"Men with wives."

"Safe men," Rusa snorted.

"Men found worthy by the Mother. There are many such. What of Teg, the miller's son? He has often said he admires you—"

She shook her head. "I will not take a husband to rut and give orders."

"There is another way."

"No. I cannot go into town—"

"Be a bower bride. Take a shadow-husband."

Her heart pounded, with awe as much as fear. "You want me to go to the valley, to be mounted like a beast—"

"Like what we are, like a true daughter of the earth. What shame can there be in it? You do not want to know the man, so be it. The Mother will see to it you do not know him, nor he you."

Shadow-husbands were not shades. The supplicants of the Mother were flesh and blood, men who made the pilgrimage to Her valley to demonstrate their adherence to Her ways. Often they did this in preparation for marriage, for men once wed did not often make that journey. The rites of the Mother were the last remnant of the Old Way—the way women had conceived before the Children of Alm had come to this land and learned the habits of the men of the North, who kept their wives close by their sides, forbidden to other men.

Rusa's hands shook as Mother Rappeleye reached out and pressed the soft leather bag of runes against her palms.

"Take my stones, the Rappeleye stones. Use them to fashion the Wheel. Let the wisdom of our mothers guide you." The old woman leaned back again and closed her eyes, shutting out the sun. "Give us a daughter to hold our land."

.   .   .

That night in her cottage, surrounded by trays of amber beads and lead bottles of vitriol, Rusa knelt on a carpet her mother had woven and laid the Wheel. Candlelight flickered in firefly golds, reds and greens from racks of vials holding the secrets of her trade. From a heavy oak chest at the foot of her bed, she retrieved her wands, wrapped in linen and dust. She picked loose the knot and folded the cloth back from four wooden staves, each as long as her forearm. They were polished and true, flat across the upper surface, with a deliberate notch in the middle and a smooth hollow at each end. A *faetha's* wands, the mark of a healer and seer. She had made them during a year spent at Aurdollen, learning the Mother's ways. With her own lore she had found each tree, with her own hands taken the wood, shaped it with knife and sand: alder, hazel, rowan, and yew. The four sacred trees of the Mother. Even as she took the wands again in her hands, she felt the wisdom she had put aside years ago in favor of her own counsel.

They spoke to her because she had made them, and because the Mother had given her the gift of bespeaking the things of earth, of wood and stone.

With a steady hand, she poured fresh birch shavings in a ring, then laid the wands upon the circle. She aligned them with the four quarters of the world: cold sky, warm earth, fire, and water. Alder first, as the first-created and beloved of the world, then yew, to open the gates of life and death. The staves crossed at right angles, their notched middles locking. Bisecting these, she laid hazel, for wisdom, and lastly rowan, for truth. With the wands set, she placed a lighted candle pot at each end, then sat back on her heels to study her work. How many years had it been? Fourteen years ago she had consulted the runes. They had not lied then. They would not lie now.

Reverently, she turned the bag and poured Mother Rappeleye's runes out onto the dense red pile of the carpet, scattering the stones across symbols of sky and earth, water and flame. She touched one blue stone, amazed at its inner fire. Runes passed from mother to daughter, though some women might own several sets. Rusa herself owned a set she had shaped the same year as she had fashioned her wands, but these . . . these runes were ancient, round with use, surely shaped by Rappeleye hands from the first stone their hill had ever yielded, and they possessed the wisdom of the ages. She laid the runes in a line and made certain she had all twenty-four.

Taking the nurse stone from around her neck, she placed the tiny figure on the carpet, face up, breasts and belly prominent. One by one, she touched the nurse stone to each softly glowing rune, watching the silver surface to see if the touch produced a shadow. Sometimes a rune's energy turned and no longer vibrated to the heart of the Mother, yielding readings that would prove false. A nurse stone revealed such aberrations by turning dark.

Healers and farmers, and the *faetha* who served the mighty, depended on their runes being true. The nurse stones Rusa so painstakingly created, first carving the stone, then steeping them in vitriol and tinctures of rare metals, ensured health and good harvests and imbued wisdom into the decisions of Kheld leaders.

Mother, she beseeched, *show me what path awaits my choice.*

Every stone was true. Rusa replaced them in the bag, rolling the smooth runes within, then reached inside. This time, she whispered her invocation.

"Birch spirit, truth diviner, this willing hand rule.

Alder everlasting, life seeker, this life finger guide.

Yew death-branch, guardian, this long finger summon.

Hazel deep-sighted, revealer of secrets, this heart finger warm.

Rowan quickener, bane of lies, this ear finger force confessions."

Drawing a breath, eyes focused on the alder wand, she slid her hand into the bag and chanted the pattern she sought:

"Nine items of knowledge show . . . this heart . . . my trouble . . . my hope . . . what bars the way . . . the place . . . the person . . . the path . . . the price . . . the outcome."

One by one, matching her movements to the words, she picked a rune from the bag and laid it in the hollow of the wand corresponding to her order, beginning with the sky-quarter and alder. She worked her way around the Wheel—laying a rune in every hollow, then sealing the reading by placing the ninth rune at the center, where all wands overlapped. As soon as the weight of the last stone left her fingers, she dropped her hands to her lap and huddled, eyes closed, dreading to learn what the Wheel might reveal.

Wand by wand, she had laid it. Stone by stone, she had watched its unfolding. Her training as a *faetha* had given her weapons of skill but no protections against belief.

She was a Rappeleye woman, from a line of mothers descended from All-Seeing Bess, the Mother Rappeleye whose runes had guided Alm to the Door and brought her people to a new world. A Rappeleye woman, gifted to divine the secrets of stone and speak to the land, to Rappeleye Hill and basalt menhirs and sacred groves. A woman who, though violated as a girl, had been fortunate in not giving birth to a child of violence, who had served the Mother well as a priestess and penitent. Since leaving Aurdollen, Rusa had functioned for many years as guardian of the Hill, protecting the oracles of others but not looking after her own. She slaved to perfect the Mother's image, but she had taken no apprentice, no husband, no child to her heart. That remained as untouched as the runestone yet to be mined in the depths of the Hill.

The rune at the center of the Wheel glowed blue, a solitary remonstration.

. . .

The Valley of Moons lay within two days of Rappeleye Hill, a long journey by foot. Rusa undertook it, not wanting to deprive her kinswomen's husbands and sons of the horses, which they needed for working the fields. Edda walked with her, well-armed with bread loaves and cheese. Rusa wore her best wool cloak, blue, the hood and hems embroidered with flowers and rune signs. Any who looked closely at the markings would know her as a Rappeleye. The women stopped first at their family oak, in the center of the grove wherein the dead were buried, and gathered some of the acorns fallen from its mighty branches. This season's crop had not yet dropped, but many from the previous year still littered the ground.

"At least our oak will continue," Edda said, patting the bulging pouch of acorns swinging from her hip. "Though properly a son should do it, I will plant these as we go."

The Mother honored those who spread her fruit.

Was it easier, Rusa wondered, to be a man, ordered to seek fertile ground upon which to cast his seed, while a woman must guard her field? Oaks ruled the fields of Amallar, stood tall upon hills, lording over lowlands rich with other trees. The oak was, of all trees, the most male, beloved of the Mother yet the very staff of the Sun. The Faeduadan, the Priests of Lud, carved their runes from oak, cast them onto the naked earth in daylight, and studied the resulting patterns of light and shadow. Always they sought to divine the future and the fate of their nation. The ruling clan of Thegn had, of late, come under the leadership of men who adhered to the cult of Lud. Less and less did Kheld-folk follow the ways of the Mother.

Rusa curled her hand within her skirt pocket, around the heavy shape of a rune. She carried it with her, the rune that every time out of three castings had come ninth to her hand and rested at the heart of the Wheel.

Laaz. The symbol for *woman*, for *moon*.

. . .

A priestess greeted them at the valley entrance, standing in the shadow of a menhir draped with garlands of white flowers. Round and red-cheeked, the woman wore a plain gown the gray color of rain clouds, fronted by a long scarlet apron. She leaned upon a staff carved with the symbols of shield, tree, and moon. A loose hood covered her hair but for a few escaped strands that lay white upon her cheek. Rusa followed her example, lifting her hood so that it concealed all but her face. She handed the priestess her handful of acorns with a murmur, hoping the Goddess would be pleased by her offering.

The priestess smiled, her blue eyes lifting brightly. "Fruit of the Rappeleye oak! That is a noble tree, child of the oak that sheltered All-Seeing Bess and gave Alm his spear."

Rusa bowed her head at the reminder of her family oak's legendary lineage.

"Come, daughter." Wielding her staff with the ease of long practice, the priestess led the way onto a stony path into the valley. Edda followed behind, a chaperone comfortable with her charge's companion. "Is it true you seek to conceive an earth-fathered child?"

It was wrong to mislead a deity, but what of a priestess? Rusa remembered the lesson of her trade—that lies surfaced when touched by truth.

"I seek to conceive, that is true. However, I do not want to see the man, or know him. Though my family depends on me for continuance, I fear I may not be a proper vessel for such a gift."

"No woman here receives a man unless she so wishes."

"I know. That is why I am here."

The priestess was silent for a minute, then asked. "Do you fear that you will conceive a child without joy?"

"I did so once before."

She had been laughing, chasing the ball he had thrown too hard, when he had caught her up in his arms and carried her kicking into the cornfield. He had thrown her down between the rows and ploughed her like one of his furrows, planting his seed. Had he watched her courses to know when her body was ripe, or had his lust been random, her misfortune a cruel chance? That day she had conceived against the Mother, in fear and pain, no joy at all. As her body swelled, the Rappeleye mothers had whispered fearfully, always around corners, when they thought she could not hear, predicting a dire future for any child so conceived. The day her body convulsed in pain, months too soon, Rusa fled the house, seeking out the field in a thunderstorm. There she stood, blood running down her legs into the dirt, until it fell from her body. Even now she remembered being filled with wild, gluttonous joy.

"The child did not live?"

"No."

"The Mother's mercy," the priestess murmured.

Rusa did not disagree. Others had said as much, at the time and for years after. Only she knew how virulently she had hated the baby growing inside her, or how happy she had been at its death. In her heart, she knew she had killed it with her hate. Unwanted, unloved, it had withered like a seedling without water or sun, until it had died. Not wanting anything to survive of the man who had raped her, she had starved it even of hope.

What she feared now was that her hate had not diminished, that it still lay in wait—and that it would kill again.

· · ·

The temple of the Great Mother emerged from a high mound crowned by oaks and ringed by ranks of the five guardian trees. The mound itself was honeycombed by passageways and chambers devoted to Her mystic rituals. A well at the heart of the temple promised to cure infertility. Penitents buried in the hill under the guidance of priestesses clawed their way forth again, reborn and cleansed of whatever ills had afflicted them. Rusa could not tell which of the men along the path had come to be cleansed and which had come to fulfill their pilgrimage. Many of the men were young, like bullocks in their prime, with eyes that followed her cloaked and modest form with a knowledge she dreaded. Just as she did not know their business, they could not know hers, and yet she felt as though it were emblazoned on her somehow for all to see. Only when she had passed into the part of the temple reserved only for women did she feel her equilibrium return.

Here the priestesses instructed her in the sacred rituals that prepared her to receive the Mother's blessing—a child fathered by a man in the Mother's name. She visited and gathered twigs from the five guardian groves, burning each kind one by one on the altar with prayers for health, wisdom, unburdening, remembrance, and strength. She bathed in the sacred pool, promising the Mother she would yield even as the earth to the sky. She anointed her skin and hair with herbs for fertility and quickening. The kind priestess who lit the lanterns they would carry on their walk to the chamber told her the man, too, prepared to perform a divine act, an act of worship. To that end, both were expected to be silent, to give that space to the deity. The deed itself would occur in darkness, in a womb of earth.

When Rusa saw the place, she recoiled. In a deep passageway beneath the hill, the priestess took away her lantern, setting it upon the floor beside a squat door framed with slabs of stone. The lintel bore red ochre symbols. A moon invoked protection. A rabbit beseeched fertility. Rusa straightened as the priestess opened a door into darkness.

It was a hole, a cavern under the earth. Damp air billowed from within, bringing with it the smell of mud and worms, of freshly turned fields and uprooted things.

I am mad to want this, Rusa thought.

She looked into the eyes of the priestess. The woman had not told Rusa her name—no priestess would, though the Mother had ordered that each thing in the world possess its own, unique name. The priestesses were themselves aspects of the Mother, interchangeable with each other and with Her. What looked back at Rusa wasn't kindness, however patient it might seem.

"The answer to all questions lies within," the priestess said.

Rusa drew a deep breath. The taste of earth clung to the air. "And if at any point I do not wish to continue?"

"You have but to call out."

With trembling hands, Rusa undid the clasps of the shift she wore, dropping it from her body. She had no need for clothing here. Though heavy with water, the air from within was warm. Ducking under the lintel with its red ochre drawings, Rusa entered. On hands and knees, she felt her way into the center, soft earth yielding beneath her fingers, then turned to raise a hand overhead, and felt the shadowy ceiling of interlaced roots. Her unbound hair spilled over her arms. Though not high enough for standing, the chamber had room enough. The door closed, cutting off light, and she filled her lungs with the Mother's breath.

The priestess had said a man would come, so she lay on her back and waited, trembling. The floor beneath her felt cool, smooth, the earth itself. Small sounds filled the surrounding silence: worms burrowing overhead, roots tunneling deeper into the earth. Animals lived thus, rabbits in burrows, shrews and lizards nesting under stones. Little by little, her body relaxed, her heart slow and breathing soft. Here, in truth, she could indeed become one with the Mother.

When the door opened again, her heart leaped and the muscles in her limbs drew taut as ropes. Light flickered for a moment, only to be blocked by the shadow of another entering the low-ceilinged chamber. The man. She heard the door close again. She heard his breathing.

In the darkness, he moved over her. Perhaps he followed her warmth, for his enveloped hers, his scent of smoke and moss folding about her even as his hands found her body and she stiffened at his touch. His hand slowed, dropped away. In that movement, she felt his puzzlement, wondering if he were mistaken. She released a ragged breath.

Again he moved, slow and deliberate. His exhalation brushed the skin just below her breasts, accompanied by a tickle tracing a path just beneath it. Warm lips, accompanied by a crisp crush of hair, told her he was bearded. The kiss shocked her and she stiffened. Unbidden, a small sound like something wounded escaped her throat. *Please*. Even she could not have said what she wanted then, for he had done nothing to be accused of, save obeying his own nature, as she had known he would.

He drew back again and she felt the bulk of him, his male weight lowering. He settled beside her. "What is it, girl?" His low whisper conveyed concern. "Are you virgin?"

She almost laughed. Any who knew her would not have asked. She had not been a virgin long enough to now remember she had ever been one. In many ways that still mattered, she was one still. He could not see, in the dark, that she was not a girl. Whether by design or oversight, his hand remained upon her hip, a warm reminder of connection.

She turned toward him, a shadow-man whose breath mingled now with hers. Here in the Mother's bosom, a single cry from her would banish him. She could shame him. What would he feel, when she sent him from her, rejected his seed? Would he shy from women, knowing that in the Mother's temple he'd been found unworthy? Or would he be angry, determined to prove his virility?

Not for me to decide, she realized. That knowledge settled over her, washing over her, acquiring a priceless power. Here in the Mother's womb, it was not for her to decide this man's worth.

Her hand found his arm, followed the hard shape of it to his shoulder, looped around his neck and drew him near until her lips touched his. They parted to hers, pliable with gratitude and purpose. He governed his caresses, being neither rough nor crude, but left no doubt as to his ardor. With wonderment, Rusa measured him with her hands, learning what she could. He was as tall as she, broad of back and shoulder, strong in the legs. His beard, full and thick, clipped close, teased her skin. He owned knowledge of a woman's body. Her scant knowledge of a man's left her surprised by turns, and she grasped at her impressions . . . how strong he was . . . how hot his masculine shaft felt against her thigh . . . how hard . . . how deep he penetrated her and how little pain there was. She expected worse, and was grateful.

He performed his service efficiently and was tender after, holding her close, keeping her warm.

Did he want as much as she that the Mother grant a child?

Head on her shadow-husband's chest, Rusa listened to his heart—its slow, steady beating. His body in the aftermath felt familiar. She invented a story for him—that his wife was barren, that he hoped the Mother would grant him a gift. That here, deep in the earth, his seed might yet take root.

She left him recumbent on the earthen floor, the fluids of their joining soaking into the Mother's being. Her thighs were slick, as they'd been before. She looked back once, when the door opened, but saw only that the arm across his chest was brown from the sun and that he had raised his head, to look after her. The door shut as soon as she cleared the threshold and stood barefooted on the cool, smooth floor. She shivered as the priestess helped her dress and placed a shawl about her shoulders.

"May your womb be blessed," the priestess said. "Earth-fathered children are favored by the Mother. Such was Alm, in the days of our mothers."

"Indeed he was." Rusa walked quickly from the passage. Another priestess would come to the chamber, but not until she had reached the temple, secure from the shadow-husband's eyes. "All-Seeing Bess, however, was not. She was a Rappeleye."

"May her line continue."

. . .

They exited the passage, stepped into open places. Night had fully fallen and their lanterns now cast golden circles before their feet, pushing aside shadows. Across the inner courtyard, women clustered around the sacred pool, waiting for the moon's image to form fully within its basin. When the image was complete, they would enter to bathe in the water's fertility.

At the door to the chamber where she and Edda would spend the night, Rusa paused for another word with the priestess. She smiled to hear her aunt's soft snores coming from the other side of the door. "You will plant the acorns, I hope."

The priestess smiled. "We would be remiss if we did not."

Rusa nodded and watched the woman walk away, her work done. Her own work, of course, had just begun. With child or not, the time had come for her to claim her place as a Rappeleye woman. She entered the room and changed into her bed gown. From the pocket of her traveling shift, she retrieved her nurse stone and looped it over her neck. The shining weight upon her breastbone brought a smile to her lips.

I will take an apprentice, she decided. *There will be no more nurse stones until I have had this babe.*

She did not know if she would make another visit to the Valley of Moons, or if she would ever take another man. Now that she was not near him, the particulars of the man who might have given her a child did not seem important. Rappeleye men ever remained in the shadows.

Maybe that was what he had been unable to accept, that man who had thrown her down that day so long ago. *You little rune hag,* he had called her. *You won't forget me.*

And so she hadn't.

Yet memory of him had faded, and now she barely recalled him ever having been. The event lingered longer than the man. When she looked into the future, her past was transparent. She placed her hand upon her belly, above the daughter foretold by her laying of the Wheel.

I will teach you to make beautiful runes.

A. C. Fisher Aldag is a wife, mother, Pagan clergyperson, writer, environmental activist, and small-time farmer who lives in Michigan. She is one of the founders of Caer na Donia y Llew, a legal Pagan church with a Cymri (Welsh, Celtic) tradition. For the past several years, she has been researching historic systems of magick, Witchcraft, folklore, and Paganism from different regions in the United Kingdom.

The Bitter Herbs of Camelot

BY A. C. FISHER ALDAG

"They said that you could help me. You know, the ladies uptown. They said you'd give me a potion, and I could get rid of it without anybody knowing."

The girl was only about thirteen, wearing plastic barrettes in her hair. She was hunched over and frightened, not only because of her condition and what her parents would do if they found out, but also because she believed that the Old Witch Woman might hex her. Without protest, the girl swallowed the cupful of sour green liquid. After she'd paid the fee and left, Peter set the coffeepot on the woodstove, opened the firebox door, and stirred up the embers. Even this small action tired him, so he sat back in the maplewood rocking chair, pulled the rough woolen blanket up over his skinny knees, and stared at the floor.

"What? Ye think that I done wrong?" Lady Sheila Todd swept the elderly cat off the table with the back of her arm. It yowled in protest and slunk under the icebox. "Ye think her papa would welcome a bastard to his table with wide-open arms and a smile?"

"No, my lady," Peter replied wearily. Apparently, she was spoiling for a fight, and he and the old tabby were the closest targets. "It's not up to me to tell you what to do."

"Bloody-damn right." She slammed a pile of graniteware dishes down on the tabletop. "Am goin' out to pick some more tansy. Set the table, an 'tis nae too much trouble." The heavy oaken door banged shut behind her.

Sighing for no reason, Peter stood and began to arrange the plates and bowls on the woven linen placemats. Her forks only had three tines. They hadn't come from any antique shop; most likely they were heirlooms. Or maybe the blacksmith in Carmelnut had crafted them just last week. The utensils were like Sheila herself— ageless.

The coffee began to perk as the sun vanished behind the trees. Night came abruptly to the Carmelnut Forest. Even here in the clearing there were only a few hours of lemony daylight, and then nearly instantaneous dark. When Peter was a little boy, this phenomenon had frightened him. Now it was almost a comfort.

He opened the door and walked down the front steps into the yard. No grass grew here; the walkways were crushed stone, and the earth was covered with woodchip mulch. Carefully tended herb beds and truck vegetable gardens were arranged to catch the limited hours of sun. He peered around the tongue-in-groove log wall. Lady Sheila was on her knees in the dirt, plucking handfuls of fern-like leaves and sprays of yellow flower heads, dropping them into a basket. Her head was bowed over her work. "It's coffee," Peter announced, "and I think the roast smells done."

She got to her feet and smoothed down her long calico skirts, and it was quite possible that she had been weeping. Peter ignored it. If she wanted to talk, she would. It wasn't very likely. Gathering the herb basket, she followed him into the cabin.

•   •   •

Tansy and rue and pennyroyal, that'll do ye. And mayhap a drop of scotch broom, and cohosh, nary the blue but the black. Afterward, ye needs must wash out your woman's place with some'at to staunch off the bleeding, lest ye get the flux. And keep it clean, mind, or you'll sicken and die. Know me a woman, she done herself to home with a coat-hanger. Bled herself dry afore dawntime. But that was when 'twas illegal. Nowadays 'tis naught agin the law, merely so costly that womenfolk on the dole can scarce afford it. And the young'uns, they needs must get the consent of their kinfolk. Half the time, 'twas a kinsman that done for 'em. Just like the gov'ment, ain't it? Passing a daft law like that. Ah, well. Worse comes to worst, they'll come to me.

•   •   •

Peter remembered his family vacation trips to their cottage in the woods. During the tedious car ride, he would sing, "We're going up to Carmelnut, to Carmelnut," over and over, until his mother begged him to stop. Just like the other kids, he'd knocked on the Old Witch Woman's door, then ran away, or put rotten fruit in her mailbox. He wasn't at all surprised when he returned after almost thirty years and she was still there, looking nearly the same age, still living in her neat little cabin in the clearing in the woods. Peter knocked, but this time he didn't run away, because he was going to ask Ms. Todd if he could fish the small rapids on her land.

When she opened the door, she had stared at him critically and said, "Canna do nothin' for ye. 'Tis beyond healing. Am sorrowed." Peter was so astonished that he had to sit down, right there on her rustic front stoop, because he hadn't told anyone in Carmelnut that he was sick. The only people who knew about it were his parents, his married sister in Detroit, and Moondoggy. Peter couldn't remember what he said to the Old Witch Woman, only that she gave him strong coffee and a clean handkerchief, and let him cry for the first time since the diagnosis.

Later he learned that Sheila was not the Old Witch Woman after all, but her daughter. Sheila had been only sixteen when her mother died, leaving her to stir the cauldron, mutter the charms, and dispense the tonics and spells. The tribespeople called her "m'lady," an honorific they used for priestesses and chiefs. Peter was surprised to learn that she hadn't married. Usually, their people had a dozen kids by the time they were thirty. Like so much else, it was something Sheila refused to discuss.

. . .

After the moon turned, another young woman came to the cabin, seeking the potion. She was wearing tight spandex leggings and a low-cut top, and her hair was dyed the color of thistle flowers. Although she wasn't long out of her teens, her skin was leathery. She sat down in a wicker chair and lit a cigarette without asking permission. Her voice was whiny, demanding. "You know what I want."

"The same thing ye done wanted the last time," Sheila answered testily. "Wait just a consarned minute. Gotta fix up a fresh batch."

The visitor dropped her money on the tabletop and swallowed the drink. "It sure doesn't taste any better."

"Dinna forget to take ye a hot bath, after 'tis gone."

"Yeah, yeah, I know."

"Wash out your woman's place good."

"I know, all right?"

"There might be some queasy, this time. Ye might sick it up."

"It never made me sick before."

"Aye. Well, it might could this time. Only works so often, afore it don't work no more." Sheila scooped up the dollars and made them disappear. Peter pretended to concentrate on washing the dishes. "Ye might wanna try some o' that birth control stuff."

"Oh, you know men. They won't wear condoms. And the foam is so messy, and the Pill makes me bloat . . ."

After the blowsy woman had departed, Sheila remarked, "She'll know from messy, when she starts in to puking. Will wish that she'd kept her legs shut."

"What makes you think that she'll, um, vomit?" wondered Peter. "I mean, nobody else ever has, right?"

"Dinna never give nobody else the wormwood and spurge, mixed in with their draught." Sheila winked, and Peter caught a glimpse of the Old Witch Woman in her smug, mirthless grin. "Them plants shall make her sick as the dog who ate roadkill."

"You're wicked," he remarked, and of course, she took it wrong. Slamming the ladle into the pot, splashing rabbit stew all over the floor, she whirled to face him.

"Oh, 'tis so very wicked, eh? And who got herself in the fam'ly way three times, by three diff'rent menfolk, afore she'd turned twenty? Am I so bloody careless, to cast off my own? Yon heifer be too stupid to breed." Sheila tossed her head, whipping her silvery hair. "Wicked, ye say? An ye think me so, take your *cowyn*[1] mores away down the road!" She threw her hands in the air, narrowly missing a hanging lantern. "Go talk to your preacher man, he'll have plenty to say about wicked."

"Sheila, please," said Peter quietly. "I'm not getting on your case, all right? I thought it was . . . appropriate. Teach her a lesson." He began to mop the spilled stew with a red checkered dishrag. "You know, she's right about one thing. Men won't wear condoms. That's how I got—how Moondoggy got—oh, hell." He smiled sourly. "She's not any more careless than I was. Too stupid to breed."

Sheila looked contrite. "Dinna say that, Peter. Ye are naught stupid, just short o' luck. The gov'ment concocted that germ for one of their wars, I read it in the paper. Then it got loose in one o' them big cities, New York or somewhere. That's how ye took sick. Just bad luck, is all."

He almost laughed then, but turned away just in time. "Yes. Well. It looks like dinner is ready, m'lady, and I think your pie is done. Should I take it out to cool?"

"Put it up in the pie-safe." Her ageless face brightened. She really was quite pretty when she smiled. "Oh, just remembered.

---

1. *cowyn*: outsider

Got ye a letter today, came to my mailbox instead o' your'n. 'Tis up there atop the pie-safe." She grinned like a little child with a secret. "Think 'tis from your insurance comp'ny. What does it say?"

"They denied me," he answered, crumpling the letter in his hands.

•　•　•

If ye must do it, at least dinna tell sweet lies about it. Call it what it is, a killing. 'Tis naught murder, like them Christers always yell about, with their Right to Live booths at the county fair. You've seen 'em there in front of the cowyn doctor office, with their signs and their blood-painted doll babies, hollerin' like they was set afire. Nae, ye canna deem it a murder, for the plentyn[2] *has not yet drawn breath. But them pro-choosers ain't got it right, neither. 'Tis more than just a scrap o' tissue, like a cancer or a wart cut off your knee. It was a killing. Will tell ye right now, I am a killer, but 'tis like killing in war time. Some thirteen-year-old girl makes a mistake, should she pay with the rest of her life? Yet after the third or fourth time, ye can hardly call it a foolish blunder again.*

•　•　•

Sheila's homey log cabin was vastly different from Peter's vacation cottage. His place had running water and electricity, for one thing. It was also overly decorated and stuffy. After his parents retired, they decided they couldn't maintain the cottage any longer, and his married sister in Detroit didn't want it, preferring to vacation on the lakeshore. "You've always loved it there in the woods, Pete. Maybe you and your, um, friend could stay there on the weekends. Wouldn't it be perfect to entertain clients?"

That was before Moondoggy left him and the senior partner at the agency had gently ushered him out the door. That was back when Peter could climb a flight of stairs without gasping. These days he spent most of his time with Sheila. Their unusual relationship had begun when she invited him for dinners, with an occa-

---

2. *plentyn*: child

sional sleepover, which evolved into him practically moving into her home.

She pretended to grouse at him: "Chop me some wood, an 'tis nary too much trouble for a fine young man like yourself. Haul up some water, won't ye, the maid took a holiday." He would just smile, for he knew how lonely Sheila really was. Many of her own tribespeople feared her. She had male visitors infrequently, and when she did, he made a point to return to his tasteful, silent, dusty cottage. The gentleman callers didn't visit overly long, and after a few days had passed, the Witch Woman would be on his doorstep, complaining that her garden tools needed oiling or the hatchets wanted sharpening. Despite her constant harangues, Peter found her little cabin quite peaceful.

Once, a tribeswoman paid her with a ceramic jug of homemade whiskey, and they'd sat around the woodstove and gotten comically drunk. "Have ye never yet had a woman, Peter m' lad?"

"Yuck," he replied, making a face. "Girls have cooties, you know. They'll put the mojo on you."

Sheila laughed, slapping her knee.

"How about you? Haven't you ever been married?"

"Once upon a time." She pretended to gag, like she'd tasted her own witch's brew. "Done put him out. He was but a foolish lad, couldna keep me."

"Like Peter, pumpkin eater? Had a wife and couldn't keep her?"

"Aye, but ye are the only Peter I know of. 'Tis naught a common moniker here in Carmelnut." She leaned over and refilled his glass.

"Why is the town called that, anyway? Carmelnut. It's an awfully dumb sounding name."

"'Tis naught truly Carmelnut at all, but Caer Mai Llunedd. House of the full moon in May." She grinned up at him, and once again, it struck him how pretty she was. "Your folk called it Camelot. But the Camelot of the old lands is gone. All that be left is Carmelnut, Indiana, America." Sheila drank deeply, and wiped her lips daintily on her apron. "And speaking o' foolish names, how come your husband be called Moondoggy? Now, that sounds downright silly."

"It's from a movie. You ever heard of *Gidget*?" She shook her head, and Peter smiled. Her people didn't even use electricity, let alone have cable television with the oldies channel. "Well, Moondoggy was this beatnik surfer guy, who always tried to avoid work, kind of like the panhandlers uptown."

"And your man, he dinna work?"

"No, he actually had a pretty good job. But he was this ethereal type, who called himself Moon Eagle. That was his 'spirit name,' you see. He did massage therapy, foot reflexology, all of that stuff." Sheila looked puzzled, not understanding half of what he said, but by then, it was more of a monologue than an explanation. Peter smiled ruefully. "So we called him Moondoggy, kind of making fun. I guess he was screwing most of his clients. Right there on the massage table. When I tested positive, he said that I gave it to *him*." Peter was drunker than he thought, for suddenly his eyes were brimming with tears. "Can you believe it? He actually thought that he caught it from me . . . "

The last he remembered, Sheila was helping him to bed. Her linens smelled like meadow flowers. The elderly tomcat jumped up and curled beside him. She covered them both with a rough woolen blanket and blew out the lantern on the bedside table. "Sweet dreams, my friend," she whispered, and that night, he slept better than he had since he was a boy.

. . .

Neither of them spoke of it, but his condition was becoming worse. Sheila no longer nagged at him to haul water from the well or carry foodstores up from the root cellar, but she still called him a cowyn laggard, born in a featherbed and raised in a bower. She taught him to card wool and spin with a distaff, to knit socks, and to whittle wooden spoons to sell to the tourists. During the long, drowsy afternoons, he sat in the maplewood rocker, and sometimes his mind would drift and his eyes would go out of focus, and he would awaken from his daydream to the Witch Woman scolding him. "You're as lazy as my worthless tomcat!" He saw the relief

164

on her face at these times, and her gladness that he woke up and moved.

Peter was staring out the window at the sun-dappled yard when he saw the horse and carriage approaching. It was brightly painted in the colors of Sheila's own tribe, driven by a woman wearing a bonnet and shawl. Just then he felt the chieftain's hand clasp his bony shoulder. "Com'on, Pete, quit your woolgathering. Get out to the privy, sweep it down good, aught looks like a pig sty!" He nodded, realizing that the visitor would not discuss her troubles before an outsider.

He could hear much of the conversation, and although he could not understand their lilting Celtic language, he could guess at the tribeswoman's dilemma. She appeared to be in late middle age, her iron-gray hair coiled on her head, her apron covering a waist thick from childbearing. Her youngsters ranged in age from a toddler who clutched at her skirt, to the shy teen boy grasping the horse bridle. Before Peter had graciously made himself scarce, the lady unconsciously rubbed her belly and hung her head like a criminal.

"She thought that her fruitful time had passed," Sheila told him later, and that was all that she said.

•   •   •

There be some o' us who can do the fertile-making magic, who can bring crops to the stony hilltop, or cause a heifer to calve, or who can get a barren woman with child. 'Tis my sorrow that I canna do aught. Sometimes, can do a healing. But mostly am skilled in the death-bringing charm. When I was a lass, my Mama told me that this was a gift, but there are days when that's downright hard to swallow. Yet when a kinswoman comes to me, a-wailing that she's in the fam'ly way once again, then my talent can be a blessing. Women with fifteen, sixteen plent[3]*, they don't need nae more. So many births wear 'em out. Mama always said it was doin' them a favor.*

Me'self, an I had me choosin', I would take the fertile magic any day.

•   •   •

3. *plent:* children

165

Some times were better than others, when Peter felt healthy and strong and able to take on the world. He hadn't returned to his cottage in nearly two weeks, but he wanted to spend this one good day doing something more productive than trudging down the road to his own land. It would be more worthwhile to go fishing at the little rapids behind Sheila's cabin. Maybe he could catch a few rainbow trout. The priestess was gone away for the afternoon, probably ministering to her people. When she came home, she'd be pleased to find that he'd fixed supper for a change. Peter had always been a good cook, but he was an even better fisherman.

His pole and lures were in the woodshed, right where he'd left them in the early spring. It was quiet and dark in the old-growth forest. The arching branches reminded him of a cathedral, the holy ground of the tribespeople. The little pathway down to the stream-let was a bit overgrown, but he noticed where feet had recently trampled the weeds. Probably kids, daring to defy the Old Witch Woman and trespass on her land.

Peter heard them talking, and he halted on the trail before they saw him. They were speaking the language of the tribe. It was Sheila and a younger man, perhaps one of her gentleman callers. Peter chuckled to himself. He would leave them alone and go fishing somewhere else. Perhaps he would spend the night in his own cottage, for the first time in weeks.

Something was wrong, though. The tribesman raised his voice in anger, and Peter could understand quite a few of the words. *Cowyn*, outsider. *Plentyn*, child. And *faggot*, that was the same in any language. Sheila shrieked a vicious answer. "Dead, 'tis dead, I tell ye! Dead! Go away!"

"Aye, m'lady," the young man retorted. Peter stood his ground, uncertain. Was she in danger? Should he go forward to rescue her, armed with only a fishing pole? Before he could decide, the tribesman shoved past him on the trail. He was ruggedly handsome, his face tattooed with their ritual designs, his hair plaited carefully, his clothes ornamented with beads and shells and bits of glass.

166

Dressed for courtship. The young man glared at Peter, spat a curse at him, then hurried away down the path.

He went to her then. Sheila was kneeling on the limestone river-bank, her long skirts pooled around her. Her hands were clenched in her lap, her silvery hair covering her face, her breath coming in harsh sobs. Tenderly, Peter raised her to her feet, allowed her to lean on him. He was weaker than he thought, and he staggered. "Come on back to the house. Please, Sheila. Let's go back home, and I'll fix us some coffee."

He led her down the trail, pausing for a moment by the well to draw up water. Dipping her apron into the bucket, Peter gently wiped her face. Then he put a protective arm around her, escorting her past the fragrant herb gardens that bordered the cabin.

"Wasn't that your husband?" he asked later.

"Need nae husband," Sheila replied with a scowl. "All men be lazy sods, useless as teats on a boar. Got me the cat to catch mice. And ye to snore and leave your socks on the floor. What should I do with a husbandman?"

"Darned if I know, Ms. Todd."

· · ·

On a bad day, Peter could scarcely rise from the blankets, but she insisted that he get up and sit in the rocking chair, to keep his lungs clear. The seat was padded with cushions to prevent any more pressure sores from developing on his skin. Peter knew that his days were numbered, because the Old Witch Woman didn't harass him at all for his slothfulness. Instead, she nagged him to eat. "Just a wee drop of this nice broth. I spent all morning cookin' it, the least ye might do is swallow a bit. You're gettin' so scrawny, a fair wind could blow ye away."

"I'm leaving my cottage to you," he informed her.

"What? Have nae use for aught, 'tis electric and such, and any-how you'll be up there soon enough. Most likely with some fine young lad from the city."

167

"Please, m'lady," Peter said hoarsely, and she spooned some of the soup into his mouth. He no longer had a stomach for coffee. "You know I'm not going to live very much longer . . . "

"Fie," she interrupted. "Just hush your baneful words. Ye will likely outlive us all. The Gods might see fit to nail me with lightning tomorrow. Or I could be uptown to Carmelnut, get hit by a car."

"Optimistic as ever." To please her, Peter swallowed another bite of the stew, although his throat seemed to close. "You could always sell it, you know."

"Hush, now, and eat up. Done took me all bloody-damn morning to cook this."

Peter did not speak for several more minutes, and she thought he had fallen asleep in the chair. Then he lifted his hand and dabbed his lips with a checkered linen napkin. "Remember this spring, when I first knocked at your door, and you told me there was nothing that could help me?"

"Aye?"

"I thought of something that you can do. If it gets too bad, you could give me some of your potions. Please. Make it painless. If it gets bad."

"Will speak of aught, an the time comes," she said, and turned back to the stove.

. . .

Done had to do aught once, when an elder had the wasting sickness, the cancer of the innards. It was the end, but her body wouldna give up and die. She was screaming with the pain of it, like hot coals was all in her belly, burning up her life. 'Twas right awful to hear. Them Christers would make this illegal, too; helping to put someone out o' their misery. They claim 'tis playing at being a god. Well, if the Gods was doing their job, they wouldn't need me.

The cowyn would likely say that I poisoned her, as I gave her the death-bringing potion. Will not tell the recipe here, nor even name the herbs, lest someone do mischief with 'em. 'Tis plenty good enough to say that it worked, and her suffering came to an end. And I would pledge that her spirit done thanked me.

.   .   .

Summer was waning, and Peter could smell autumn in the air. Funny how he'd never noticed it in the city, even though he'd often had lunch outdoors at a street-vendor's cart, or taken long walks at sunset with Moondoggy. Here in Carmelnut, Peter could scent the difference in the forest, although the leaves had yet to change color. The sunlight fought its way through the trees, and it was dusk by four thirty in the afternoon. This no longer dismayed him, like it had when he was a boy.

He had gotten so weak that he could barely push open the heavy oaken front door. It was a long and arduous journey to the privy, so Sheila had set up a chamber pot for him indoors. It was another one of her new-old antiques, timeless as the Witch Woman herself; it could have been crafted yesterday, or it might be as arcane as the woodlands. It humiliated him to use it, knowing that she had to clean up after him, so whenever he felt strong enough, he would slowly make his way down the crushed limestone path to the outhouse.

Today when he shuffled around the tongue-in-groove log wall, he found Sheila kneeling on the ground near the yellow tansy flowers in the herb bed. She startled when she saw him, hastily turning away and wiping her sleeve across her eyes, so he knew that she had been weeping again.

"What's the matter, Lady Sheila?"

"Must be the pollen, a-makin' me sneeze."

"Probably. Now if you'll excuse me, I was headed for the bathroom." Peter took a step and swayed, and had to put his hand on the rough cabin wall to steady himself. He managed to make it to the privy and back, although the journey took nearly half an hour.

Sheila was waiting for him near the herb garden. "Ye look a mite bit peaked," she observed. "Abide here for a piece, an ye will." She went to the edge of the clearing, almost into the woods. In a few moments she returned, dragging an old wooden bench. "Here, have ye a seat."

"You know, when you sell my cottage, you could afford to buy some new lawn furniture. Something that doesn't stick splinters in your butt." He smiled, and she could see every fragile bone of his skull.

"How do ye know that ye will naught outlive me? Am older than ye, and will likely drop dead first. Then ye must sell off my land. Or mayhap you'll keep it for the fishing. If the bloody gov'ment dinna snatch it for taxes, that is."

"Please. I'm leaving you the cottage. You can sell it. Use the money for something that will help out your tribe, your people, like a scholarship or something."

"The tribe is good as dead," Sheila replied bitterly. "Nae daughter to follow me, to rule when I'm gone. My people be dead, like the Camelot in the old land. Look. Look here, Peter." She knelt once again in the herb bed, parted the feathery tansy leaves, and placed her palms against the damp earth. "'Tis here that my *plent* do sleep."

Peter thought that he had misunderstood. Her child slept here, in the herb garden? No, she must mean children. The word *plent* was plural; otherwise she would have said, "Here my *plentyn* sleeps." But that still didn't make any sense. He did not comprehend what she was trying to tell him . . .

And then in a moment, he understood.

"Was naught never able to bring forth," Sheila explained in a defeated voice. "No living plent. One was stillborn. Them others dinna quicken past their third month."

Her own babies had fertilized the herb garden. The death-bringing plants were watered by the priestess's tears.

. . .

The leaves drifted down in the Carmelnut Forest, somber brown oak and bright scarlet maple and sun-yellow beech. Peter didn't know where he'd caught the darn cold; there hadn't been any visitors for almost a fortnight. It made him so weak that he couldn't get up out of bed. His skin was covered with lesions, but they didn't hurt him. The Witch Woman fed him and washed him and changed his soiled bedding, and she scolded him like she had all summer long. "Sit up now, afore your lungs fill up with ill humors. Look here, ye got a letter from your sister in Dee-troit. Sit up here now and read it to me." Sheila didn't wait for a reply before she tore the envelope open. "So, what's she got to say for herself?"

"'Dear Pete. I hope you are having fun on your vacation. How is the weather there? I'm glad you were able to spend the summer at the cottage. It was always your favorite place to go, even more than the lakeshore. I remember when we were kids, and you used to sing "We're going up to Carmelnut" until Mom wanted to tape your mouth shut.'" He rolled his eyes and smiled. "'I know how much you always loved those spooky old woods. And speaking of which, do you remember . . .'" He trailed off. The letter said, "'. . . do you remember that one lady who lived in the cabin? We used to call her the Old Witch Woman. God, she was scary. She always gave me the creeps. We used to think that she caught little children and ate them for dinner . . .'"

"I'm tired now, m'lady. I'll read you the rest of it tomorrow, okay?"

.   .   .

Peter was shaking with chills from the fever, and his skin felt hot to the touch. One moment he was freezing, and the next, thrashing about and throwing off the covers. The elderly tabby slept on the pillow beside him, paws curled beneath its chin, tail twitching vigilantly. Sheila put more wood on the fire and bathed him with rose water, but the fever would not break. Long about evening, he awakened and looked up at her. His breath was coming thick and gummy from his lungs.

"It's almost over," he rasped.

"We'll have nae such talk, ere it hex ye, foolish cowyn lad." She forced a straw between his parched lips, but he swallowed very little of the healing concoction. "An ye speak such curses aloud, 'twill come true."

"It's time. Time for the other . . . potion."

"Nae, I'll hear naught such a thing. Would ye like me to go uptown and fetch ye the preacher man?"

"No thanks. He'll only tell us how wicked we are." Peter smiled weakly. "I just want . . . " His voice was so thready, she had to bend close to listen. "I just wanted you to know, this time here in Camelot with you—this was the best time of my whole life."

"You'll be havin' plenty more good times, afore ye grow old."

She had to spoon-feed him the dark herbal mixture. Much of it ran from the corner of his mouth, dribbling onto the white linen pillow sham. Clucking, she dabbed at his sunken cheek with a red checkered towel. "Want'cha to know, Sheel . . . th' *best* time . . . "

"Sweet dreams, my dear one." With a backward sweep of her arm, she sent the tomcat scurrying from the bed. The Witch Woman lay down beside her friend Peter, covered him gently with the coarse woolen blanket, and held his hand as he fell asleep.

A. L. Waldron is a young writer from Vancouver, Washington. She considers herself a pantheist or agnostic who is interested in Paganism, Buddhism, and Gnosticism. She will be attending Evergreen State College, after which she hopes to pursue a career in political science or, in order to deepen her understanding of ancient religions and cultures, anthropology.

We Have Come Home

BY A. L. WALDRON

Golden-red sand seeped between my toes like the thick earth of Mars. Yet this was not the red world I had lived upon since my childhood, worshipping a strange war god. Nor was this the sea of Europa, or the secret gardens on Ceres. In the starships that carried us from world to world, we revered Chaos, and prayed that she would preserve us in the void.

This place, this world called Aeaea, was strange to me. Starships burned like shooting stars through her golden night. Our own ship rested in the port, while teachers, hundreds of children, and I gathered by the ocean. We raised our eyes to a bright arch looming over the port. Upon it, in blue, glowing letters, was scribed: *Sapiens dominabitur astris.*

A student of mine, a young boy named Elliot, walked up beside me, and curling his fingers with mine, asked, "Ms. Sotiria, wasn't Aeaea the island of a witch?"

"It was," I said, surprised. "Elliot, who told you that?"

"Read it somewhere," he said. "Oddy-Oddy . . . *Oddy-sy*. You gave me it to read when we were on the ship and I was sick, remember? But do you think she was one of the old witches, like the ones from England?"

"Who, Circe? Circe was long before *those* witches," I explained to him. Near us, three girls plunged into the water and screamed. They crawled back onto the beach, shivering. "When being a witch wasn't so strange. But there is always natural magick, and that we know well."

"If Romans and Greeks got their magick from Earth, then how did the witch get her magick from Aeaea?" Elliot asked. "It doesn't make sense."

"That's not exactly how it goes, Elliot. It's something called relative pantheism," I said, but the words simply went over the boy's head. "You'll understand when you're older."

"Maybe," Elliot said. He knelt down and sifted his other hand through the sand. "But I know that Aeaea is supposed to be like Earth, isn't it? Is that why everyone wants to come here? 'Cause we don't have to burn its skies or dig into the ground? We did that on Mars so we could live there, right?"

It was easy to forget that human beings were not nomads, native to the abyss, but that we had come from a small, blue star named Earth. The star maps we knew were charted from Earth, yet on Aeaea the skies were inconceivable and strange. No maps had been drawn of these stars, no constellations created except for those by children, pressing their faces against the glass windows and crying out animals and shapes as if they were cloudwatching.

"Elliot," I said, "could you imagine the old Greeks having knowledge of the power of Venus's storms? Do you think they could contain their greed if they knew of all Dis's treasures held in the asteroid belt?"

"I don't understand, Ms. Sotiria."

"That's all right. Never mind what I said." I sighed. "I don't even know what I'm talking about. Sometimes, whenever I look around, and I think about how we, as humans, change these cold deserts into new Americas, I just wonder if we're supposed to be here."

"Who says that?" rumbled a voice.

Approaching Elliot and me was a man in his late fifties, with a dark, heavy beard. Melvin Stravos spoke to us in his deep, articulate accent. "Who says that humanity is not doing exactly what it is meant to do?"

"Mr. Stravos, all Ms. Sotiria was saying," Elliot defended, although not sure of himself, "is that maybe it isn't right."

"Morally?" he inquired, raising a brow. "No, no. There is nothing wrong with turning a rock into a flowerbed. Terraforming is an art, but, you know that, right, Ms. Sotiria?"

"Well, no, Melvin. That's not what I mean," I said. "I did not say it was wrong—just strange. Not right in the way that fish shouldn't grow wings and fly."

"Living on Mars can give one such an alienated, illogical feeling." Stravos said. "I lived there for ten years up until now, Ms. Sotiria. You know that. That incident made me change the way I see things. It made me want to see more—more than I'd ever done before. But look at me! I'm getting old, and my lungs are giving out. Now, Earth is where everything begins. Gods help me, I'm going there one day, no matter how crowded it gets."

"Why are you here with us, then?" I asked.

"I can never stay in a place for too long, and besides—" Stravos pulled a white box out of his pocket and placed a cigarette in between his lips. "How many humans are out there now?"

"Fifty billion?" Elliot asked.

"Thirty-eight," I corrected him, and looked to Stravos. "I understand your point, Melvin: overpopulation, colonization. It's been done a thousand times over and over again. But it just feels strange, doesn't it? You have to admit. These other places just aren't our home."

"I guess it would be appropriate for me to ask you, then," Stravos said. "Why are you here with us?"

I didn't know what to say to this. Stravos slid the cigarette out of his mouth and pointed its smoldering tip at the port.

"Look there, Sophia. See what it says? *Sapiens dominabitur astris.* Do you know what that means?"

I read the fluorescent blue letters. "The wise person shall have dominion over the stars."

I turned away from the arch and looked to the yellow horizon. Darkness wheeled through the sky, carrying the moons into the sunrise.

"Dominion over the stars." Stravos smiled. "And humans, or homo sapiens, are the wise men. We no longer live in a society of idolatry, with the gods of money, sex, and power, but rather in one of astrolatry—worlds, science, knowledge, and life. Humans, not the gods, now reign over the stars. But still, we all worship immortality, don't we?"

A strand of sun streamed over the sea, bathing the sleeping city behind us in a gray glow. Lights flickered on like waking fireflies.

"And this is what it is all about, isn't it?" Stravos said. "This spreading. We are keeping humanity immortal." He exhaled, and breathed in the tobacco. "Well, I have something to attend to, something not including children, thank gods. I will speak to you later, Sophia."

Elliot and I watched as Stravos waved goodbye, leaving to join the other adults nearer to the port. Elliot whispered something to me.

"What was that?" I asked.

"Gilgamesh," he said.

Pausing, I tightened my grip on his hand.

"Since when did I teach Sumerian mythology?"

"Read it somewhere," Elliot said. "Don't remember, though. Ms. Sotiria?"

"Yes?"

"I'm tired. My stomach hurts and I want to go back home."

"Oh, honey." I knelt down, and Elliot clutched my shoulder. I wrapped my arms around him, cooing, "We were in the Chaos for a long time, I know, but maybe one day you'll be able to go back. Just think what Mars will be like when you're my age! Can you imagine?"

"Why did Mommy send me away?" he cried, his face red with sobbing. "She hates me! She doesn't want me anymore!"

"Elliot," I sighed, "your mommy is coming in a different ship, that's all. You went with us so you could be with your schoolmates, remember? You wouldn't want to be on one of the adult ships anyway. They're terribly boring. They don't have play structures or anything."

He giggled, but his wet eyes still glistened.

"When will they be here, Ms. Sotiria?"

"I don't know," I admitted. "But we won't separate, Elliot. We won't leave anybody behind. We're like a family, you know?"

"My family is in Tharsis." Elliot wiped his eyes with his sleeve. "And I want to go back home."

I smiled at him.

"Elliot, I know Aeaea seems strange now, but soon it'll be home. You'll love the new school, all the play sets and toys and—"

A starship whistled overhead. Children screamed, waving their arms.

"—Mars will be just another red star." Elliot and I gazed over the ocean in childish wonder. "And soon, Aeaea will become another one. It'll just keep on going like that until we reach the edge of Chaos."

"And what then?" Elliot asked.

"We'll be immortal."

· · ·

"What do you think Earth looks like?"

Glass-eyed children gazed over me, with fiddling hands and the innocence of the seven-year-olds they were. The classroom was silent, until a small girl named Lynn lifted her arm. "Round?" she chirped.

The class giggled. Lynn blushed.

"Well, yes. It is round." I said. "But what do you think it is like to be an Earth person? I don't think any of us come from there, right?"

One of the boys, Edwin, raised a dark hand. "My grandpa was born in Australia."

"Did you hear that? Australia," I said, as the children made quiet, awed sounds. "We're going to draw what we think Earth is like, just to get Mars off of our minds. The paper is over there . . . "

A dozen little bodies crowded around the paper bins, formed into circles of three, and began to draw. Lynn tugged at my skirt.

"Yes? Are you having trouble?"

Lynn folded her fingers and tapped the floor.

"I don't want to draw Earth." she said. "I want to draw dinosaurs."

"We'll draw dinosaurs another day," I said, attempting to smile. "Just sit with Rosa, and I promise you that we'll do what you want one day, okay?"

Lynn sighed, and sat down at one of the small tables.

"Remember, you are supposed to draw what you think it's like to be on Earth."

Holding my arms behind my back, I walked up behind my students. Over their shoulders I saw white mountains, red deserts, orange skies (sometimes with two moons in the sky; "Earth has one moon," I had to remind them), and the Great Wall of China and the Eiffel Tower.

"Rosa, who is that?" I asked the chubby, red-haired girl. Rosa turned her freckled face up from her drawing of a green woman, and said, "It's Mama Earth. Do you like it, Ms. Sotiria?"

"I do."

"See mine?"

Elliot raised his picture. What appeared to be a mother, father, and child holding hands were surrounded by gray boxes.

"Why's the sky blue?" another boy taunted. "That's just stupid."

"Yeah, Elliot, that's so dumb-looking."

"It's really blue!" he exclaimed. "I promise, I swear to the gods! My mom told me so!"

"You're a liar," Rosa sneered. "You've been everywhere, Ms. Sotiria! He's a liar, isn't he?"

Before I could explain that I'd never been to Earth, Lynn rose, hanging her head. She held out a piece of paper to me, and then stormed through the door.

The students leaped up to see what Lynn had drawn, but I held the paper above their heads: a red comet plummeting into the dead ground, buildings and people burning in the flames. I folded the paper.

"Wait! Look on the other side, Ms. Sotiria." Elliot said, tugging on my skirt and pointing. "See?"

I flipped the paper around, and found there, crumpled and creased, what Lynn had wanted me to see: a dozen women and men, as dark as earth with corn-yellow hair, floating in the blue. Their arms surrounded people holding baskets of corn and grains, flowers, goats, and sheep. These words were written in the clouds: *I don't want the stars.*

"What does it say?" the children chimed. "What does it say? Isn't she in trouble?"

"I think it is time for everyone to go outside. Put on your playing shoes, though, okay?" I said, no louder than a whisper. They gathered at the cubbies, pulling out toys, snacks, and shoes.

"Rosa, do you need help?"

"No, Ms. Sotiria."

I walked them as far as the door, and yelled into the playground, "If any of you need me, just call!"

"Ms. Sotiria?"

The quiet voice rose from behind me. Lynn looked up like a frightened animal, her straggly blond hair flecked in red dirt.

"Where'd you go, honey?" I asked.

She sniffled. "Mars."

"Mars?"

"Come with me."

Lynn guided me out of the classroom and into the hall. We walked through the inner courtyard, where three teachers sat, holding small, glowing screens. I knelt on a step.

"We can sit here, Lynn."

"No we can't," she argued. "I have to show you something."

"Sophia?" David Kole, a lanky man in a brown sweater, looked up from his device. "Come here. No, no, just let the girl sit there. It's not for her to know."

I cast a glance to Lynn, but she had folded her arms and hidden her face. David motioned me closer, and whispered, almost gravely, "They aren't coming back."

My heart bounded.

"Who isn't coming back?"

A woman with long chestnut hair named Francine touched my arm and said, "The ships, Sophie. The starships aren't coming."

"Why?" I exclaimed. The others hushed me. "Francine, are you joking with me?"

She shook her head.

"But what about my students! W-why aren't they coming? Are they just delayed, or did—"

"Calm down, there," the older woman, Marisse Maud, cackled. "Listen to him before you do something stupid."

David sighed, turned off the screen, and slipped it into his pocket. Lynn made a high-pitched squeal. It took me a moment to recognize it as crying.

"Sophia, they will never come. There are no delays, no mistakes. Nothing." David stated, his voice solemn. Francine tightened her grip on my arm. "There was a malfunction in the light-speed field around the ship. The sudden halt caused it to implode. They barely reached past the belt before being crushed in the vacuum."

"Crushed?" My voice shook. "Crushed in the Chaos? But w-what do we do? How do you expect me to tell this to my kids?"

The old woman sighed. "That's just it, Sophia. You don't."

White explosions played in my mind's eye like a film: my lungs halting, gasping for air in the vacuum, whistling, screaming, and cold impact. Ice glistening like glass in Europa's black sea, luring me into its depths as I clung to a metal panel . . .

Their faces blurred into pale, ghastly shapes.

"But we just can't tell these children that their parents are coming when they never will!"

David furrowed his brows. Europa's stars glistened over his head. I heard myself from five years ago, screaming, *How could they? How could the gods be so indifferent and cruel?*

"Is it any better to tell them that their parents are never coming?" David said. "That Chaos killed them?"

"No, but—"

Little fingers grasped my hand. In my memory, a man's hands reached into the cold water, lifting me, screaming.

"Ms. Sotiria!" Lynn cried, red in the face. "Come on! I have to show you!"

"Please, Lynn," I gritted my teeth. Again, I saw the explosions. "Now is not the time. Go on the play—"

"No!" she yelled. "I'm not going to play! I know what happened about the starship, but I want to show you—"

"Lynn! Go outside!"

My screams echoed against the courtyard walls. Memories of the crash vanished, and silence folded around us so heavily that we could not even hear the sound of our own breathing.

"Lynn, I—"

The little girl stepped back, releasing her quivering hand. She fled, her hair fluttering like a long, golden wing. I crumbled, burying my face in my hands.

"It's okay," Francine assured me. "Sometimes you have to speak your mind—"

"It's not that!" I cried. "It's not that at all. Just half an hour ago, I instructed my students to draw what they thought Earth looked like—and do you know what they drew?"

I sucked in my breath.

"Mars. It looked like Mars. All red and mountainous with black and green and orange skies. But Lynn, she made a blue sky and put gods in it. It was like they were having a festival, the way they did thousands of years ago."

"Sophia, really—"

"She said, 'I don't want the stars.' Can you believe that? Can you believe there is a child who only wants simplicity? Yet in this era, that's one thing that we can't give her! All she wants are gods and a family, and now she can't have either!"

We heard the rattle of a man clearing his throat. Melvin Stravos strode down the concrete steps to stand over us. His thick fingers played over a green book.

"I wanted to question you on the morality of informing the students of this . . . tragedy. My own students know already—quick as Mercury, they are."

"Your students are almost adults," Marisse said. I began to tread toward the sound of laughing children outside. "What are they, eighteen? Melvin, we're taking care of children."

"Babies, for me," Francine muttered. "I love them, but they don't have to know anything for a long time."

I leaned against the stone doorway, casting a final glance back at the teachers. My fingers played with the ribbon on my blouse.

"It doesn't matter," David Kole interrupted, folding his glasses into his pocket. "They are all orphans now."

· · ·

Golden skies warmed the playground, as if the sun had filled the heavens, winking on the plastic structures and the sweating foreheads of children. Redheaded Rosa pushed a dark boy on the swing. A dozen little girls spun around on a carousel. Boys crawled up the slides when supervisors turned their heads. Near the field, Elliot and two other boys sat in a circle, eating sandwiches and playing with hovering tops.

All of them were orphans.

All of them were alone and oblivious.

I walked over to the boys, leaned over them. Pity sank in my chest. "Did you see where Lynn went?"

Elliot gave me a concerned look. His friends simply turned their heads from side to side.

"I watched her go into the field," he said. "Just disappeared."

I looked over the red tips of the grass. The stalks were bent in the shape of little feet.

"Thank you, boys."

"Can I come?"

"Just stay here, Elliot. I wouldn't want to lose you."

Too, my mind added, but I shook the word from my consciousness. I stepped into the field, red grass crackling under my feet. As if I had entered a dream, the grasses muffled all sound but for my own calls.

"Lynn! Lynn Henderson, answer me! Lynn!"

The echo of a bell rang across the field, and moments later, emptiness. I contemplated whether or not to turn back, but the grass continued to crunch as I moved forward.

"Lynn Henderson, where on Aeaea are you? Lynn!"

A small voice replied, "Mars."

I parted the stalks ahead of me, and found a small, circular clearing. Lynn sat on the red earth, her legs curled up to her chin, white blouse dirtied. Dead candles and rocks were scattered about her like fallen soldiers. Lynn's tears dappled her face, but she smiled.

"I found Mars, Ms. Sotiria. We never left it." I knelt to her, reaching out my hand and touching her head. "Mommy's still here, and daddy too. And Ares and Earth and Jupiter and Venus and Diana! They're not gone, and they didn't die. Ms. Sotiria?"

"Yes?"

"Why didn't the gods like Mars?"

Aeaea's golden sky captured my gaze as I remembered that old, red world. Nothing like its god, Mars was cold, quiet, and peaceful, with dry riverbeds, man-made seas, blue sunsets, and lambent, scarlet deserts.

"Mars was not very kind," I explained. "He was the god of war."

Lynn cocked her head to the side.

"What's *war*?"

"War is something that no longer exists," I said. "Humans don't go to war anymore, so neither do our gods. Expansion and knowledge are the true competitions between peoples. I know, you don't understand. However, one god did like Mars. Her name was Venus."

Lynn blinked.

"Oh," she sighed. "I think I knew that. But Ms. Sotiria, if Mars was mean, why was I always told that Father Mars makes the crops and fields grow, and that he protects us?"

"That is what he first was, and that is what he has returned to being."

"I-I miss . . . " Lynn stuttered, tears breaking her voice. "I miss Father Mars. I miss how it turns blue when the sun sets. I thought that when Mommy and Daddy came back, they would bring Mars too."

I realized that, while Lynn's children would be raised to revere a new goddess named Aeaea, Lynn could never stop loving Father Mars. I, too, could never love the Earth my family came from. Even Melvin Stravos understood this yearning, and as much as he detested human crowding, he always wanted to go back. Worship was nostalgia, a need for home.

"Have you ever heard the phrase, 'Home is where the heart is?'"

"No, Ms. Sotiria." she said. "But I don't care, 'cause I am not going back. I'm going to stay here forever."

I sighed. "Just remember it, okay?"

Faraway bells chimed over the field. Wind whispered through the grasses, playing with our hair. Pollen fluttered over my face as I headed away from the clearing, when Lynn tossed a toy at my back.

"Tell them," Lynn called. "Tell them our parents aren't coming."

I turned around, closing my eyes.

"It's more complicated than that."

"Tell them. They need to know, Ms. Sotiria. Like they need to know that Earth's sky is blue."

I picked up the toy.

"All of us will have to spend one last day on Mars. One more day in childhood, and then we have to move on. I'm bringing the class here, and I'll tell them."

"I want to go home."

"Me too."

. . .

My feet glided across the field like Mercury's winged ankles, over the empty playground and courtyards. Panting, pressing up against the classroom door, I heard a man speaking.

"Melvin?" I gasped, sweeping through the door. "I'm sorry, I didn't mean to be so late."

Stravos looked up from the picture book across his lap. The children sat around him, turning their bright, curious eyes at me. He smiled. "Ms. Sotiria, I'm glad you're here. Would you like to sit down? I hope you don't mind me taking over—"

My fists clenched, shaking with nerves. I shook my head, trying to clear the emotions away. How could I tell *children* that their parents were dead? How could I do this and still believe myself to be compassionate? *It was inhumane*, something in me whispered.

I spoke, in a more powerful voice than I knew myself to have. "Stand aside, Mr. Stravos."

"What's wrong?" Rosa asked. "Your eyes are all red."

I did not see these children as belonging to someone else anymore. I thought them my own, with a love as strong as Ops for her own babies. Who could see their own children's dreams devoured by the heavens and time?

"Today, there was . . . what I m-mean is . . . " I stuttered. My blood drummed in my ears.

"Do you want me to handle this?" Stravos interrupted. "If you can't, that is."

"Would you?" I clapped my hands together, but shook my head. "No. No, never mind. It's fine. I can do it myself."

"Do what?" Elliot asked.

"Mr. Stravos, everybody, I need you to follow me." I said, and Stravos gave me a concerned look. "Please, it's just out in the field."

I exhaled and Stravos smiled. "Sophia, it's okay. We'll go."

He cleared his throat, and set aside the picture book. The children bounced to their feet, and we walked out of the classroom. They whispered fearfully as we entered that strange, grassy field, and trod into Lynn's sanctuary.

"Hi, Ms. Sotiria," Lynn piped, her eyes lowered.

"Would everybody sit down?"

Little heads nodded, strangely quiet and solemn for seven-year-olds. Stravos, with his black tweed jacket and green book, towered beside me like a wise, old titan. His eyes darkened, and he spoke in a voice calm and deep.

"A tragedy has occurred today," he began. "There was nothing we could do to prevent it, nothing any human or god could do."

"Was it the witch?" Elliot cried. "Did Circe get somebody? Turn them into pigs?"

Rosa gasped, and the class giggled.

"Not a witch," I said. "Above our world, and every world, there is a beautiful, black void called Chaos. Out of her, everything came: gods, people, and stars. But Chaos isn't like those things she made. She has no soul, really. She is indifferent.

"Indifferent," I repeated. "Meaning, unlike people, she can't care or feel. At times, she hurts us. A few hours ago, a starship from Mars took off into the sky, but that light around it—what makes us be able to go so fast in such a big place—faded away. There were people inside. We knew them, we loved them. I was friends with them. They raised you."

"Ms. Sotiria, are you saying—"

"Nobody is coming home. No one is going to come into the port. Nobody is coming."

My voice resonated quietly in the clearing, over the bowed heads of my sobbing children.

"What about Father Mars?" cried a boy. "Why didn't he do anything?"

"It was not Father Mars, James. Sometimes the gods, including Chaos, are sweet, blessing us with suns and beautiful worlds, friends, family, and loved ones."

"But for this kindness to exist," Stravos said as he rumbled beside me, "so must cruelty and this indifference we talked about. This tragedy is not our own fault, but the fault of nature and a consequence of adventure and curiosity. For this day, this one last day, we will pray to Father Mars, but then we must come to terms with the fact that he no longer watches over us, and that as long as we are under Aeaea's skies, we are under her divine providence. So we must say goodbye to the mothers and fathers we left behind, and tread bravely into our new lives."

"One more moment here, and then we will leave this all behind."

Stravos and I strode into the red grasses. Elliot rose and clasped onto my fingers. He murmured, "I'm ready."

Lynn took his hand, Rosa hers, and soon we had become a chain: a trail of children connected only by their quivering hands, trusting, following each other through the red field. Hands interlaced and a humming passed through the grasses—whimpering, weeping, howling little bodies shivering tears. Small voices rose:

> "We approach the sacred grove,
> With hearts and minds and flesh and bone,
> Join us now in ways of old,
> We have come home."

"Thank you for helping me, Melvin," I whispered.

He smiled, and rumbled softly, "I was glad to, just as I was glad to help you on Europa."

My heart jumped with the image of flashing metal and ice. I shook my head, willed the fear away, and asked, "How long ago was that? Five years?" He nodded. "I'm sorry. I don't like to think about it. The whole experience of the crash just horrified me. I didn't want to learn about terraforming anymore. I couldn't even stand the idea of traveling to other places, especially in starships. I guess that's why I became a teacher like you, so that I could just stay in one place."

Stravos laughed.

"Because I'm such a sedentary creature? You well knew I traveled—quite a bit when I was young. Didn't you take my anthropology class in your senior year?"

"I did, and I remember. I guess teaching just seemed like a very domesticated and stable life to me."

"Why did you come to Aeaea then?" he asked. "You didn't have to."

"It was them," I said, and squeezed Elliot's palm. "All my students. Teaching is where I feel comfortable. It's my home, you know?"

"I know."

"And maybe the gods knew that they would need a mother." Elliot pressed himself up against my hip. "Things seem to turn out like this," I continued. "With purpose, you could say. And about the crash, Melvin, I just wanted to thank you. For a long time I tried, but I . . . "

"Couldn't? Ha, I understand. People have told me that I'm . . . what is that word? Intimidating?" Stravos hesitated for a moment, and slipped the old, green book he was carrying into his pocket: *The Art of Happiness.*

I smiled.

"If you hadn't pulled me out, I would have—"

Stravos set his hands on my shoulders. "Leave it behind in the clearing, with everything else."

Our footsteps and voices crackled, the sun sinking into a sky of molten bronze. We approached the school as the heavens shadowed themselves, but no one was waiting for us.

We had no one to come home to.

Paula R. Stiles is a forty-one-year-old American whose SF and fantasy stories have appeared in Neometropolis, Not One of Us, Strange Horizons, Black Gate, Writers of the Future, *the zombie anthology* History is Dead, Hub Magazine, Far Sector, *and* Transmitter. *A former EMT and aquaculture extension agent in Cameroon for the Peace Corps, she recently completed a PhD in Scotland on the Knights Templar in Spain. Under the pseudonym "Peter Ferrer," Paula has co-written two mystery/SF novels,* Fraterfamilias *and its sequel* Confraternitas, *for Virtual Tales, about an artist and his shaman brother on the run for murder in pre-9/11 New York. She follows a Christian syncretist path, leaning toward Gnostic and occult disciplines. Her stories also often reflect her strong interest in Siberian and prehistoric shamanism. Visit her website at http://www.geocities.com/rpcv.geo/other.html.*

Seabird

by paula r. stiles

I landed my seaplane in the Los Angeles harbor. I'd called it "Seabird" after my daughter, Nib. As I taxied in, the Customs agents met me at the dock. L.A. was still a big port down south, a big city of four million people, and I was a little guy in a little plane, but they paid attention. The Customs agents came out in hazmat suits while I was mooring my plane to the dock. I had to raise my arms and let them run Geiger counters over me, probably checking for a weather-control device on the sly. Then they patted me down and sprayed disinfectant all over my jeans and leather jacket, in my face and hair, making me choke and cough.

I thought of the limpid, green waters of the Arctic coast, where the glaciers calved into the sea with a sliding crack you could hear for miles. No such clarity down here. The harbor looked filthy brown. Oil slicks, maybe. They still bought our oil. We still had some.

The South had tried to invade us for it, but soon discovered that the North's weather-control tech trumped even nukes. One tornado summer and one very bad hurricane season later, the two sides had reached a truce that still worked twenty-six years later. Sort of.

"Christ's sake, guys," I said. "It's cold up there. Not like we got anything all *that* exotic."

They didn't answer me directly, but once they finished, they nodded and stepped away. They pulled off their helmets. One fingered my passport and plane registration while the other one quizzed me. "Please state the nature of your visit, Mr. Bingham."

"I'm here to visit my daughter. My wife . . . ex-wife's aware I'm coming."

"That's an awful long way to come for a parental visit."

I shrugged. "I live a long way away. She's my daughter. I make it down when I can."

The guy didn't crack a smile. Were Customs agents trained to do that? He nodded at his partner, who spread open my passport and stamped it.

The Customs guys gave me back my passport. The Southern visa on it was marked "Special," but it wasn't nearly as pretty as the shaman's stamp I had from their Northern counterparts. I gave the agents a disgusted look. "Nobody's really getting injected with Neanderthal DNA up north, you know. And we're not cannibals or baby-killers, either." That was their latest rumor: that we were turning ourselves into evolutionary throwbacks. It had been making its way across the subarctic grapevine for months, everybody getting a big laugh out of it. Down here, it wasn't so funny.

"Sorry," the guy who'd stamped my passport said. "It's a new protocol for AC professionals." He didn't look sorry. "Especially ones with families. They get weird ideas about parental custody."

"Okay." It wasn't okay, but I didn't want to waste any more time or goodwill before I got to see my daughter.

One of the guys gave me a funny look. "What *is* an 'AC professional,' anyway?"

I shrugged, wondering how I could squirm out of that question. They had a funny attitude about altered consciousnesses here, let alone professionals who manipulated them. Maybe they had the idea that I was trained in weather-control tech. I was, but not exactly in the way that they thought I was.

"Oh, you know, we're like psychics," I said, unable to find anything less lame. "We tell people's fortunes and things like that."

They looked skeptical but let me go. I took a taxi through the city; it cost a fortune. It always surprised me how they kept the infrastructure going, even while complaining nonstop about the incipient disaster that was coming any time, any day, to wipe humanity off the face of the planet. At least nobody was talking about global warming anymore, not with a new ice age settling in for the long haul.

The city looked shabby, with glittering, earthquake-proofed high rises, as delicate-looking as metal lace, built right next to crumbling, rambling shacks cobbled together from earthquake-shattered cement and rebar. I wondered if they knew how bad it looked, or cared. Oh, sure, we had our trash dumps on the permafrost next to every settlement, but we didn't sprawl. There weren't enough of us to sprawl. Not even our collections of machine corpses ("My museum of spare parts," as a fellow aviator liked to put it) made much of an impression on the Northern landscape.

The taxi left me off at my ex's housing complex. I'd once lived here. As I went up the steps two at a time the way I used to do, I didn't see anybody around. Gloria had said to come in the afternoon, so I'd tried to time my flight plan as well as I could to match her rigid schedule. She always complained that I made her juggle. I knocked on the door. Nothing. As I came back down the steps, I looked up and down the street.

"Daddy!" A small meteor hit me at waist height and spun me around. I grabbed at it in reflex and looked down.

"Nib!" I lifted her up in my arms. My little seabird, piping on the wind.

She wrapped her arms and legs around me as I gave her a big hug and kiss. She smelled like lavender soap. "Mommy said you'd come. I've been waiting. I got a watch for Christmas. I've been counting the days and the hours and the minutes and the seconds. See?" She held up a cheap, old wind-up watch to my ear.

I glanced at the watch. "Uff da, you're heavy, girl. Is the house open? Let's go in the house."

"We can go around the back," she said. "The door's open. Ed's out in the yard."

"Well, that's good." Who the hell was Ed? The babysitter? My replacement? Then I remembered—he was the new boyfriend of about six months. The cop. I hadn't really thought that Gloria would leave Nib alone and neglected, but the small, jealous part of me that I couldn't suppress, the part that was angry that I hadn't seen my daughter in three years, wished I didn't need a chaperone. I carried Nib around the back and let her slip to the ground by the gate. She opened it and ushered me through.

A tall, rangy guy with short, dark hair like a seal's pelt was digging at something in the backyard with a hoe. Ed, I presumed. He looked up as we came in. He smiled; it seemed genuine. He must have been the first person besides Nib since my arrival down south who wasn't treating me like a leper. He came forward to shake my hand. "You must be Matt," he said. "Nib's been really looking forward to your visit."

My mouth twitched in bitter amusement. Nope. My wife hadn't forgiven me yet. "I take it Gloria doesn't have much to say about me."

The smile faded. Oh, she did, but nothing good. "Well, you're the ex. I like to take anything she says with a grain of salt." He seemed too nice to be with Gloria. But then, everybody thought I was a nice guy, too. Gloria could be sweet—at first. I bet she'd used Nib ruthlessly, to reel him in.

"Mommy calls you a 'sumbitch polar bear,'" Nib said. She frowned. "That's a bad word, 'sumbitch,' isn't it?"

Ed and I exchanged that kind of look adults do when they're in a damned-if-you-do-damned-if-you-don't situation with kids. Whatever we said, it would get us in big trouble with Gloria. "Mommy just gets tired sometimes, honey," Ed said, going for the middle ground.

Nib nodded. "Yeah, it's a bad word."

I tousled her hair. "Don't worry about that, sweetie. I'm here, now. I brought you a present." I crouched in front of her and pulled off my backpack, setting it on the ground. "From the North."

Ed got a "Gloria won't be happy with that" look on his face, but I ignored it, especially since Nib's face was lighting up like the Northern Lights. "I'll go inside and get us some drinks, give you two some time together," he said, retreating. I watched him go, more than a little surprised. Gloria had made a point of telling me he was a cop—and how reliable he was. The unspoken flip side, of course, had been how reliable I wasn't. He shouldn't have been trusting me. But maybe I had an ally I hadn't anticipated in Ed. Or he was testing me, seeing if I'd run with Nib. Hell, I'd thought of it, but dropped it as a dumb idea. Not like it would be hard to stop us before we got back to the plane. And Southerners were already nervous about the rumors that we liked to shanghai kids to the North to solve our population problem.

Nib reached out and touched my beard. "You do look kinda like a polar bear."

"You like bears?" I said.

She nodded. "I only ever saw them at the zoo. I have dreams about them, but Mommy doesn't like it."

My mouth went dry. She was dreaming about the North, a place she'd never seen? This was a new wrinkle that Gloria, of course, hadn't mentioned. I'd have to proceed carefully. I fished out a present. It was small, but I'd taken a lot of time over it. I handed it over. "Here you go, sweetie."

As I watched her open it, I reached out to stroke the side of her face, savoring the delight when she spotted the necklace and pendant—a small, ivory figurine on a leather cord. "It's mammoth tusk," I said. "You can find it all over the North, and you can get it for free. But I carved that myself. It's for you."

"Is that a seal?" she said, feeling the ivory.

"Mmhmm. Took me over a year, working away at it every day." I tried to suppress the thrill at her recognition. She was a smart little girl who went to school; that was all. Of course she'd know what a seal looked like, even the crude shape that I'd made, though I had to say that it looked good once I'd polished it. *Down, boy. No way in hell would Gloria let you take her back. Especially if she's like you.* "I've got some pictures of the North, too, if you'd like to see them. And some discs of music. Lots of drums and stuff."

"Ooh," she said, but the pendant still distracted her. I helped her put it on, pulling the leather thong over her head. "Did you really carve this?"

"Yup. I sure did." I stroked her hair, basking in her pleasure. It had been so long. I'd missed so much. How could I miss more of it? But I'd been in the South less than twenty-four hours and already it was making me antsy. I couldn't stay down here and I couldn't just abandon my daughter. Three years was already too long. "You know, up north we use these for things like rituals."

Her eyes lit up. "Really? I tried to read about that, but my teachers tell me it's Big People stuff."

"It's Big People stuff up there, too. But it helps if you start learning about it when you're little." I knew I shouldn't tell her. It was illegal down here to involve minors in Alternate Consciousness manipulation, especially in something like farsight or weather control. But I was good at it—even some of the "theoretical" stuff—and she was interested. And she was my daughter. To be an AC professional, to be a shaman, brought you into close connection with the idea of continuity. Not necessarily your kids, because a lot of shamans remained celibate most of their lives. But you wanted to pass on your hard-won knowledge to someone. Though I'd been born and raised in the South, I'd grown up near the snowline and had premonitions for years—dreams, second sight, trances. My "weirdness," as my ex put it, had shattered my marriage.

The final straw was our trip to the beach. Mud flats extended for miles outward up and down the coast, but this was one of the few beaches left. Gloria was being a real bitch and it was pissing me off. I went out to the water's edge to clear my head. As I looked out at the horizon, I "saw" a lightning storm blowing up, hot and roiling blue under the sun. I gathered up Nib, insisting that we all pack up and go home, with a cloudless blue sky overhead. Gloria was furious with me.

When a lightning storm blew up off the coast a few hours later, her mood didn't improve, not even when the reports came in that two people had been struck by lightning and died. Gloria accused me right then and there of causing the storm. My teeth had been itching all day from the subsonic approach of the thunder, so I wasn't in the best of moods. It turned into a screaming fight. After I said that she had no proof, that she was basically accusing me of witchcraft, and how crazy would that make her look, she finally shut up. But our marriage was over.

When I moved up north and started working for a charter-plane company, I apprenticed with an old woman whom I still saw from time to time when I dropped off supplies in her settlement. We all wandered up there, postmodern hunter-gatherers. Normally, getting a permanent visa in the North took ten years, but with my weather-spotting skills, I'd got one in three. That was what the shaman's stamp had won me. They'd welcome a child of mine.

I squelched that thought again. Gloria really wouldn't let Nib go. Besides, she needed Nib. Why should she be deprived of her daughter the way she'd deprived me of mine? As angry as I was, I couldn't do that to her.

Raised voices came from the house. "I told you not to leave them alone!" filtered through the screen door on the back porch. Gloria didn't sound any different after three years. Some things, some people, never changed.

Nib shoved my pendant under her sweatshirt and stood up. "That's Mom," she said matter-of-factly.

Gloria came stomping out onto the porch. "Honnneeeyyy," she wheedled at Nib. "Come here. Come here, now." Nib look resigned, but she went, dragging her heels. No, some things really didn't change. Gloria grabbed her up in a hug and practically dragged her up the porch steps, then pushed her into the house. I'd never seen Gloria raise her hand to Nib, or even her voice. But I'd never seen anyone use affection as aggressively as she did, either. If Nib was any indication, it might as well have been physical abuse. But I was in no position to protest, not without a lot more concrete evidence than my daughter's general unhappiness.

If you could get her up north, you could argue her case there . . .

Gloria came back outside. She smiled. It looked brittle. "You're here early."

"I came when you said to come." I'd wanted to avoid a precipitous arrival to avoid an equally precipitous departure.

The smile vanished. "You always have to cause a problem, don't you?"

Christ. It felt just like yesterday. Her yelling and me trying to dodge it. She was very good at seeming to care so much while making everyone around her feel like shit. I didn't think any of us were quite real to her. We were spearcarriers on the stage of her life.

I spread my hands. "I don't want any trouble, Gloria. I just came down to see Nib—Nora—as we arranged."

Gloria folded one arm under the other, twiddling at her hair. Nervous as a cat and skinny as ever. If she sensed anything of her surroundings that didn't directly involve her, I'd have been shocked. "Yeah, all right. I just was expecting you later."

Ed came out onto the porch behind her. "Hey, Matt, I fixed up the couch for you. Is that okay?"

"Sure. Why not?" Gloria's face tightened. Seemed Ed wasn't quite the reliable bastard Gloria had made him out to be. Even though my own stomach tightened in response, I couldn't help a small satisfaction. I usually slept in a tent or a shelter, and I'd been sleeping in my plane for the past couple of days. A couch would be luxury. "Thanks for putting me up."

Once inside, I was less thrilled about the tightness in my chest. The house seemed a lot bigger on the outside than it did on the inside. Gloria smiled sourly at me. "Still having problems with claustrophobia?"

That sounded like Gloria's favorite paradox after "When did you stop beating your wife?" "No," I said. She didn't look convinced. I could see trouble there, but I let it lie for now. Not like I could do anything about it. This was her world, no matter how imperfectly she functioned in it, and I had to play by her rules, at least for now.

"I don't really understand why a caveman like you would hate enclosed spaces so much," Gloria said. It was as if she had to push it, as if she couldn't help herself.

"I'm in the open air a lot," I said. "You get used to that, not a house." I fished for neutral ground. "Nib—Nora looks good. She's in second grade now, right?"

"She's doing well," Ed said. "Very bright. All her report cards say so. It's a good school." Gloria looked sour. She was even going to deny me this. I tried to breathe down my anger. It wouldn't help. Gloria was my daughter's mother. I'd picked her as my lifemate and as the mother of my child. It wasn't Nib's fault I'd chosen badly. I had to work with Gloria, love it or not.

"Come see my room, Daddy," Nib said, grabbing my hand. She dragged me up the stairs to a room at the north end of the house. I wondered if she'd chosen one with a view to the north or if it had been an accident. Nib pushed open the door and pulled me inside.

The room had that "just picked up" air about it, a room cleaned by a child on her own. Not as neat as the kid might think, but a good effort. The bright yellow bedspread was covered with smiling sunflowers. A big stuffed walrus sat on the bed. I remembered sending it to her one Christmas.

Nib got down on her hands and knees, fishing for something under the bed. She pulled out a dark green backpack. Unzipping it, she pulled out a star map. "I started looking at stars at night, after you wrote me that letter about them," she said.

"You can read my letters?" I couldn't imagine Gloria reading to her.

"Mmhmm. Ed helped me with the hard parts."

"Good for Ed." I felt a stab of jealousy, but tried not to let it get to me. If he'd read my letters to her and was offering me the couch, maybe he wasn't so bad. I wouldn't have gone so far as to see him as an ally, though.

I looked around the room. It was a little too bright and cheery for Nib. I noticed a plastic container over by the window. "Is that a terrarium?"

"It's a bug house," she said. I wondered if she understood the slang for that, then told myself sternly that I wouldn't laugh either way. "I put a praying mantis in it." She frowned. "I put some other bugs in it, but the praying mantis ate them."

I bent over and stared through the plastic into the bug house. A small, mottled-brown mantis cocked its triangular head and eyed me back. Early for the season, even this far south. But it had probably hatched from a case laid last fall. They grew up fast, almost like kids. "Mantises do that. They're carnivores. Carnivores eat other animals. Mantises eat other insects."

"Do you have a lot of bugs up north?"

"In the summer we do. Lots of mosquitoes. Big enough to carry away small chi—um, livestock." I crouched beside her and put my arm around her shoulders. She snuggled up close. "We have a very short summer. Everything has to rush through whatever it wants to get done. If people get lost, we have trouble finding them in the summer because so much is hopping and growing and the land has turned to mud. We have to rely on electronic equipment more because even a sha—because you can get lost against the green or in a sudden storm." I'd almost slipped up there. Gloria wouldn't appreciate my mentioning I was a shaman to Nib. Bad enough to admit to the officials down here that I was an "Alternate Consciousness professional." As if calling it by some neuropsychological gobbledygook would make it less scary. "In the winter, things are more stark. You can really see stuff against the snow, and you can travel faster over snow than mud. But then, people can get buried in snowdrifts and there's less food if you get lost, and you can freeze. The plants stop growing and the trees and a lot of the animals sort of go to sleep."

"What do you do up there?" She was wide-eyed, ready to be impressed.

"I fly things back and forth between settlements. I have a seaplane, and I pick things up from one place and fly them out to another. Most of us live on the coast. I take people places when they need to get there quick, and I also help find people when they're in trouble." It wasn't a lie. Being a shaman wouldn't really be a full-time living, even once I got established. "I'm pretty busy."

"I'd like to see it, the North," she said.

I didn't know how to answer that. I'd hoped she'd be glad to see me, but to want to go with me . . . surely, that was just a vision. Going with me must have seemed like Never-Never Land. She didn't know the realities of the North. I should have told her, made it clear so she'd know better and stay home.

Instead, I said, "I'd like you to see it, too."

"Mommy won't let me, will she?" Nib said.

I didn't know how to dance around that. "No, I think she'd miss you too much."

. . .

I spent the next two nights on the couchbed. The arrangement lacked privacy, but I'd slept on cement floors in the past. I could take it. I also began to notice things—like how Nib crept around her own house with her shoulders hunched and how Gloria always seemed to be angry with her, or at least disapproving, even when Nib wasn't doing anything, even when she wasn't in the room. Ed would watch them, then look at me and shake his head. But he said nothing. Nib would come in and Gloria would grab her and hug her. I couldn't fault her for that. But then she would start in on her, whining about how Nib had tracked dirt into the kitchen, or caught another bug to feed her praying mantis. Gloria hated bugs. And she loathed dirt, especially since the house only got running water for a couple of hours per week.

At five a.m. every morning, Nib snuck down the stairs to see me. Of course I was glad that she wanted to be with me. I attributed her enthusiasm, or tried to, to the novelty of seeing me again. To a seven-year-old, the mom who was with her every day must have seemed like old news, while the glamorous dad coming down from the North would seem like the coolest guy around.

But there were other things. School had only a week left, which seemed to relieve Nib. It turned out she was being bullied at school. The other kids thought she was "weird," which was a code word that most immigrants to the North understood. We'd all heard it enough to know what it meant.

I tried to broach the subject with Gloria, but she got tense and said, "Nora's having a little trouble socializing in her new grade. She'll be fine by the beginning of the next school year. I had a long talk with her teacher." As if talk would solve everything.

I tried to let it go, especially since the last day of the school year was coming up. The next day, Ed called, saying he couldn't pick up Nib at school as usual, and Gloria was at work. Could I do it?

"Yeah, sure," I said. It was a few blocks away. Didn't seem hard. I strolled over there, arriving just as school got out. As I approached the school, I saw Nib, cornered at one end of the schoolyard. Not a teacher in sight, of course. They never did seem to notice the uninnocent activities of bullies.

I broke into a run, not saying a word, so that I got up behind them without their noticing me. They surrounded her in a jeering ring. "Hey!" I said, right behind them.

The look on Nib's face—and the way the other four kids jumped—was worth whatever shit I was about to get. They all turned in confusion. Embarrassment warred with defiance in their swaggers. I didn't waste time tipping the scales in my favor. I fished my passport out of my pocket and showed it to them. I flipped it open to my shaman's stamp, flashing rainbow sunlight in their faces. "You know what this means?"

They all looked shocked. *Witch*, their faces said. *Bringer of fire, brimstone, and nuclear rain.*

I pointed at Nib. "She's my daughter. You mess with her again, I'll turn you all into radioactive toadstools, got it?" They all nodded, eyes wide. "Go away before I lose my temper. Do it now."

They fell over their own feet obeying me. I hadn't trained so hard to scare bad seeds, but I decided I'd settle for it when I saw the look on Nib's face. "You okay?" I said. She nodded. "Let's go home. I don't think those kids will bother you again for a while."

"There are always others," she said. But her face told me a different story. While she was too proud to hug me there or hold my hand on the way home, I could tell that I couldn't have looked a bigger hero in her eyes if I'd ridden in on a polar bear, shaking a thunderbolt.

Gloria was less impressed. "What are you trying to do, you son of a bitch?" she said as soon as I told her what had happened once she got home from work. "Get Nora expelled? They don't let just anybody into school anymore, you know."

Yeah, only the followers and the degenerates. The free public school of our childhoods was long gone, part of a culture pushed south and broken up by the ice. "For Christ's sake, Gloria, she was being bullied. I'm trying to protect her. Has it ever occurred to you to take your daughter's side instead of caving to every piece of moraine out there?"

The look on her face told me I'd gone too far. Not like that was hard. "I don't want you to take Nora outside of the house from now on."

"Fine." We stomped off in different directions. Ed gave me an apologetic shrug as I brushed past him on my way out of the kitchen. *Thanks bunches, Ed.*

The next day, I sat crosslegged out in the backyard with Nib in my lap and my arms around her. It was a cloudy day, but I didn't sense any bad weather coming. "I want you to look around the yard," I told her. "Take as long as you want." She took several minutes to do it, though her attention was as dragonfly-quick as any kid her age.

When she finished, I said, "Are you ready?" She nodded. "Good. I'm going to cover your eyes." I put my hands over her eyes. "Now, tell me as many things as you can remember."

She listed them off, starting with the obvious, of course. Things that moved and big things—birds, grass, the stand of small trees in the back by the fence. She didn't mention the hole there beside a large tree that led out into an empty field. It seemed obvious to me, but that didn't matter. She'd build up her concentration later. You had to be gentle with kids and not expect them to know things automatically. If they could have taken care of themselves, we wouldn't have needed to be good parents to raise them.

"I can't remember everything," she complained, when she ran out after five things. It had started misting overhead.

"It's okay, sweetie. You don't have to push it. It's not a test. It's just an exercise to help you build up your concentration." I'd have to watch this black-and-white thinking they'd been trying to drum into her head down here. Followers, indeed. I rubbed my face against the back of her head. There were twigs in her hair—she'd been climbing the big tree an hour ago—and it smelled of soap. It was darker and straighter than I remembered, too. When she was a baby, she'd been a curly redhead. "Now, I want you to try this: think of one of the things that you listed and try to connect it to another thing. Can you see a connection?"

"The bird in the tree?" she guessed.

"Yep. Very good." We went through a few others. Tree and ground. Grass and ground. Ground and fence. As she did, the weather started to clear and a blue patch of sky appeared overhead. I heard noises from the house, but I was so distracted with Nib that I assumed they were Ed. If I hadn't been distracted, I would have noticed that the noises were too short and abrupt for what of Ed's lanky style I'd seen so far.

"What are you two doing?" Gloria said sharply behind me. Nib started and broke out of my grip, jumping up out of my arms and skipping away a few feet. When she turned, she looked nervous, the seal pendant once again hidden under her shirt. I thought she might be sleeping with it at night.

"It's okay, honey," I said, even though I felt an acid pit in my stomach. Gloria made me as tense as she did Nib. I got up and turned around. "We were just playing a game."

"A Northern game?" Gloria said sourly.

"Something like that, just one that kids play."

"It wouldn't have anything to do with weather control, would it?" The sour note deepened.

"No." It figured Gloria would find a way to make blue sky a bad thing. I brushed dirt off my pants, stepping in front of Nib as she scampered back to the tree and climbed it.

Gloria wasn't ready to give it up. "Because if it were, that kind of game is illegal down here."

"I know that, Gloria. Don't blame her. I just wanted to teach her something that was appropriate to her age." In other words, I didn't want to tell her how horrible and red in tooth and claw the North was, like in Southern fantasies. It was a harsh place and it didn't play favorites. Either you needed to be up there or you left or you died.

Gloria pushed herself off the railing she'd just been gripping. "Come inside. We need to talk."

"Okay." I turned to Nib. I could just see her face through the tree's leaves. She knew how to hide, a useful skill up north, even if we were lacking in trees in a lot of areas. "I'll be right back."

Gloria waved at her. "Stay inside the yard, honey. We'll be in the kitchen, okay?"

I followed Gloria inside, trying to ignore the clenching in my stomach. I wasn't the kind of guy who liked to dominate his wife—or ex-wife—for fun. Gloria used to accuse me of all kinds of things, especially once I started changing. I started getting antsy in enclosed spaces and crowds, started longing for cold silence

Seabird

and white spaces the way I was wishing right now that I could be anywhere but in this kitchen. Gloria had thought it was another woman. Maybe it would have been easier if it had been a woman, or something else external.

Gloria took a position next to the sink, her hand on the counter. I folded my arms, then decided that was too confrontational and stood with my back to the refrigerator, my hands flat against the door. I'd talked down vodka-swilling, knife-wielding drunks in the North with less tension. "What's up?"

She smiled sunnily at me and then said, "Whatever you're doing with Nora, I want you to stop."

I should have known the bullying incident was the last straw. "I'm trying to get to know her again. That's all." I started to fold my arms again, but forced them down to my sides. "Gloria, I'm not doing anything that would hurt her. I swear. I just want to make up for lost time."

She frowned. At least she'd ditched the positive outlook. "That's not what I'm seeing here, Matt. What I'm seeing is you practicing your mumbo-jumbo on my daughter, things that will get us all in trouble."

"She wants to know about the North, about what I do. I'm showing it to her." The silence grew cold between us. Gloria's knickknacks covered the walls, but I couldn't see anything of my daughter in this kitchen. If I went upstairs and looked through Nib's room again, would I see anything of hers that wasn't hidden under the bed or inside of a plastic terrarium?

"I'm not doing anything dangerous with her, Gloria. I know the risks." Better than she ever could.

Ed came into the kitchen, a neutral look on his face. "Anything wrong?"

"We're just having a conversation," I said. I didn't need two against one.

"I'm allowing this visit only because of Nora," Gloria said in that tone of voice that made the listener feel guilty for making her

204

sacrifice so much. "I'd prefer it if you made things as easy as possible."

I should have known it wouldn't last. "How long?"

She raised her hands. "Don't be like that, Matt—"

I pushed myself off the counter and she shrank back. "Drop the act, Gloria. You don't want me here. This is just a big inconvenience for you. How long do I get?"

She let her hands drop. "I'd like for you to go now. Please. You can stay down south for the term of your visa, but I want you out of here."

My head flaming inside, I took a step toward her. "You . . . bitch."

A male voice somewhere, unimportant, was saying my name. All I saw was Gloria's face, torn between fear and some weird triumph. "Go ahead, big man! Hit me! You always wanted to do it!"

I took another step. I'd never raised a hand to her, but if she thought I'd stop at just that . . . somewhere to the north, I heard thunder.

"Daddy!" A little hand slipped into mine and tugged on it. "Daddy, come with me! Come see something!"

The red haze faded. Dazed, I looked down at my daughter. She looked scared. "Come with me, Daddy. I want to show you something."

Gloria was yelling, but her voice seemed tinny and small. I let Nib pull me past her mother, out the kitchen door and down the steps. The misting rain had started up again, but Nib ignored it. "Come see," she said, lowering her voice to a whisper. "Come see!"

She led me over to the tree and looked up into the leaves. "There's a hole in the fence. Do you see it?"

She'd noticed it? "Of course. I thought you didn't."

She tucked her hair behind her ear. "Take me with you, Daddy." She looked up at me. "I want to go with you. I want to go north. We can go tonight."

"Nora!" Gloria shouted from the porch steps.

"Please?" Nib's eyes were huge in the shadow of the tree. I knew that tone of desperation. I'd heard it in my own voice enough times before I went north.

"Nora! Come here!" Gloria screamed Nib's name, as if she could hear Nib's little voice, for once.

"I'll wait for you! Come to the hole by the tree," Nib whispered. Ducking her head, she turned before I could answer her, or even speak. She scampered back to her mother. Gloria grabbed her and yanked her into the house. The screen door crashed shut like a trap.

.   .   .

Ed drove me back to the seaplane in his hydrogen-converted rattle-trap of a car. "You sure you don't want to stay at a hotel?" he said.

"It's fine," I said. It wasn't, but I'd had enough of Southern hospitality. I'd rather sleep in my own seaplane.

"I'm sorry about Gloria. You freaked her out, that's all. Stay a few more days. I'll talk to her."

"Do you think Nora's happy?" I was tired of being nice and indirect.

Ed sighed. "Gloria tries, Matt. She really does. She's trying; you're trying. It's nobody's fault."

I stared at him, even as he kept his eyes on the road. "Do you think my daughter's happy, Ed?" His face twitched, but he didn't answer.

I settled back in my seat and folded my arms. "That's what I thought."

We drove the rest of the way in silence. As we pulled into the harbor parking lot, Ed said, "Gloria was pretty upset when we left. She'll probably take one of her pills to calm down. I bet she'll sleep until noon tomorrow." He finally turned his head and met my eyes. Damned if he didn't wink at me. "Just so you know."

.   .   .

I didn't sleep much that night. When I did, I had bad dreams. Nib was calling, "Wait for me, Daddy! Wait for me by the big tree." Her voice trailed off into the high call of a seabird that woke me as it flew over the plane. I saw what I had to do, what was best for my daughter.

Before dawn, I got a taxi back into town. The weather had cleared overnight, with a promise of warmth later once the sun rose. A good day to fly home.

I had the guy drop me off a block down from Gloria and Ed's house. I told him to wait. The field was easy to find but not so easy to get into. The houses stuck together as if ignoring the wasteland behind them. I had to get down into a small gully off an alleyway to find the back of Gloria's house. The hole in the wooden fence was at the top of the ravine and half-obscured with weeds. I cleared them away and crawled through. Settling myself down on my belly, I waited.

A few minutes later, a small figure with a full backpack slipped out the back door and trotted across the lawn right to the big tree. Nib crouched beside me as I pushed myself up. I gathered her up in a big hug.

"I let the praying mantis go," she whispered in my ear. "And I brought my watch. See?"

When I pulled back, I saw she was wearing the seal pendant out on her shirt.

Black Doe

by vylar kaftan

The child died at dawn. First Wife was too ill to tend her son, so Trayja closed his eyelids and painted them as his mother would have done. She wiped the vomit from his mouth and kissed his lips. Then, as Second Wives must, she mixed herbs with ground reindeer antler and sprinkled them over his body. When Goros came to beat her with a stick, she said, *"N'rit tosk." I am responsible.* By law he could not touch her, and so they came before the Council.

By this time Khee had recovered. She shouted at the Councilmen and shook her heavy beaded necklace. "She killed my child. Ingkak, boy-child—son of Goros, hero of the Great War. He drank her blood soup and died."

The seven Councilmen sat like glaciers. They wore embroidered skin shirts and breeches with three stripes of beadwork on each leg. The men half-circled the fire—their boots on their knees, their palms upturned. Trayja thought they looked foolish. Any man with a club could kill them all before they could untangle themselves. Trayja lifted her eyes past Khee. She stared through the hut's door at the distant hills. The autumn wind whistled across the tundra. She grieved for their shared son too, but done was done. Wishing wouldn't fix her careless mistake.

Khee stomped her foot. "Second Wife has always envied me. She wanted me dead too—the murderess!" She broke into wild sobs. "Murderess, monster—"

"Control your hysterics, or we will make you leave," said Ruk, the eldest. He was blood-kin to Trayja through her mother and had always been kind to her. "Keep your peace. Goros, be sure of this."

"It is my honor," Goros replied. He touched Khee's shoulder and drew her behind him. She glared over his shoulder like an angry beaver at its dam.

Ruk nodded, but didn't stand. "Trayja. You invoked the Old Ways with your words. Are you sure you wish to commit to this?"

"*N'rit tosk,*" she repeated, clasping herself in her arms. She was as tall as any man, but she felt small here.

Ruk spoke softly. "I would counsel you otherwise, kinswoman."

"I know how to make blood soup. Goros brought me the doe. I drained her and mixed the blood with fresh milk. I soaked *turap* bark in it overnight, as I should have." Trayja closed her eyes, her nose filled with the soup's meaty smell. Nothing else in the Tribe-lands smelled like it. She opened her eyes again, her voice harsh. "But I didn't cool it outside before serving it. I kept it in the hut. The hut was so cold . . . I thought it would be enough. I didn't know the soup would spoil."

Ruk frowned and curled his fingers. Before he could speak, Khee screamed, "She kept Anishuywa from blessing the soup! And in punishment he has taken my child—and almost took me. She would be First Wife!"

"I would not!" shouted Trayja, clenching her fists.

The women faced each other, with Goros between them like a wall. Trayja took a deep breath. Khee wasn't worth losing her remaining status. Trayja dropped her hands and said, "I would once have been First Wife to another man. That is true. But with my father's dishonorable death, I know my place. Fear not, Khee. I have no wish to displace you." *Not with Goros, certainly*, she thought. Her hands curled into fists again.

"It should have been you that died," the older woman hissed.

Ruk's voice rang like an eagle's cry. "Khee, you are dismissed."

Khee glared at Trayja, then strode out the door. Goros watched as she went, but didn't follow. He frowned at Trayja like she was one of his hunting-spears thrown astray. Goros never lost his temper, even when beating her. He would be a Council member someday.

The Councilmen remained impassive. Ruk glanced around the half-circle at their faces. "Trayja, you know that blood soup must be properly chilled. Anishuywa does not approach fires. This child, had he lived, would have grown feeble. His *jurra* would be weak—the cold would kill him. This is why boy-children and their mothers must drink blood soup before the child is fully weaned. Anishuywa commanded it to the first hunters on the plains. So the songs go, and so it has been since before any of us remember."

"This is why I am responsible," insisted Trayja. "And I want *jarusk*. The Old Justice."

Ruk said nothing, but his head fell. He unfolded his legs gracefully and stood at full height, just below Trayja's shoulder. "So be it. Goroska Trayja, you are exiled for two years. At the end of that time, your return must be earned. *Gri kor sortok*."

The decision fell like a hailstone on her head. Exile she had expected, but *sortok*—and she must declare such status to any village she visited? She would die. Ruk knew it too, and his eyes lowered. He added, "You may leave in the morning. I will send my blessings with you, and a luckstone. Anishuywa protects those who invoke the Old Ways."

211

Trayja bowed her head, hiding her face behind a curtain of thick black hair—her one beauty, for which Goros had chosen her. A luckstone wouldn't be enough.

.   .   .

Trayja waited at the village's edge, having slept uneasily and packed quickly. Winter was coming. The late-morning sun crept over the horizon. She carried little—dried seal meat, a bone knife, a small spear, tinder and flint. She would need fire to survive—she was no boy, weaned with blood soup. Anishuywa was a god for men. Like other women, Trayja had Kamulankuk—the buxom Mother. If she were as fat as the Goddess, Trayja thought, she could live for two years without needing food.

Ruk approached, clutching his fur-lined hood close to his face. The luckstone glowed faintly in his gloved palm. "Child, why have you chosen this?"

Trayja didn't respond. She pocketed the stone, slipping it between her fingers. Perhaps it would do her some good.

Ruk touched her cheek. "Was it truly so bad, being wife to Goros?"

She turned away, not wanting to see the compassion in his eyes. She saw no use in speaking of the past. What was done was done. Goros—and the poor child. She squeezed the stone.

Ruk's soft voice carried through the wind. "You are full of *jurra*, child. Such energy. Would that you had been my daughter. I would have found you a better mate."

"Had you been my father, I would have been someone's First Wife," Trayja snapped.

"Bitterness will hurt you," he said. "Trayja, I will pray for you. Where will you go?"

Where indeed? While she had never loved Goros, the Yugulek village was the only home she had known. But she'd considered carefully last night, as she lay without sleeping on the bear furs of her bed.

"I will go to the mountain shrine," she said, looking toward the mountain's crest. The snowy peak glittered against the gray sky.

"But you are *sortok*. The gods—"

"Are the only ones who might speak with me." She brought her eyes back to Ruk. "I will visit the shrine. If I go to another village, they'll only turn me out. If I go to the gods . . . "

Ruk shook his head. "Be careful. Do not anger them." He stared at her without blinking. Trayja guessed that he was memorizing her face. Most likely he asked where she was going so he'd know where to look for her body.

Trayja had little patience for goodbyes, but she respected Ruk. She touched her forehead to his and walked away. She gripped the luckstone in her palm, the carvings of its thousandfold blessings intangible through her gloves.

· · ·

The mountain shrine was six days' journey by foot. Trayja kept a swift pace, grateful for the clear autumn skies. Her feet crunched over the icy ground, snug in their deerskin boots. At night she sheltered under a rock outcropping and built a fire from dead bramble bushes. She ate dried fish and slept fitfully with a rock under her hip.

On the second day, her muscles ached and she slowed her pace. At midday she passed a reindeer herd, which bounded away at her approach. The god Anishuywa would be racing across the plains in this weather—his antlers held high, his snow-white fur shining, his proud stride tearing across the white landscape. Trayja strained her eyes looking for Anishuywa, but these were ordinary brown beasts. That night, she found no shelter, so she huddled inside her coat as the hunters did, and entered *shuruk* sleep—waking just often enough to pace a quick circle and sleep again instantly.

It kept her blood moving, but exhausted her. She woke bleary-eyed and weak. She chewed some meat strips and began walking again. She oriented herself by the frozen slope and went east toward the mountain—knowing that somewhere ahead of her sat a hut of the Tribespeople. Goros had mentioned it once. Several huts stood on the tundra like sentinels. The Tribes took turns supplying them with food and firewood. Any huntsman might shelter there if caught unaware by a storm.

The plain sloped into the river valley, interrupted by leafless trees stretching skyward like antlers. The hut stood by the river. The valley's far wall stretched up the mountain, where the people of the Old Ways had built a shrine to the gods. It was in this valley that Trayja's father had slain a pregnant doe. A careless mistake— but it cost him his life, and Trayja her status. And now another mistake had sent her into exile. *It's done*, she told herself. Dwelling on it was useless.

Lost in thought, Trayja tripped as something caught her boot. She tumbled down the slope, sliding against rocks and bramble bushes. "*Surk!*" she cried out, fearing she'd break her neck. Pain shot through her right ankle. Her feet skidded ahead as she grabbed a tree trunk. The luckstone slipped from her pocket and vanished into the snow.

Trayja righted herself and leaned on her ankle. Icicle-sharp pain burst through her leg. "Anishuywa, Kamulankuk," she muttered, drawing her hood close. She eased down the slope, favoring her ankle. It was dark when she reached the bottom and hobbled into the hut. A fire pit and woodpile stood in the hut's center. In the corner, a ratted fur lay on a pile of moldy cloth. Too tired to build a fire, she lay down, trusting the walls to shelter her. She slept for almost a day.

When she woke, her ankle had swollen to purple tenderness. The wind rattled the walls. Trayja built a fire, curled up under the blanket, and wondered where she'd get more food. She thought about Goros and Khee, warm together in their home, and she pressed her fist into her palm. If the gods wouldn't help her, she'd travel far away—somewhere so far that *sortok* meant nothing, if such a place existed. She'd find a way to rely on no one but herself.

That evening, a hunter entered the cabin. His red-striped hood marked him as Inatu—a tribe Trayja knew little of. He looked surprised to see her. "*Klauto gikt?*" he asked, and she shook her head without understanding. "*Sortok*," she answered, and he nodded and said no more. He lay down by the fire and slept. Trayja clutched her knife all night—*sortok* had no rights, especially alone with a strange man. In the morning he left without speaking, leaving a sack of dried meat, a flask of milk, and a broken bone. The message was clear—*be well in your travels, but don't stay.*

Trayja devoured the meat. She stretched her leg, hoping to see the ankle healed, but it hadn't. She had no choice but to remain. She spent a week there, praying the hunter didn't return. On the second day she vomited when she woke, but thought little of it until the week had nearly passed. That night, she crawled to the door and looked at the sky. A new moon, barely present—her *kamu-koremtak* should have come upon her. Her breasts ached at the thought, and she grew dizzy. Two days later, she knew: she bore Goros's child in her belly.

Trayja screamed into the lice-infested blanket. She punched the wall until her knuckles bled. She wished Goros's child would burst from her body stone-dead. Hungry, she ate some meat and promptly vomited. She remembered the dead boy-child. Khee was right. "It should have been me, child," she whispered.

In despair, she slept again, and in the morning woke with numb resolution. As soon as she was well, she would go to the mountain shrine. Only the gods could help her now. She rubbed her ankle and decided that three days would be enough. She looked outside to check the weather. In the distance a pair of hunters headed her way.

Trayja's heart raced. She decided to wait for them, hoping they would be as kind as the last man. In case they weren't, she gathered all the food into her pack. She sat on the bed, knife in hand. When the hunters arrived, they drew their own knives. They were Karaiki, a people who traded with Trayja's own. For a moment Trayja considered not saying anything, but her honor compelled her: "*Sortok.*"

One man spit. The other spoke Yugulek. "Get out."

Trayja limped toward the mountain. An old trail circled the base, and the journey was easy at first. But the path steepened, overgrown with shrubs. No one kept the Old Ways anymore—they worshipped the gods from comfortable huts. She stumbled up the hill, supporting herself with branches. Burrs scratched her deerskin gloves, and dark red berries stained her coat. She sheltered the first night under an oddly shaped rock, and the next night slept *shuruk* again. Her tongue was dry and her head ached. She hadn't urinated in a day. She sipped some milk, but conserved her supply.

Finally Trayja approached the shrine. Above her head, the rock crested to a white peak. The shrine itself lay half-buried in snow. Frozen mud walls held mosaics, with thousands of rocks worn smooth in icy streams. Two statues stood before her: a snow-white reindeer buck with thirteen-point horns, and a jet-black woman with flowing hair and outstretched arms—the fattest, most beautiful woman she'd ever seen. At the shrine's center stood a smooth bone basin tied with frozen sinew. When Trayja touched the basin's clear ice, it shimmered. The gods were here—but whether they'd listen was another question.

She knelt at the altar and drew her knife. "Anishuywa, Kamulankuk. I give you all that I have left." Her frozen fingers clutched the knife against her temple. She grabbed her long black hair, tore it against the knife's sharp edge, and draped it on the altar like an unwound rope. She trimmed wisps from her neck and added them to the offering. When she finished, she removed a glove and touched her stubbly head. Now she truly looked *sortok*, she thought, and laughed. But the laugh turned bitter. The statues remained silent. She was a fool to think the gods would speak with her.

Angry, she pulled her hood over her head and stared at the altar. She thought about leaving, but she had nowhere left to go. As she watched, a single strand of hair lifted itself and coiled through the air. It danced a circle and drifted into the Goddess's outstretched hand. Before Trayja could blink, there stood Kamulankuk in her ample glory, laughing like someone had just told a great joke.

"My daughter," she said, smiling. Her stomach rippled as she leaned down and pressed her forehead to Trayja's. A halo of soft hair tickled Trayja's face. "My lovely, beautiful daughter."

Trayja dropped the bone knife. Kamulankuk laughed again, and warmth filled Trayja. The Goddess said, "What, you don't think you're beautiful?"

"I'm too thin," said Trayja, when she found her voice. "And I have no hair."

"Nonsense. You're lovely as you are."

Trayja stared at her, wondering if she dreamed from exhaustion and pain. Perhaps she was entering the Long Sleep. If so—what was done was done. She would address the Goddess as she wished. "Wealthy One," she said, "I am *sortok*. I prepared blood soup badly, and a boy-child died. I will perform any task you set in order to earn forgiveness."

The Goddess stepped back and folded her arms. "Do you regret your actions?"

"I do," said Trayja, but as she spoke she felt resentment surging. She shouldn't have been making blood soup at all. She should have been a First Wife. It wasn't her fault that her father had been dishonorable. Yet she had paid the price. *The boy-child paid*, she reminded herself, and bowed her head. "I regret the death of the innocent child. *N'rit tosk.*"

"If you earned this forgiveness, would you return home? To your people and your husband?"

Trayja opened her mouth and closed it again. Finally, she said, "I would do my duty, as it pleases you." As she spoke, she clenched her fists. She missed the only home she knew. But even if she earned her way back, she'd still have to live with Goros—and bear his child, which by law would be considered mainly Khee's.

The Goddess laughed. "And what would please *you*, child?"

"Freedom," Trayja said, looking over the mountain's edge at the valley. "I want to stop paying for other people's mistakes. I'd rather pay for my own."

Kamulankuk touched Trayja's hood. The hood slipped back, and warm hands stroked Trayja's shorn head. "Freedom is also a terrible burden, child—yes, I know your heart, and I hear you. You can't survive as independently as you'd like. But I'll let you taste freedom for a time. Because there's something you must do—for me, and for my beloved Anishuywa."

"What do you need?"

"Three tasks. You will know them when the time comes. Do you accept?"

Trayja wondered if she could refuse. She suspected Kamulankuk would accept the answer—and leave her to die on the tundra. Refusing the Goddess would certainly shorten her exile, although not the way she liked. *"N'rit garisk." I accept.*

Kamulankuk smiled. "I'll grant you freedom. Just remember the price must be paid."

The Goddess vanished. The shrine disappeared into darkness. The only light came from the icy altar where Trayja's hair lay. She jumped to her feet and gripped her knife. Her whole body pulsed with each heartbeat. A strange wind blew through the shrine. The black hair rose from the altar and spiraled around itself.

Something slammed into Trayja's back, knocking her onto her hands and knees. The hair splintered into thousands of fragments and swarmed toward her like an insect cloud. Hair burrowed into her skin and covered her in thick black fur. Antlers burst from her head. Her cry became a snort. Cold air entered her widening nostrils, warming as it filled her lungs. As her body expanded and her legs lengthened, she wondered, *What about the child inside me?*

After that, she stopped thinking. She had never felt so alive. *Kore, kore, kore!* She leaped through the darkness, landing on the mountain path. She bounded away, her proud antlers honoring the sky as her tough hooves praised the earth. She dug through the snow to a lichen patch, ate her fill, and raced away through the valley. The slope that tricked human feet was natural for hooves. She leaped over the crevice and sped across the plain to where she'd seen the reindeer.

The herd grazed at a frozen lakeshore. A few enormous bucks paced the herd's edges. Delicate brown does guarded their nearly grown fawns. At Trayja's approach, they scattered. The bucks circled her. She presented herself—antlers raised, tail erect—as they sniffed her scent. After a while the largest buck snorted and nuzzled her neck. Other bucks walked away, satisfied at the judgment. The buck touched his nose to her ears. Trayja licked him. Any buck might mate with her, once she entered heat. This one's strong neck and powerful hindquarters pleased her. When she was ready, he would come to her. Trayja felt free for the first time since her father's death.

Thank you, Kamulankuk. Trayja snorted and tossed her head, smelling the tundra soil. She turned toward the mountain to offer her prayers. A snow-white reindeer stood alone, outlined against the gray rock. The God gazed at her, patient as winter. Trayja lowered her antlers, realizing the first task required of her. It tore at her—her first taste of freedom, interrupted by duty. But she had promised the Goddess.

Dipping her antlers to the buck before her, she slipped away and trotted up the mountain to Anishuywa. He turned his head at her approach and did not acknowledge her. She touched her antlers to the ground, wanting to run away. The God would demand too much, she was sure. He'd want submission. He'd require everything from her—all she had fought for, and her newfound freedom.

Anishuywa nuzzled her and lifted her head with his antlers. She forgot her fears in his presence. His eyes were gray, like winter skies in the few precious hours of daylight. Despite her pregnancy, the desire in his eyes drove her into heat. She pressed her face to the snow and gave herself to him fully. She climaxed with a human's knowledge and an animal's honesty.

The entire winter afterward, when she grazed and migrated with the herd—her belly growing heavy with child—she would see the few hours of daylight, and a name would return to her: *Anishuywa.* Her body trembled with delight—so much so that her legs wavered beneath her, and all she could do was remember.

· · ·

When her time came, Trayja found a small cave near a frozen stream. She lay on a lichen bed. Before her stood Anishuywa, white and bold, watching his child's birth. Behind her knelt Kamulankuk's vast form, receiving the child into her warm embrace. As the wind blew outside, Trayja pushed and grunted. The Goddess stroked her flank, singing about the world's creation in a language long forgotten. After a few hours, Trayja produced a beautiful young doe. She licked her daughter's brown head and sniffed her tiny tail. Kamulankuk stroked the fawn's ears, and Anishuywa dipped his antlers to her.

But Trayja's pains continued. Her instincts screamed trouble. She pushed again, and another child burst from her—human, a baby boy-child with thick black hair on his head. Kamulankuk caught him and struck his back. The boy wailed. Anishuywa nuzzled the squalling infant.

Trayja looked at Kamulankuk in wonder. "My children," she said in reindeer language. "How is this possible? Goros's son living inside me all this time—"

"The fawn is Goros's daughter," said Kamulankuk, grinning. "She transformed with you. She'll be brave and clever. The boy is Anishuywa's. He's a spirit child—and your spirit is still human. He'll be a great healer."

Trayja pressed her nose to the boy's belly. She murmured Old Language prayers for her children's health. When she raised her head, the gods had vanished. She was alone with her fawn and her baby.

Days passed as she recovered her strength. She called her daughter Jat and her son Urag. Her daughter grew strong. Shortly after birth, the fawn wobbled onto her feet and explored the cave. Jat poked her nose into each corner and sniffed at the entrance until Trayja snorted to call her back.

Urag worried her. He suckled at her belly but lacked strength to draw milk. The child couldn't handle the cold as reindeer could. Trayja curled around him, but it wasn't enough. As Jat grew, Urag weakened. One morning, as the boy lay shivering, Trayja realized her second task. She bowed her antlers with grief—how terrible, to need someone she hated—but she would do this task for her son.

She left her babies alone—praying they'd be safe—and scoured the tundra for a bramble patch. When she found one, she chewed it until her gums bled. By afternoon, she'd torn a long vine spiked with thorns and spring flowers. She took one end in her mouth and dragged it back to the cave. Trayja wedged the bramble's end in a crevice. She picked up Urag, who cried out as her teeth marked his skin. She balanced the child on her back and stepped across the vine. She twisted her body and ducked her head to catch another bramble loop. By late morning, she had managed to strap Urag in place for the journey ahead.

Trayja set off for the Yugulek village, with Jat trotting behind her. Urag cried of hunger, but soon he slept. She kept a fast pace. It was nightfall when they approached the village. It smelled stronger than she remembered. A pyre burned at the village's edge. On the nearby altar lay the deceased one's possessions—for purification before reuse. Ruk's best spear lay on top of his beaded pants. Trayja dipped her antlers in deference to the Long Sleep. *Mene anishorok, Hirska Ruk.* Done was done. The reminder made her task easier.

Trayja approached the hut of Goros and Khee. The smell of deer stew wafted through the air, making her choke. She wanted to run, but Urag needed her. She touched Jat's nose, urging her to stay back. Then Trayja snorted and tapped her hoof against the door.

Goros opened it, spear in hand. He nearly dropped his weapon. Khee screamed. Trayja would have laughed at their cowardice, but she grieved too deeply. She knelt, revealing the baby strapped to her back.

No one moved. Goros reached toward the child, then drew his hand away as if he might be a spirit. Khee muttered, "Anishuywa, Kamulankuk," as she tapped her thighs in prayer. She was rounder than before, yet had no child at her breast—Trayja thought she must have borne and lost one recently. Yes. She'd been right to bring her son here. If only he might remember her, she would be content.

Goros fetched a knife. Trayja flinched, fearing he might harm her—but no, he cut the boy loose. Khee took the child and suckled him. Trayja looked away, not wanting to lose her son to Khee—but he must live with his own kind. She stood again, commanding Goros with a look. *Guard this child, or I will kill you.* Goros blinked, and Trayja wondered what he understood. He bowed his head.

"*Anikala su gabki,*" he whispered. *Sacred black doe.*

It would have to be enough. She left the village with her daughter, head held high. She glanced back, and saw her people had gathered at the village's edge. They talked among themselves. Some prayed or sang as she departed. The black doe, she thought. Anishuywa's mate. A story would be made tonight.

. . .

In the coming season, Trayja and Jat explored the muddy plains, their hooves softened with summertime. Jat grew into a beautiful young reindeer. Almost an adult, she was Trayja's friend in a way a human child took years to achieve. Trayja shed her antlers in a bramble bush and regrew them from itchy nubs. Jat's horns grew like her mother's over the summer, until both had velvety eleven-point sets.

They migrated with the herd that winter, and returned in spring. Trayja taught her daughter the tricks of human hunters. Her daughter listened, wide-eyed, and remembered what she heard. Reindeer-born Jat could hear the earth. Sometimes she'd share secrets, like how ice could sing and how rocks decided a river's flow. Often she understood things that mystified Trayja. Once in late autumn, as they drank from a nearly frozen valley stream, Trayja told her daughter that does were only hunted when boy-children were weaned.

"But why?" asked Jat, her ears flicked back.

"It is Anishuywa's will," said Trayja. "A boy-child weaned with blood soup earns divine *jurra.* Anishuywa's power helps him withstand ice and cold. This is one of the Old Ways."

"That's not what the land says," Jat told her.

"Anishuywa commanded it to the first hunters."

"He commanded that hunters drink the doe's spirit. Not her blood."

Trayja was surprised to discover that "spirit" and "blood" were different words for reindeer. She called both *jurra*. She knew that spirit was more than physical warmth, but she had never separated them so clearly. "You're sure?" she asked.

"In the Old Ways people understood that these words were different."

Trayja lifted her head. She looked across the river toward the plain where the herd grazed. "You think Anishuywa wishes for humans to stop making blood soup?"

Jat tipped her antlers. "I think humans no longer hear the earth, and so they cannot understand the will of Anishuywa."

Trayja considered as she drank again. She'd always figured that she and her daughter would become human again, once she'd completed her service to Kamulankuk and Anishuywa. Perhaps that was the greater purpose she served—somehow, she would end the misunderstanding.

She looked at the vast, gray sky. Seasons had passed. Soon she could return to her village, if she'd earned it. Her son would be nearly weaned. Someone would make blood soup for him—but it wouldn't be Trayja. After two years as a doe, she could never make blood soup again. But this third task for Anishuywa—each task had been harder than the one preceding it, and—

A group of hunters headed toward the herd—and Trayja understood the gods' plan. She raked the dirt with a hoof. "No," she said to the sky. "No, you won't take my daughter."

The tundra didn't respond. Furious, Trayja raced across the plain toward the hunters. She would kill Goros before he could have her daughter. Behind her she heard Jat's hooves pounding, following her out of confusion. Trayja whirled around and snorted a command: *stay*. Her daughter halted, tilting her head in question. Trayja sprinted toward the hunters but didn't see Goros. She circled around the herd, wondering how she could possibly defy the gods' will. On instinct, she ran back to Jat.

Goros had split away from the other hunters, seeking strays. Jat stood near a mossy patch, ignorant of the threat. Goros aimed his spear. Trayja bellowed. She lowered her antlers and charged. At the noise, Jat raised her head and leaped away. Goros yelled and threw his spear. Trayja made the only choice possible. With a great jump, she landed between the spear and her daughter.

The spear struck her flank. Blood poured down her fur, staining the lichen beneath her. She staggered and sank to the ground. Pain blinded her. She heard Jat running and Goros swearing. Hands touched her—familiar ones. Her husband's hands. She kicked weakly, knowing he'd slash her throat.

But he caressed her body's length, his hands gentle against her rough fur. "*Anikala su gabki*—great black doe, you who brought me my son—I swear it was an accident," he whispered. "*N'rit tosk*. I will save you if I can."

Trayja lashed out at him, but Goros dodged her kicks. He knelt beside her and pulled the spear from her flesh. Her blood surged around his hands as he pressed the wound. Trayja bellowed, but Goros pinned her to the ground. "Hold still, beautiful one," he said. "I swear by Anishuywa himself that I will not harm you."

Trayja snorted, too tired to resist. Goros stripped off his sealskin coat. He wrapped her flank and tied the coat underneath her stomach. He jumped away as she struggled to her feet. As she loped stiffly away, he called, "*Gabkuraki*, Anikala."

He had blessed her in the ancient way. Trayja stumbled across the plain to find her daughter. *Goros will freeze without his coat*, she realized. To her surprise she hoped that a storm would not approach.

· · ·

Trayja met her daughter over the next hill. With Jat's guidance, she stumbled to the cave where she'd birthed her children. She tore at Goros's coat until it fell away. It had done its work—the wound had sealed. She prayed it would heal cleanly. Trayja stared at the discarded coat, remembering Goros's kindness to her despite not knowing who she was. Without his help, she would have died. It was hard to accept.

The next day, her body grew hot despite the chilly air. After sniffing the wound, Jat snorted anxiously and licked Trayja's neck. She brought moss and berries, but Trayja had no appetite. Then Jat brought water in her mouth, and Trayja drank, knowing she would die without it. The water tasted like her daughter's scent as it splashed across her muzzle.

Trayja fought the fever, but it was strong. As she burned, she slipped into deeper sleep. She no longer heard her daughter's snorts. She lost track of daylight as winter darkness took the land. Once she woke to realize Jat had vanished without leaving food. Her flank ached, and she noticed a bald patch where none had been before.

"Anishuywa, Kamulankuk," she murmured. Confused, she slept again. She dreamed of the God lying with her, his white head soft against her belly. The Goddess stroked her back and whispered into her fur. "Child, child, you knew there would be a price."

"I knew," she said in her dream, speaking both reindeer and Yugulek at the same time. "I knew there would be a price. But it's too high."

"The price must be paid. You know what must be done, daughter."

Trayja did. She remembered Anishuywa's great gift to her. She'd been waiting all her life for this moment without knowing it. She wanted to touch her antlers to his, but she couldn't move. "Wealthy One, I do know. Kamulankuk . . . I've asked you for so much, and not done as you wished. I'm sorry. I ask only one small thing more. So I can finish your tasks."

The Goddess touched her forehead to Trayja's. "What do you ask, child?"

"I need the strength to stand."

The Goddess smiled, the expression spreading across her face like melting ice. "Granted, daughter. But that strength was already yours."

Trayja woke. She was alone in the cave, still burning with fever. She pressed her forelegs to the ground and lifted herself on her haunches. She raised herself to her feet, slowly lifting her antlers until she looked straight ahead. "Anishuywa," she whispered. "Kamulankuk." The names gave her strength.

She left the cave, aching with every step. Snow covered the plain, and the herd was gone. She trudged westward, watching for wolves, and headed toward the Yugulek village. She stumbled on a rock and fell. Her wound tore open. Blood trickled down her leg and matted her fur. She remembered the day when she'd hurt her ankle on the mountain slope. It seemed like three lifetimes past.

Trayja forced herself to her feet. She had her freedom. She would do this on her own. A cold wind cut through her thick hide. The village huts lay across the plain ahead of her. *Keep moving, keep moving.* The village looked impossibly far away. Each step took more strength than the last. She walked until she could move no more, and then she collapsed. What little strength she had left was gone.

She lay in a stupor, and then smelled something familiar. *My daughter*—she opened her eyes. Jat stood before her, a clump of black fur clutched in her mouth. Behind her stood Goros, Khee, and the child Urag. Trayja struggled to stand, but failed. Jat dropped the fur and licked her nose. "I've brought them, Mother. Let them help you. You don't have to fight alone."

Trayja snorted weakly, wanting nothing to do with Goros. But Jat nuzzled her insistently. "His people worship you now. They say you brought a sacred healer to their village. Please, Mother. Trust me. Let them help you, because I can't."

I don't need any help, Trayja wanted to protest. But Jat had been so brave—to go to the village, where a man might kill her, and bring—

Her nose fell forward. Goros stroked her head. He wore the beaded pants of a Councilman. "Stay with us, *Anikala su gabki*. This child—he has power. He can heal you, as he has healed others in our village. Khee, bring the child."

Trayja tried to kick, but her legs wouldn't move. Small hands touched her flank. She wouldn't take help from Goros, but from Urag—*my son, my child*. He kissed her fur. She wanted to reach for him but was too weak. She reached for her son with her spirit. The world spun when they touched.

Urag, the God's son. She remembered his feeble attempts to drink her milk. But now he drank her fully. Urag lapped at the *jurra* streaming down her flank. The wound sealed underneath his tongue and vanished. Her fever floated away as her son drank the blood soup only she could provide.

She closed her eyes, her burden lifted. Her body shrank and transformed. When Urag finished, Trayja lay naked in the snow in Goros's arms. Her son snuggled at her hip, and her daughter sniffed her hair. She had never been more content.

"Anishuywa, Kamulankuk," whispered Goros, his eyes wide. He touched Trayja's cheek. "You've earned a return and more, Second Wife. I don't feel I'm worthy of you."

Khee drummed her hands on her thighs and added, "I'll do penance. I've treated you badly."

At Trayja's hip, Urag sat up straight. From his tiny body spoke a deep voice that rumbled like an avalanche. "Hear me now, for I speak Anishuywa's truth. With this *jurra* I drink, I complete the circle. No more reindeer shall die for the boy-children of your people. I call on you to obey my true command: all sons of your people shall befriend a reindeer doe and learn her ways, that they might someday treasure their own wives as deeply."

The boy fell silent. A moment later, he was laughing like any newly weaned child. Trayja scooped him into her arms. How could she have thought to live without him? The day she'd asked to be alone seemed very long ago. Jat licked the boy's neck. "Urag, my son," said Trayja. "You'll be a great Councilman one day, with the wisdom of the reindeer."

"So the God commands," whispered Khee.

"Trayja, blessed one," said Goros, "will you come home with us?"

Trayja looked at her husband and his primary wife. Her anger was gone, and seemed small compared to what she'd witnessed. They'd cared for her son, and Goros had saved her life on the plain. Still, Kamulankuk's freedom ran in her blood. She could never return to their household. "I will not stay in Yugulek," she said, "but I will dwell on the mountain with my son—where my daughter can visit freely without fear or danger. I will guard the shrine and keep it clean. Those who honor the reindeer may bring me food and supplies. And I will have another husband if it pleases me, or none if it does not."

"So be it, black doe," said Goros. He took off his coat and wrapped it around her. Khee offered her own gloves and soft boots. Trayja accepted their gifts. Done was done. She picked up her son and touched her daughter's soft neck. The five of them walked toward the Yugulek village, snow crunching underfoot. Trayja looked up at the night sky. The clouds looked like antlers. Somewhere, the Goddess was laughing.